BEE COUNTY COLLEGE
DATE DUE

18626

E
185
.S84

Stone
Black political power
in America

18626

E
185
.S84

Stone
Black political power in
America

BLACK
POLITICAL
POWER
IN
AMERICA

Also by Chuck Stone

TELL IT LIKE IT IS

BLACK POLITICAL POWER IN AMERICA

BY

CHUCK STONE

The Bobbs-Merrill Company

INDIANAPOLIS / NEW YORK

The Bobbs-Merrill Company, Inc.
A Subsidiary of Howard W. Sams & Co., Inc.
Publishers / Indianapolis • Kansas City • New York
Copyright © 1968 by C. Sumner Stone
ALL RIGHTS RESERVED
Library of Congress catalogue card number 68-29291
Printed in the United States of America
FIRST PRINTING

To my dad, Charles Sumner Stone, Sr., whose shrewd insight into human nature helped me to understand what motivates politicians, and to my son, Charles Sumner Stone, III, whose generation of blacks will wield far more political power than any previous generation and who, his father can now hope, will achieve the highest political office in the noble fulfillment of true black power.

Acknowledgments

Without the advice, assistance, and, above all, the encouragement of close friends, *Black Political Power in America* could not have been completed. I also owe an unpayable debt of gratitude to people like Ernest Calloway of St. Louis whose analysis of local black political developments in many areas saved many hours of research. Frank Wallick, a neighbor and close friend, operated a virtual "one-man clipping service," sending me articles and newspaper clips on black politics which I might have overlooked.

In the course of completing a book, an author naturally works closely with his editor. But in Bob Ockene, editor for Bobbs Merrill, I acquired a good friend, one who not only had tremendous insight into what I was trying to say, but who sympathized deeply with the dream of an ultimately open society in America.

Then, there was Teri Calabrese. Her perceptive criticisms and her finely honed editing clarified concepts and sentence structures. Those alone would have contributed significantly to the book's polished manuscript, but Teri also spent long hours typing several of the book's chapters. I relied heavily on the professionalism of her judgments.

Finally, it is my wife, Louise, who enabled me to survive the ordeal of completing what at times seemed an impossible project. It was her suggestion that the Stones "tighten their belts" and undergo whatever financial hardships we must to complete the book. Without her patience and devotion, this could not have been done.

I also acknowledge with warmest appreciation the various publishers, newspapers and magazines which so graciously permitted me to quote from their published sources.

Contents

BLACK

POLITICAL

POWER

IN

AMERICA

CHAPTER ONE

The Nonhistory of Black Political Power

> Throughout history, the powers of single black men flash here and there like falling stars, and die sometimes before the world had rightly gauged their brightness. Here in America, in the few days since Emancipation, the black man's turning hither and thither in hesitant and doubtful striving has often made his very strength to lose effectiveness, to seem like absence of power, like weakness.
> . . . The power of the ballot we need in sheer self-defense—else what shall save us from a second slavery?
>
> —W. E. B. DU BOIS,
> The Souls of Black Folk, pp. 17, 22

The history of the United States is a history of white people, written by white people and immortalized for white people.

The roles of black people* in the American historical process have been recounted in miserly footnotes and gratuitous asides. Only the accomplishments of white politicians, white statesmen, and white captains of industry have been chronicled. If, perchance, some audacious black man miraculously crashed through the made-in-America color barriers or even dared to help turn the tide of history, he has been briefly paragraphed among thousands of pages, all hailing the glories that were white. Only white people have been legitimatized as makers of American history. Black people have become its instruments.

White people have likewise decided who shall speak on black history in

---

* At the time of this writing, "negroes" and "black people" are only two of several terms in common usage. I will use these words interchangeably. The word "negro" is not capitalized in order to be consistent with the words "white" and "black."

public panels or seminars and what negro historians should be published or accepted. A recent case of white racism determining the black scholar's approach to black history occurred on February 15, 1968, when a Jewish Congressman, James H. Scheuer, convened a one-day conference on negro history and culture. Scheuer, a conservative on civil rights, carefully selected a group of black nonhistorians, with one exception, to discuss black history. Chosen by the Bronx Congressman were two representatives of the racially conservative Urban League (neither of whom was a historian), a white history professor who has written about the "negro problem," and several other persons who were not historians.

The plight of the black historian, then, becomes one of white selectivity and acceptance. As long as there are Scheuers in positions of responsibility determining who shall be heard on this critical topic, the black community will receive a distorted view of its life history.

Chairing one of the Scheuer panels was a distinguished black historian, Dr. Charles Wesley. Other prominent black historians who have distinguished themselves—for instance, Dr. John Hope Franklin and Lerone Bennett—were not participants. The criterion for invitation appeared to be that you were either white or a very "safe negro" if black.

"Safe negroes" predominate because they wish to survive. This can only be done through passive acquiescence in the pattern of racial discrimination.

If any race is ripped from the womb of its heritage, enslaved, and then pounded into the dungeons of subhumanity by a civilization that equates blackness with racial inferiority, the race will quickly take on that civilization's value judgments of itself. For hundreds of years, black people were told each day by American white institutions, a white press, a white judicial system, and white governments that they were a subculture of illegitimate children in the family of mankind. The message was repeated and enforced by the armed might of the state and the cowardly vigilantes of white mobs. Eventually, black people came to believe this white conception of themselves, and they took on the white majority's assessment of them.

Historically, members of the black race have been regarded as children. The prototype was Topsy in *Uncle Tom's Cabin*. Negroes were regarded as a race of singers, dancers, and shiftless workers led by ministers, social workers, and professional "negro leaders." If any negro did somehow acquire the political acumen of a Disraeli, the oratorical eloquence of a William Jennings Bryan, or the business expertise of a Henry Ford, he was still a "nigger." He remained a "nigger" to his own people, and the rise to political power was a climb over the jagged rocks of white oppression and a black self-concept of inferiority.

As Irish Catholics have traditionally acclaimed the "Irish politician" as a proud symbol of their ethnic power and immortal place in American history, black politicians have been rejected with equal disdain by blacks and whites.

Politicians control governments, and governments wield power. White America has never possessed sufficient emotional maturity or sense of democracy to allocate political power to black America. It has been far more reassuring to cling to an assiduously nourished cultural image of black people as an indolent, carefree, fun-loving people, clapping their hands and shooting one another on Saturday nights, rather than to view them as a race with the capacity to be politicians and businessmen.

With the exception of the ten glorious years of Black Reconstruction, 1867-77, when black state legislators and public officials laid the foundation for much of today's social legislation, black politicians have been assigned no prominent place in the making of American politics. American history, written by white historians, has ignored black politicians and black businessmen. Books and stories about 'great negroes" or "famous negroes" have invariably described the lives of singers, dancers, professional athletes, ministers, social workers, educators, and "negro leaders"—never the first negro U.S. Senator, Congressman, state Supreme Court Justice, distinguished public official, or diplomat.

One of the country's early administrators of philanthropy on behalf of negroes and one of the first in a long, gray line of white "experts" on black people, Edwin R. Embree, wrote a book, 13 Against the Odds. Included were the biographies of two singers, a boxer, three writers, two educators, a minister, and a professional "negro leader." No negro politician. His was just one of many patronizing literary essays that were to trot out the overworked clichés of the meek and humble George Washington Carver, the ex-slave who became a great scientist, honored for his submissiveness as much as for his genius; white America's most favorite "negro leader" of all, Booker T. Washington, and Marian Anderson, the brilliant contralto whose retiring personality and humility inspired pages of adoring white prose.

Few essays or history books honored those black revolutionaries Nat Turner, Gabriel Prosser, and Denmark Vesey, who sought to overturn the citadels of white racism, or those black politicians P. B. S. Pinchback, Robert B. Eliott, and Oscar DePriest, who understood the mechanics of political power and tried to make it work to the advantage of black people.

But if white historians and writers found little significance in the contributions of black politicians, black writers were equally guilty. A people whose self-concept is largely derived from the cultural definitions of a white majority will naturally accept the absence of power in their subordinate status. To do otherwise would be to challenge the majority's values and question their authenticity. Very few black people, at least those concerned with survival, were prepared to leave the sanctuary of the psychological plantation to which they had been consigned all their lives and to dissemble the logic of white judgments. Black writers thus adopted the same socio-neurotic value judgments of "outstanding negroes" or "famous negroes" as their white counterparts. In their books and articles about outstanding negroes, black writers simply ignored black politicians. They were invisible.

In his book *The Lonesome Road*, the gifted and brilliant black writer J. Saunders Redding recounted the lives of thirteen "outstanding negroes" —including three professional "negro leaders," a writer, a boxer, a singer, and a doctor. Even that sensitive soul who was one of the first to sing of the beauty of black people, the late "poet laureate of the black people," Langston Hughes, was affected by this cultural blind spot. In two of his books, *Famous American Negroes* and *Famous Negro Heroes of America*, which delineate the great achievements of seventeen black men and women and sixteen negro men and women respectively, only the second book contained the biography of one black politician. This was Robert Smalls, a Congressman whose fame was enshrined not by his political exploits but by his capture of a Confederate gunboat, which he delivered to the Union Army during the Civil War.

A scholar no less distinguished than the late Dr. E. Franklin Frazier, chairman of the Sociology Department of Howard University and a prolific writer on negro life and history, dismisses the negro's involvement with politics in his monumental text, *The Negro in the United States*. Of a total of 767 pages, only five pages are devoted to the negro in politics during and after Reconstruction, and a stingy two pages sum up political leaders. Nowhere does Frazier assess the impact of black political leaders, either on the national or local level, nor does he accord any importance to the impact of the black vote and its influence or even noninfluence in achieving its demands for full equality. In *The Negro in the United States*, the black politician is an "invisible man."

In a more recent textbook, *The Negro in America*, by Dr. Earl Spangler, an effort is made to place the negro in a proper context in American history. In this ninety-three-page book, written for school courses in civics or history, a half-page discussion is devoted to the black politician's role during Reconstruction, and seven pages describe his political activities as both politician and administrator in the Federal government. But there is no recitation of any of the highlights of the growth of the black vote and where it was a decisive force in local and national elections.

In yet another recent textbook, *The Negro in American Life* by Mabel Morsbach, published in 1966, the last chapter, "The Search for Equality 1945-1966," contains *eight* pages on the activities of black sports heroes and *one* page on black politicians.

A far more critical failure to recognize the black politician's contribution to American history appears in the book, *World's Great Men of Color II* by the late J. A. Rogers, generally regarded as one of the most knowledgeable black historians of all time. Describing outstanding black men and women in Europe, South and Central America, the West Indies and the United States, the book recites the accomplishments of twenty-four black Americans. *Not one is a politician.* The twenty-four are: Estevanico (discoverer), Nat Turner (leader of a slave revolt), Frederick Douglass (national leader), Jan Ernest Matzeliger (inventor), Peter Jackson (fighter), Paul Laurence Dunbar (poet), Bert Williams (entertainer), Booker T. Washington (national leader), William Monroe Trotter (writer), W.E.B. Du Bois (author and scholar), Marcus Garvey (black nationalist leader), Hubert Harrison (educator), Ernest Everett (biologist), Arthur Schomberg (historian), Henry Ossawa Turner (painter), George Washington Carver (scientist), Jack Johnson (prize fighter), Matthew A. Henson (discoverer), Roland Hayes (singer), Carter G. Woodson (historian), Paul Robeson (musician and singer), C. C. Spaulding (businessman), Marian Anderson (singer) and Joe Louis (prize fighter).

Whatever crucial role black politicians and public officials have played in helping to shape American history has been obscured not only by lack of recognition by both blacks and whites, but by the lily-white history books in schools and colleges which relegated the negro's importance in American civilization to a bitter, brief fling with slavery.

It is understandable, then, why negroes have been unable to find heroes among black politicians or even businessmen. Politicians and businessmen in a nation governed by the political ethic of the ballot and the capitalistic ethic of the dollar are the authentic power brokers in American society. Negroes have been taught from the beginning of their American noncitizenship as slaves to their second-class citizenship as cultural subordinates that power is a commodity reserved for white people and that "Right, as the world goes, is only in question between equals in power, while the strong do what they can and the weak suffer what they must."*

America was a democracy founded to protect the rights of white people. Black people were only three-fifths human, according to the U.S. Constitution. From its inception, the United States was really a political composite of two cultures: a white-supremacist, superordinate culture of technological efficiency, political democracy, and economic mobility and a black subculture of social disorganization, political servitude, and poverty.

Small wonder black people should find it easy and almost mandatory to accept the white majority's assessment of their leaders. In a special August 22, 1966, *Newsweek* edition titled "Black and White," the magazine published a national poll taken among "rank-and-file" negroes and that amorphous, changing, self-perpetuated body of self-designees known as the "negro leadership." The poll ranked negro leaders according to the degree of approbation among both groups.

* "The Melian Conference" in *The Peloponnesian War, the Complete Writings of Thucydides.* New York: Modern Library, 1951, p. 331.

The only negro politician ranked in the first sixteen was Adam Clayton Powell, who placed tenth. Rated above him by "rank and-file' negroes as their leaders were an athlete, Jackie Robinson, in third place; a comedian, Dick Gregory, in fourth place, and a state NAACP official, Charles Evers of Mississippi, in sixth place. The country's most famous and probably most powerful negro union leader, A. Philip Randolph, was ranked eleventh.

Among the so-called leadership group, the ranking varied significantly, with the exception of number one, the late Reverend Martin Luther King, Jr., who was rated first by both groups. But the "leadership group" ranked Randolph second (compared with the "rank-and-file" rating of the University of Mississippi's first negro student, James Meredith, second). Thurgood Marshall, former NAACP legal strategist and, at that time, a member of the U.S. Circuit Court of Appeals, was third, and James Farmer, former head of the Congress of Racial Equality (CORE) fourth. Like the "rank and file," the "leadership group" ranked Adam Clayton Powell tenth.

There is probably no other ethnic group in America that would accept athletes, comedians, and retired civil-rights leaders over politicians as its principal leaders.

Leaders command power. They motivate society and cause social change. They dominate the power elite and influence its decisions. They control the decision-making processes of government and dispense jobs and money. With the exception of Powell, none of the "leaders" listed by either group could qualify as power brokers of social change, political power, or economic control. This is because negroes have never understood the raw dimensions of political power. Only very recently has the façade of invisibility been stripped away from the black politician. With all his shortcomings and weaknesses, the black politician is finally becoming a prophet with honor in his own land.

Perhaps it was no accident of history that 1967, a year of historic breakthroughs for black political power—the appointment of the first black U.S. Supreme Court Justice and the election of black mayors in two of America's largest cities—was the year the first black politician won the Spingarn Medal. The Spingarn Medal is awarded annually by the NAACP to a negro whose outstanding achievements merit special tribute. In 1967, Edward W. Brooke, U.S. Senator from Massachusetts and the first black Senator since 1881, was honored. He was the first black politician to win the Medal in its fifty-two-year history.

Before this, the Spingarn Medal had been awarded to four singers, two actors, two musicians, an athlete, five writers, a historian, and seven civil-rights leaders—the most numerous category of all. In 1964, the board of directors of the NAACP had been so desperate for an awardee, and so unable to understand the monumental political events of the time, that they presented the Spingarn Medal to the NAACP's own executive director,

Roy Wilkins. This act has rarely been equalled for bankruptcy of vision and organizational incest by any organization.

But the NAACP, guided, financed, and controlled by whites, was not permitted to honor the black heroes who dealt in the acquisition and distribution of power—Oscar S. DePriest, at the time of the election the first black Congressman in twenty-eight years; Arthur W. Mitchell, first Democratic black Congressman in the history of America; William L. Dawson, first black committee chairman in Congress; Adam Clayton Powell, first black Congressman from the country's largest city, New York; Hulan Jack, first black Manhattan Borough President and highest black municipal or state elective official; J. Ernest Wilkins, first black subcabinet member; Archibald J. Carey, Jr., first black to head a Federal committee on government employment; A. Leon Higginbotham, Jr., first black member of a Federal regulatory agency; Howard Jenkins, Jr., first black member of one of the most powerful Federal agencies, the National Labor Relations Board; and Mrs. Constance Baker Motley, first black woman Federal judge.

The list is inexhaustible and so is the inferiority complex of the NAACP. But the era of "Black Power" and the rise of black militancy that called for the resignation of the NAACP's white president emboldened the civil-rights organization to honor somebody besides a black actor, singer, musician, or writer. It had taken the organization fifty-two years to discover black politicians.

If the NAACP boarded the black political-power express slowly, other black institutions and organizations were also gradually waking from their racial somnolence. One was *Ebony* magazine.

Ebony, one of America's most successful negro business ventures, made a million dollars (and by 1967, achieved a circulation of one million) by playing down negro militancy, muffling its pleas for negro equality with the muted tones of Uncle Tom eloquence, and denying the beauty of blackness by filling its pages with ads extolling the white virtues of a "lighter, brighter skin" and "straight hair." Whenever *Ebony* wanted to get militant, it trotted out one of its historians, who reported how militant and angry negroes were hundreds of years ago, or it reported, a few months after the fact, the events of some successful demonstration or "March." *Ebony* was never in the vanguard of the "negro revolution." An apostle of *ex post facto* militancy, it rode in the caboose as a frightened passenger, praying that white businessmen would continue to love it enough to buy more full-page color ads.

In its September 1963 issue celebrating the one hundredth anniversary of the Emancipation Proclamation (a truly historic issue), *Ebony* listed the election of the first negro in Congress, Hiram Rhoades Revel, as one of the "10 Most Dramatic Events in Negro History."

In this same issue, the magazine also listed what it considered to be

America's "100 most influential Negroes." The largest number, twenty-three, came under the political category; five Congressmen, one state senator, six judges, two elected public officials, six appointed public officials, and three political leaders. Compared with the other categories—eleven ministers, ten educators, nine publishers, eight entertainers, and eight businessmen—the negro politician seemed finally to have gained a long-denied recognition.

The "white-out" on black politicians and their crucial importance in many phases of American history as well as contemporary social change may be ending. Black politicians will only gain ascendancy into the decision-making councils of America and membership into the most exclusive club in America, the power elite, in direct proportion as black people themselves are ready to accord black politicians the respect, affection and fellowship other ethnic groups have given to their politicians.

No matter how stained his hands, how sullied his reputation, or how unpopular his manner, if the black politician has played power politics with the same relentless and unconscionable efficiency as white politicians, he will soon be accepted by black people as have the most important power brokers in society. Just as the Irish Catholics have affectionately clasped to their breasts James Michael Curley and William O'Dwyer, the Italians Carmine DeSapio, and the Jews Jake Arvey and Jacob Javits, black people are just beginning to revel in the astute machinations of William L. Dawson, Adam Clayton Powell, and J. Raymond Jones.

In a nation that owes its viability to politics, black politicians will continue to grow in prestige and numbers, and their stars will not fall before the world has "rightly gauged their brightness." The age of demonstrations has passed, and the age of the ballot is upon the black man. It is the tool of survival, and, as Du Bois said: "The power of the ballot we need in sheer self-defense—else what shall save us from a second slavery?"

CHAPTER TWO

The Era of Black Power: Paradise Regained

I shall be content if those shall pronounce my History who desire to give a view of events as they really did happen, and they are very likely, in accordance with human nature, to repeat themselves at some future time—if not exactly the same, yet very similar.

—THUCYDIDES

No segment of humanity has ever escaped the universal laws of history.

If the white storytellers of America's growth have sketched a "separate but equal" treatment of events for posterity, history has nonetheless been made with an unfaltering will of its own. If history has repeated itself—and who can deny that it has?—it has done so equally for both whites and blacks.

For black people in America, history repeated itself in 1967. It was a year of dramatic political breakthroughs, the optimistic beginning of a new era of political power for a mournfully powerless people.

A black man was appointed by the President as the new Commissioner or "mayor" of the nation's capital, Washington, D.C.

Two black men were elected mayors of two of the country's largest cities.

A black man was sworn in as the first black U.S. Supreme Court Justice, and three black men became the first state legislators in three states of the former Confederacy for the first time since Reconstruction.

Not since 1870 had any one year struck such a status-quo-shaking blow for black political equality. That was the year black people were elected to several high political offices for the first time since they had been dragged to this country in chains:

The first black U.S. Senator, Hiram Rhoades Revel, was elected from Mississippi.

11

The first two black U.S. Congressmen were elected, Joseph H. Rainey from South Carolina and Jefferson P. Long from Georgia.

The first black justice of a state supreme court, Jonathan Jasper Wright, Associate Justice of the South Carolina Supreme Court and the only negro to hold such a high judicial post in any state in the history of the nation.

The first black lieutenant governor of a state, Alonzo J. Ransier of South Carolina.

The first black mayor of an American city, Robert H. Wood of Natchez, Mississippi.

It was the beginning of seven full years of elected black officials, distributed liberally throughout the hitherto all-white power structure of Southern politics. The distinguished black scholar W. E. B. Du Bois called them the "mystic years." They were the forerunners of more years that were to produce a total of twenty black Congressmen, two black Senators, a black acting governor, six lieutenant governors, two state treasurers, three state secretaries of states, and three superintendents of education.

As an electrifying year of change in the black man's political fortunes, 1967 paralleled 1870. Until 1967, black political power had been measured solely by the black vote as a "balance of power" to elect friendly white officials or black legislators from predominantly all-black districts.

This tradition was abruptly shattered in 1967. A new mood of blackness bear-hugged the black community. A revolutionary cry, "Black Power," first heard in the summer of 1966, was being listened to by some negroes, although most rejected its strident militancy for fear of offending their white contemporaries.

But if Black Power meant different things—black pride, black violence, racism in reverse, black revolution, black political power—to different people, it meant just one thing to aspiring black politicians: that they, too, could become mayor, governor, or Senator. A new compulsion for political activity began to be felt by black people.

Banding together with a sophisticated unity steeped in black pride, black people acquired a new dimension of political power by:

Electing the first black mayor, Carl Burton Stokes, of America's eighth-largest city, Cleveland, Ohio.

Electing the first black mayor, Richard Gordon Hatcher, of America's seventieth-largest city, Gary, Indiana, the "Steel City."

Electing black men for the first time since Reconstruction to the state legislatures of Mississippi, Louisiana, and Virginia—Robert Clark from Holmes County, Mississippi; Ernest N. Morial from New Orleans, Louisiana; and Dr. W. Ferguson Reid from Richmond, Virginia.

Providing the margin of victory in the defeat of a "white backlash" candidate for mayor of Boston and simultaneously electing the first negro, a Harvard Law School student, Thomas I. Adkins.* to the Boston City Council.

Running a black man, Hugh Frost, vice president of the board of education, as the Republican candidate for mayor of Youngstown, Ohio (he was defeated, probably because he was a Republican in a heavily Democratic town, not because he was black); running a negro, Tennessee state legislator A. W. Willis, for mayor in the Memphis Democratic primary (he placed fourth and was defeated)

Electing negroes for the first time to a number of public offices as disparate as the Kentucky state senate (a woman), the Seattle city council, a Waterloo, Iowa, court judgeship, and a school commission in Pittsfield, Massachusetts

Emboldening Dr. Reginald Hawkins, a distinguished black civic leader in Raleigh, North Carolina, to declare his candidacy for governor of that state in 1968 on the Democratic ticket.

If the years 1870-77 could be characterized as "Black Power in Dixie,"** then 1967 was that philosophy's most successful expression in the twentieth century. This resurgence of Black Power was the most revolutionary fact of American politics in 1967. And it represented history repeating the events of 1870, the year black people saw their first political representatives in public offices of any kind in substantial numbers.

Certain events had led up to this dramatic breakthrough in 1967. One undoubtedly was the 1966 election of the first negro U.S. Senator since 1881. The impact of Edward W. Brooke's victory in Massachusetts was given the national spotlight again when he was sworn in at the beginning of the Ninetieth Congress in January 1967. Another event lending impetus to the development of black political power was the June 13, 1967, appointment of the former NAACP legal counsel, Thurgood Marshall, first black justice to the United States Supreme Court.

Brooke's swearing-in and Marshall's appointment helped to provide a

---

* The Boston City Council dates back to 1909. Negroes were members of the Boston Common Council which antedates the Boston City Council. The first negro member of the Boston Common Council was George L. Ruffin, who was elected in 1895. Ruffin was a Republican. Boston's negroes tended to concentrate in the West End colony, and, by 1885, they represented more than half of the Republican voters in the old Ward Nine.

Negroes had a total of ten Council members until 1895.

In 1909, the last year before the Common Council was reorganized out of existence and the various wards gerrymandered by the Irish Democrats to knock out negro political power once and for all, Ward Ten's negro representative in the Council, J. Henderson Allston, was actually the senior member of the Common Council by virtue of his election from the old Ward Nine in 1895, and he presided at the opening session of the Council and welcomed the newcomers.

** In Before the Mayflower, by Lerone Bennett.

political climate in which a black man could be more than just a representative of black people—he could represent and govern whites as well.

Both events were omens of a change in the black political fortunes. But 1967 held out its share of political misfortunes for black people as well. The year began as if America were going to embark on a journey of vengeful political repression of negroes instead of one hastening their political progress. The U.S. House of Representatives, frightened and angered by the sprawling popularity of the Black Power concept among negroes, summarily excluded from the Ninetieth Congress Representative Adam Clayton Powell, chairman of the Education and Labor Committee, one of the country's most powerful negro politicians and an early exponent of Black Power. It was the first legislative "white backlash" to be organized against a black politician since the Reconstruction, when the U.S. Senate refused to seat the dutifully elected Senator from Louisiana, P. B. S. Pinchback, in 1876, because, like Powell, he was an arrogant, light-skinned, handsome darkie.

The 1967 summer of black rebellions in thirty-five major cities, culminating in two massive black-generated insurrections in Newark and Detroit, had pushed negro-white relations to the brink of total alienation. The white population of Ohio's tenth largest city, Springfield, was not sufficiently impressed and educated by its history-making first black mayor, elected in 1965, so that they repealed the city's fair-housing ordinance and barred the city's governing commission from enacting any similar legislation in the future.

However, despite a majority mood in the country that told pollsters "negroes are moving too fast," despite a slackening of Congressional concern for civil rights, black people responded to the new radicalism in the civil-rights movement, Black Power, by translating it into reality at the ballot box. They simply went out and elected black mayors.

If this unexpected cresting of Black Power distressed whites, black people calmly embraced their newly acquired bastion of negotiating from "situations of strength." Just as the Irish, the Italians, the Jews, and the Poles had long played the game of ethnic politics to the excruciating hilt of ethnic solidarity, negroes, as good American traditionalists, were finally having their turn.

Jewish voters had often crossed party lines to elect Jewish candidates, despite repeated denials from Jewish leaders that any such thing as a "Jewish bloc" existed. (The Liberal Party of New York State is tacitly accepted by all professional politicians as the "Jewish Party" without anybody ever saying so publicly.) Irish Catholic voters had unfailingly secured the control of political machines in the big cities as if Irish politicians had received a special mandate from God. Italian-American voters were the electoral insurance for the breakthroughs of Italian public officials as a "balanced ticket" in New York City and State came to include by definition an Italian along with an Irish Catholic and a Jew. Polish-Americans loyally guaranteed the election of Polish-American public officials, even from districts where they did not constitute a majority.

These ethnic groups all enjoyed a common denominator of existence—their white skin. Cuddled in folksy togetherness under the protective myth of the "melting pot," these same ethnic groups merchandised another myth —that ethnic-bloc voting to elect a member of their own group to high political office was simply a legitimate extension of the American dream. Ethnic clannishness was forgivable so long as it masqueraded in the cloak of Americanism as practiced by whites.

Yet similar bloc-voting efforts by black people to elect black people always collided with the stone wall of white supremacy. Black political unity was condemned as "racism in reverse" by Jewish-owned newspapers and Irish Catholic columnists. What had been good for the white goose yesterday was not regarded as sauce for the black gander today.

For the most part, black people docilely accepted this charade with its invidious distinctions between white and black. In so doing, they countenanced a civil-rights struggle governed more by the interracial niceties of hand-holding marches than by a Machiavellian quest for true economic and political power.

True, the civil rights movement was scarred by murders, and the violence imparted a battlefield flavor to the movement's activities. Yet, black people refused to react violently in the early years of the "freedom struggle." Despite the church bombings, the police brutality, the unpunished murders of civil rights workers and the frequent listlessness of the Federal government, the movement was essentially a series of peaceful sit-ins, protest marches where the anthem "We Shall Overcome" was sung, and hand-clapping revival meetings.

It was only when the black youth of the ghetto became convinced that this approach was nonproductive that the black rebellions began to sweep through American cities. Beginning in the summer of 1964 in New York City's crowded ghettoes, Harlem and Bedford-Stuyvesant, "race riots" soon destroyed entire black neighborhoods in 83 major cities.

Only one black man in America clung to the violence-tarnished dream that the technique of nonviolence in massive marches and demonstrations could still achieve results.

The Rev. Martin Luther King, Jr., one of the few black charismatic national leaders in America, stood almost alone as he criss-crossed America in pursuit of black equality through nonviolence. An eloquent and moving orator, he preached a doctrine of love and forgiveness that an increasing number of black and white people ceased to hear.

On April 4, 1968, while standing on the second-floor porch of a motel in Memphis, Tennessee, he was killed by a sniper.

While a grief-stricken country immediately went into a period of national mourning, turmoil erupted in the black communities of more than one hundred twenty-five American cities.

King had been a necessary product of his time, when the country's blacks and whites both found it easier to swoon to King's 1963 rhapsody in front of the Lincoln Memorial—"I Have a Dream"—than to organize behind such pragmatic admonishments as Congressman William L. Dawson's (to a Chicago South Side audience in 1956) to get out the vote—"Don't get mad. Get smart."

Still, the rampant emotionalism in the movement did serve a limited purpose at a time when emotionalism was all the country could deal with. It enabled blacks and whites to work together in common cause. At all times, in all organizations and in all strategies, the emphasis was on integration Integration defined the goal, determined the method, and established the tradition.

Two words ruptured that tradition

Black Power.

The slogan became an immediate cause of national friction. Black Power scorched itself into the American conscience with devastating rapidity. It divided the nat on, rallied a race to its banner, and was blamed for the cataclysmic upheavals of racial violence in American cities. But like the many slogans before it which had been woven into the fabric of American democracy, Black Power continued a tradition.

American history can almost be catalogued by the compelling solidarity and abrasive disaffections that have defeated Presidents, started wars, launched crusades, united the nation, partitioned regions, and subjugated races: "Don't Tread on Me'—"54' 40' or Fight — 'Rum, Romanism, and Rebellion'—'Manifest Destiny"—"Remember the *Maine*"—"He Kept Us Out of War'—"New Deal"—"McCarthyism"—"States Rights."

Black Power was as American as all of them. And it did what any notable social motto does: It forced a national reassessment of America's shortcomings during a crisis. Perhaps it was the tension crammed way in which Black Power was born, rather than the scary implications of those two little words, that traumatized America. It was June 1966. Deep in the South during a protest march of black militants Student Nonviolent Coordinating Committee chieftain Stokely Carmichael started a chant· "Black Power! We want Black Power!"

It quickly caught on and spread to other cities, other protest marches, other demonstrations. In the two "long, hot summers" of 1966 and 1967, Black Power was screamed in the explosions of black rebellions, erroneously labeled as "race riots"* by the white press.

Dr. Alvin F. Poussaint, assistant professor of psychiatry at Tufts Medical

* A "race riot" is a violent confrontation between races. It must involve physical battle between at least two races.

School and a former Southern field director for the Medical Committee for Human Rights, described, in a 1967 *New York Times* article about how "The White Press Distorts News," the development of the Black Power movement. Wrote Poussaint:

In this country, these media are almost entirely white-controlled and are directed primarily to a white audience which ranges from avowed racial bigots to white liberals, many of whom are plagued with unconscious, latent racism. These people tend to see racial issues in accordance with their own economic, social and psychological vested interests.

White newsmen, with these same interests, often unconsciously slant and deliver news in such a way as to appeal to the sentiments of their readers. Thus newsmen not only influence but reflect the climate of race relations in American society.

I recall the Meredith March through Mississippi in June 1966 when the "Black Power" slogan was popularized by the white press. Reporters, predominantly white, from every major newspaper and TV station in the country, were covering this event. Talking to reporters on the opening days, I remember that many were frightened and resentful that they were assigned to this "senseless and foolish march." They were angry with the leaders and other demonstrators who were ultimately responsible for their predicament.

The newsmen complained that they were "bored" and that there was really no good "copy" to send back to their newspapers. They were anxiously searching for stories that would appeal to their readers back home.

When a few young civil rights workers sporadically began to yell "black power"—one of the many improvised chants that are typically heard in civil rights demonstrations—the white press saw their opportunity for news and projected the slogan all over America. Perhaps because of their own anger at the marchers and their overt or unconscious racism, the slogan was projected as sinister, savage and violent.

Thus, to the American public, egged on by a confused and bitter white press, Black Power was equated overnight with black violence and black revolution. The white press blamed the black rebellions on Black Power, even though the insurrections in eight major cities, including New York City, in the summer of 1964 and in thirty-five cities, including the Los Angeles Watts rebellion, in the summer of 1965 all occurred before Black Power was chanted in the summer of 1966.

The black militants and revolutionaries were quick to take advantage of this press-orchestrated hysteria. Sensing they had "Whitey" on the run, the black militants moved from one extreme posture to another. Black Power had been initially expressed by black people as the need for the empowerment of the black community and the development of black pride. But the white press took over and publicized the strange new doctrine as a tool for black retaliation and the annihilation of whites.

It was easy to pull off this exercise in journalistic irresponsibility. The doctrine's two most articulate—and most mobile—advocates, Stokely Carmichael and H. Rap Brown, preached the need for black people both to develop more pride in themselves and to massively retaliate with guns when attacked by whites. Brown's advice wrote the daily headlines and determined the editorials. Carmichael's speeches were covered efficiently by the press.*

But Black Power was resented by many whites as "un-American" for other more subtle reasons. Besides its terrifying overtones of violent retaliation, Black Power broke an unwritten law of the American democratic ethic. It did not disguise its ends in polite political rhetoric.

During the past hundred years, the Irish, the Italians, the Jews, the Poles, and other ethnic groups had painstakingly and almost surreptitiously built their ethnic power bases in politics and business. They had never publicly described their goal as the pursuit and acquisition of power. They simply went out and elected ethnic candidates with solid ethnic votes, controlled political machines, built ethnic-dominated businesses, and gathered enormous ethnic power on behalf of their respective groups. Rarely did these groups publicly create the impression that the unlovely scramble for power was that group's principal commitment in life. After all, the Rotary Club was not founded to help the businessman make a bigger profit and more money, but to further the Rotary ideal of "service to the community."

Negroes became the great spoilers of the American myth. By openly and

---

* On April 4, 1967, Stokely Carmichael, speaking before a group of students at all-negro Miles College in Birmingham, Alabama, declared: "To hell with the laws of the United States. . . . If you don't wake up, man, your brothers in the ghettoes are going to wake up with matches. . . . If a white man tries to walk over you, kill him. One match and you can retaliate. Burn, baby, burn."

In a series of speeches on negro college campuses during the spring of 1967, Carmichael discussed a broad and diversified interpretation of black power which included political and economic power for black people and a reaffirmation of black pride in black ancestry. But only his repeated mention of violence—sometimes brief and fleeting—came through and obscured his other variations. At Texas Southern, he developed a theme of black pride: "We must stand up and say 'our noses are wide, our lips are thick, our hair is nappy, we are black and beautiful.' At the white University of Texas, however, Carmichael moved to a political posture for Black Power: "Hopefully, the strength of black power will be felt in the national elections of 1972—it's at least a five-year organization plan."

At Bethune-Cookman College, a negro institution in Florida, Carmichael's interpretation of Black Power became *"la négritude"*: "Are you studying German? If you know Swahili, you can talk to your African brothers and the white men won't know what you're talking about."

At Florida A. & M., another negro university, Carmichael's posture was one of black resistance to both the draft and violence: "The first few black men who tell their draft boards, 'Hell, no, we won't go,' might wind up in jail, but we'd soon get it so negroes wouldn't have to be drafted. . . . If a white man hits you, break him. . . . If a hunky tries to shoot you, kill him before God gets the news."

H. Rap Brown, while not making Carmichael's delicate philosophical distinctions on Black Power, has nonetheless been equally explicit about the need for black self-defense and black retaliation. At a Black People's Party rally in Harlem for Adam Clayton Powell on November 12, 1967, Brown discussed the Plainfield, N.J., rebellion and said: "One stinking breath, bad-smelling honkie was killed. That was the only death. . . . The man won't bother black folks there because over forty rifles disappeared from the armory there and they know the brothers have them and will use them. Force is the only thing the honkie understands. That's how he got everything he has—by taking it."

notoriously advocating Black Power for black people, they had sacked the democratic fantasy of the "melting pot" (into which negroes had never melted). It was more American to foster the self-serving fiction that an ethnic group did not necessarily have to survive within a pluralistic America by taking care of its own first.

But if Black Power was condemned with a near unanimity in the white community, it found no early welcome in the black community either. Goaded by the plantation mentality of white editorials and the "we-wuz-robbed" chagrin of white liberals, the negro Establishment picked up its water buckets of accommodation and threw soothing words of denunciation on the fire of Black Power, precisely as they had been ordered to do by the white contributors controlling their organizations. Prominent negro leaders from the ex-radical turned Uncle Tom Bayard Rustin to the two men dubbed in the black community the Gold Dust Twins of negro spokesman-ship, Roy Wilkins and Whitney Young, all decried Black Power. Wilkins described it as "racism in reverse" and Young bitterly criticized it as "black separatism."

More than a slight suspicion exists that the black leaders were responding to the same sociological syndrome toward the color *black* as had whites. If this new thrust toward black self-sufficiency had only been titled "black pride," or "colored self-help," or even "negro power," some of the offensive connotations in its name might have been lessened.

Historically, the word black has accumulated a string of pejorative associations in the Western culture: black art, blackball, black book, black death, blackguard, black hand, blacklist, black magic, blackmail, Black Maria, black market, and black sheep. Compounding the latent hostility in this new term was the juxtaposition of the word *power*, which implied force and might and righteousness of purpose. How could anything black be righteous? At the other end of this color spectrum of morality was the racial superordination implicit in the cultural concept of white. The happiest and most secure existence is characterized by the expression "free, white, and twenty-one."

Advertising has subtly endowed white with approbation. "The Good Guys are always on the White Horse" was a recent slogan for a whisky of that name. "You can tell they're good guys because they all wear white hats," sang a television commercial. *Ebony* magazine became famous for its ads extolling the merits of a "lighter, brighter skin." (This in a periodical devoted to raising the standards of the black community. To *Ebony*, the standards of the white community with all its implicit racism were the standards the black community should adopt.)

Lewis C. Copeland, in an article, "The Negro as a Contrast Conception,"* described how the two colors polarized American society:

* From "Race Relations and the Race Problem" edited by Edgar T. Thompson (Durham, N C., Duke University Press, 1939).

As a natural outcome of the juxtaposition of two divergent ethnic groups, white people have sharply distinguished themselves from black people. . . . In fact, one may speak of the Negro as a "contrast conception."

. . . In popular thought black and white have become conceptual antipodes. The black man and his appurtenances stand as the antithesis of the character and properties of the white man. The conception makes of the Negro a counterrace. The black race serves as a foil for the white race, by which the character of the latter is made all the more impressive.

. . . The contradistinction between white and black is still an important element in Southern thought and literature.

. . . We can now understand some elusive aspects of the diametrically opposite way white and Negro women are regarded. The white woman is one of the most conspicuous symbols of white racial values. She stands for the home, domestic relations and intimate contacts. To protect her is to make secure the inner social circle and to forestall race mixture. Thus, she is made to exemplify the virtues of the race and is enshrouded with the symbols of purity. Her status is made all the more exalted by the conceptual polarity of comparison with the black woman. In contrast to the ennoblement of white women, Negro women stand as the symbol of degradation. Here, above all, the distinction is absolute. There can be no basis of comparison between the two. Everywhere in public one sees and hears the contrast implied in the terms, "white ladies" and "colored women." In white parlance the Negro is not ordinarily a lady or a gentleman.*

A psychologically powerless people, unschooled in the subtleties of political machinations and propaganda, are inclined toward a raw honesty when they finally do decide to acquire power. The cry ' Black Power" was a necessary first step. The second step was to legitimatize the cry. It was taken on September 3, 1966, when Representative Adam Clayton Powell, Chairman of the U.S. House Education and Labor Committee and one of the country's few militant black politicians, convened a Black Power Planning Conference at the Rayburn House Office Building which drew 169 representatives of sixty-four organizations in thirty-seven cities and eighteen states. Less than one year later, on July 17, 1967, the first National Conference of Black Power was held in Newark, N.J., only three days after that city had exhausted itself in a five-day binge of violence which killed twenty-six and injured 1004.

Although it took place in a battle-scarred city, more than a thousand representatives of 228 organizations in 127 cities attended the conference. The conference was one of Black Power's first triumphs. Of the more than eighty resolutions passed by the Conference, eleven dealt with politics. Specifically demanded were an immediate tripling of negro representation in Congress; the election of negro mayors in cities where negroes are a majority in the population (for instance, Washington, D.C., 66 per cent; Gary, Ind., 55 per

---

* For one of the most gifted excursions into the historical significance of white as a color of purity, beauty, truth, righteousness, excellence, and supremacy, read Chapter 42, "The Whiteness of the Whale," in Herman Melville's *Moby Dick.*

cent; Newark, N.J., 53 per cent and Richmond, Va., 51 per cent), a greater proportion of negro state and city office holders in top jobs; and more negroes in high-level positions of responsibility in the Federal government. The Conference also specifically addressed itself to the exclusion of Representative Adam Clayton Powell and called for his reseating and the restoration of his chairmanship as well as the defeat of those Congressmen who led the fight against him.

The conference, hailed as a success in a few black quarters and denounced as a racist adventure in most white quarters, quickly radiated into the black community. Bushy bearded militants, angry young teen-agers, unemployed mothers on welfare, government employees, pipe smoking college professors, and conservatively dressed businessmen all found an element of identity with the many-splendored meanings of Black Power. Interpretations ranged from the radicalism of a separate nation and violent black revolution to the comparative moderation of black economic self-help and black political bossism.

With the widening of Black Power's circle of acceptability among black people, some of the most rock-ribbed antagonists of the concept began to guardedly sing new praises of this doctrine. While they were unable to change their tune completely, the cacophony of their dissent was modulated. Republican Senator Edward W. Brooke, who, by his own analysis, "happens to be negro," struck the first note in the new chorus in a major address before the National Urban League in Portland, Ore., on August 31, 1967, by declaring: "I am not an advocate of Black Power in the sense that the term has come to mean violence. But power as the ability to change conditions so that opportunities are opened, right respected and enforced, and a man's future made secure, is the essence of the democratic process. The poor, especially the Negro poor, must become full participants in that process." That statement teetered perilously close to a qualified endorsement of Black Power and many press reports said so. The door to a newer understanding of Black Power was now ajar. A group of eighty black ministers meeting in Dallas from various cities to launch the National Committee of Negro Churchmen served notice that they would be urging negro churches to involve themselves with certain aspects of the Black Power movement. Look magazine, in a November 1967 issue, ran the headline "Black Power Hits the Campuses" on its front cover, to describe a story about the growing racial cohesion of black students on white college campuses. But it was the November 1967 elections which finally clothed Black Power in its new mantle of respectability. The unexpected haberdashers? The white press. Almost singlehandedly responsible for an earlier equation of Black Power with black violence, the white press this time peered deeper into the well of the phrase's surface and unearthed a treasury of new equations. One was political power.

The *New York Times*, in a story on a negro running for mayor in wealthy Westchester County, slanted its headline with the editorial conclusion: "Black Power Test Due in Mt. Vernon." As far as the editors of the *Times* were concerned, Black Power obviously meant political power.

This conclusion carried over into the analyses and reports in the days following the history-shaking November 1967 elections. The authentic voice of air-waves conservatism, news commentator Paul Harvey, said that if Black Power had any validity, it was to be found in the election of negro mayors in two major American cities. Even that model of journalistic restraint Joseph Alsop was unable to contain his excitement and exulted: "Mayors-elect Stokes and Hatcher represent 'Black Power' in the best American tradition—and thank God for it!"

Time magazine's postelection cover story on Cleveland Mayor-elect Carl B. Stokes was titled "The Real Black Power."

The *Chicago Daily News*, in its November 9, 1967, lead editorial, "The New Black Power," solemnly intoned: "And there will be those who quail before Tuesday's assertion of black power. But this is a new kind of black power—an infinitely better, more promising kind than the one Stokely Carmichael has been talking about. The black power demonstrated in Cleveland and Gary Tuesday was legitimate power wielded in a legitimate way by an important minority of Americans."

The final exercise in the national dignification of Black Power came from one of its earliest and most bitter assailants, the *New York Times*. More than most publications in America, the *New York Times* has encountered severe emotional stress in attempting to understand and report objectively on Black Power. The *Times* has a history of opposing the political efforts of negroes—in particular those seeking to advance through bloc voting and the acquisition of top political appointments on an ethnic basis. Its strident opposition to Black Power was a continuation of this posture, although the *Times* went through several changes on Black Power before deciding that the concept was a disturbingly nasty doctrine meriting an all-out editorial war. In a July 22, 1967, editorial titled "Black Phoenix," the *Times* declared, "The words 'black power' suggest chauvinism and militancy for some dark purpose. They need not. . . . Up to now, the most shrill voices have left the impression that 'black power' stood for a defeatist form of race separation and violence, as opposed to integration and non-violence. . . . A new phoenix of hope could rise from the ashes of Newark if something more than a mere echo of the cry 'black power' were to be heard." Two days later, the *Times* switched. In a lead editorial titled "Black Racism," the newspaper condemned the National Conference on Black Power as a "racist" meeting where the delegates "merely spoke about revolution."

In its November 12, 1967, editorial, " 'Black Power' and the Elections," the *Times* rejoiced, "Last Tuesday's elections in Cleveland, Gary and parts of the South translated 'black power,' that mischievous and opaque slogan, into the only meaningful terms it can have: political success achieved through the democratic process."

Time magazine, in an attempt to further sanitize Black Power, wrote one of its essays on the concept and lifted it into a stratosphere of meaningless philosophical abstraction.

America's white press, which had originally reacted to Black Power with the drab fear of violence, had now come full circle and renovated the slogan with a fresh coat of respectability. This was accomplished by the discovery of two new equations: Black Power equals political power and Black Power is black pride. Most white people felt reasonably certain they could live in comfort with these new interpretations.

If whites were slow in adjusting to the revolutionary ethic of Black Power, blacks were beset with no such difficulty. Even those who opposed the cadences of violence in Black Power readily embraced its injunction to "think black." To think black was to elect black officials. To elect black officials was to acquire political power—or black power. Black politicians who either had to seek white votes to get elected or had to continue to do business with white-controlled political machines did not openly advocate Black Power. But the vast majority of them let it be known to black militants that they were happy about its implications for expanded political support among the black electorate.

For negroes, then, a new sense of their political capabilities was articulated by Black Power. The phrase, when put into practice, was a confirmation of negroes' belief that they did, indeed, hold power to do more than simply elect friendly white public officials and black legislators from predominantly black districts. Black Power, if intelligently used, could also elect negroes to previously barred high office. As has been historically true whenever men fought for freedom, any slogan that appeals to a people's self-esteem or a nation's patriotism will prevail, despite that slogan's belligerence of expression. Black Power had prevailed, and the elections of November 1967 became a testimonial to its success.

Not since the Black Reconstruction year of 1870 had black people savored the fruit of national black political power. That feast was to last only until 1877, when America's first white backlash rose up in organized anger and began the purge of blackness from Southern politics. "Black Power in Dixie" was quickly followed by a political dark age for negroes. Nationally, a powerless and almost faceless existence for the black politician was decreed. This ninety-year blackout was to last until 1967, when negroes were to score their series of triumphant firsts and regain a measure of political power.

On balance, 1967's spectacular victories for black political power far outweighed its defeats and setbacks, with one exception—the exclusion of Representative Adam Clayton Powell from the House of Representatives on March 10, 1967.

Powell had been accused of misusing funds from the Education and Labor Committee, of which he had been chairman for five years, maintaining his estranged wife on the committee payroll, even though by her public "confession" she had done no committee work in a year, and defying the New York State courts in a civil action brought against him for libel. Negroes were embittered by Powell's exclusion, not necessarily because they believed him to be a paragon of spotless virtue, but because he had become the most successful public symbol of the kind of political power they were convinced ran America. As one of two black chairmen of a Congressional committee (the other was the former warhorse of yesterday's political battle and now a silent octogenarian, Representative William L. Dawson of Chicago, Ill., head of the Committee on Government Operations), Powell ran his committee, conducted his personal life, and played politics with a flamboyant arrogance and a stylish grandeur that tickled his black brothers but infuriated his political peers into spasms of apoplexy.

Furthermore, negroes almost unanimously believed that their Black Panache's refusal to "Tom" and to say "I'm sorry" for his imputed transgressions, and his early identification with the Black Power movement were the real causes for his Congressional unfrocking. That his peccadillos were sanctimoniously held up by other Congressmen as reasons responsible for Powell's exclusion was cynically rejected by blacks—and many whites—who pointed to similar excesses by other Congressmen, all of which had been publicized in many national publications. But these Congressmen were white, and Powell was black.

If Powell's political assassination in March 1967 presaged an anticipated political dark age for negroes, the black rebellions in major cities reinforced their fears. The summer of violence of 1967 was by far the worst of the three "long hot summers" of 1965, 1966 and 1967, when a total of eighty-three major cities were racked by the black rebellions. Many black leaders felt that the black violence would alienate white friends and stiffen white resistance to further black gains.

In the summer of 1967, Newark, N.J., and, less than two weeks later, Detroit, the country's fifth largest city, became erupting volcanoes of black fury. When Detroit's destructive anger had subsided, forty-two had died, 386 had been injured, and 5557 arrested. The pattern of black rebellions was repeated in those same hot months in 1967 in thirty-five cities from Boston, Mass., and Hartford, Conn., to Tampa, Fla., and Wichita, Kan. As shouts of "Black Power" were heard with a rambunctious frequency during the rebellions, as rioters tended to ignore stores with "Black Power" or "soul brother" scrawled across their windows, white America became convinced this new politics of violence had incubated in the Black Power move-ment. Forgotten was Watts, Los Angeles, which, in August 1965, had helped to inaugurate this insurrectionist phase of the "Negro Revolution" a full ten months before the cry of Black Power had even been heard in the land.

In response to the spreading black militancy, an equally proliferating white backlash belched in public-opinion polls and editorials that negroes had now "gone too far, too fast." White liberals, disenchanted by the tacit racial abrasiveness of Black Power, parted company with their militant black brothers, and the civil-rights movement slowly began to unravel at its inte-grated seams.

Then, the black emphasis and the white concern abruptly shifted. Almost overnight, the nation became intrigued with the sudden mushrooming of negro politicians running for mayor in major cities. While some of these candidates were not taken seriously by either blacks or whites (Chicago, Philadelphia), black candidacies in Cleveland, Gary, Youngstown, and Memphis were blessed with solid organizational backing and financial sup-port in the black communities.

The black vote, until then, had been only a voting bloc to ensure the election of their liberal white friends or their own black representatives. Now, a group of politicians was proclaiming its ability to govern both whites and blacks. This was a radical departure from established roles traditionally reserved for black politicians. With isolated exceptions, black politicians had rarely played any definitive role in the determination of public policy, the dispensation of jobs, the administration of government, the selection of political candidates, and, most important of all, the control of the entire political process. As will be discussed in Chapter Eight, "The Irish, the Italians, the Jews, and the Poles," total control of the political process and its machines—or, at the very minimum, proportionate control of these apparatuses based upon the percentage of the ethnic group in the popula-tion—has always been the primary goal of these groups in America. Even where they have not been in a majority or were not even a significant minority, they have been able to exercise political power far out of propor-tion to their percentage in the population. It was now time for negroes at least to begin thinking along the same lines.

While no one can safely predict the course of events in the years ahead, it can be stated accurately that the Black Power movement was at the least a compelling factor in the march toward greater political power.

In an allegedly pluralistic society, Black Power was, indeed, Paradise Re-gained after a "white-out" of ninety years.

CHAPTER THREE

Up from Slavery

I am just as much opposed to Booker Washington as a voter, with all his Anglo-Saxon reenforcements, as I am to the coconut-headed, chocolate-colored, typical little coon, Andy Dotson, who blacks my shoes every morning. Neither is fit to perform the supreme function of citizenship.

—JAMES K. VARDAMAN,
Mississippi Senator, 1913-1919

White America has never been quite able to escape the hangover from its obscene love affair with slavery.

As a nation, it has passed laws guaranteeing racial equality and issued proclamations, preached sermons, and published tracts pledging fidelity to the equality of man. Most of them have had little effect, and the sentiment expressed by Mississippi Senator Vardaman that black people are hardly "fit to perform the supreme function of citizenship" was harbored by most white Americans. Even today it could find hearty support.

The dominant fact of the political history of America's black people is slavery.

Every account of the black man in America begins with the subordination of the black man as an animal without privilege or respect. What distinguished him from all other immigrants was his black skin. The white indentured servant could eventually purchase his freedom and, with his white skin, merge into amorphous anonymity, undistinguishable from the most distinguished white statesman. This the black man could never do. His black skin set him apart, and it became the rationalization for white supremacy, the ethic upon which America was founded and built.

The Declaration of Independence was silent about the plight of black people. They, in fact, were not considered human. This was substantiated in Article I, Section 2, Paragraph 3 of the Constitution which declared that the electorate "shall be determined by adding to the whole Number of free

Persons, including those bound to Service for a Term of Years, and excluding Indians not taxed, three-fifths of all other Persons."

A slave was considered only three-fifths of a human being. While constitutionally slaves could not vote, several states nevertheless passed laws restricting suffrage to white males: Delaware in 1792; Kentucky in 1799; Ohio in 1803; New Jersey in 1807; Maryland in 1810; Louisiana in 1812; Connecticut in 1814 (the only New England state to do so); Tennessee in 1834; North Carolina in 1835; Pennsylvania in 1838; and Florida in 1845.

Probably the first confrontation between black men demanding their right to vote and the white officialdom of America occurred in 1778:

> The Negro's right to the franchise is said to have been established by the test case of Paul and John Cuffe in 1778. These two thrifty Negroes, of whom the former, Paul Cuffe, was a successful shipowner and far-ranging navigator, were called upon by the town of Dartmouth, not far from Boston, to pay a personal tax. They demurred, contending that inasmuch as they were not allowed to vote, they should not be held to pay taxes. After protracted argument, the town authorities admitted that taxpaying and the privilege of voting should go together.*

This was an exceptional case. Until their emancipation in 1863, black people were slaves, subhumans without the privileges, rights, or prerogatives of citizenship. While most slaves were treated with the same degree of kindness that one might treat a favorite dog, large numbers were brutalized unmercifully, flogged, beaten, or murdered at will.

The Abolitionists led the propaganda fight for black manumission; they carried on their fight mostly in the North before white audiences in an effort to win sympathy. Public opinion slowly began to stiffen against the excesses of slavery, and when the Civil War erupted, many white men viewed it as a necessary evil in the fight for freedom.

Abraham Lincoln, the sixteenth President, has been remembered kindly in history as the Great Emancipator, a benevolent, compassionate man who abhorred slavery. This is not completely true. Lincoln unlocked the chains of slavery only after he realized that his effort to preserve the Union had failed.

Whereas the Civil War began on April 11, 1861, when Fort Sumter in South Carolina was fired upon, Lincoln did not free America's three million slaves until January 1, 1863. He had hoped for some compromise to forestall the outbreak of hostilities between white brothers over black nonbrothers. Because this concern dominated his thinking, he waited until he was convinced no other solution was possible. As proof of his lack of compassion for the black slaves, Lincoln publicly took one of the most Machiavellian postures toward freedom ever uttered by an American President. Responding to a public letter written to him by Horace Greeley, editor of the *New York Herald Tribune*, titled "The Prayer of Twenty Millions," Lincoln wrote:

* John Daniels, *In Freedom's Birthplace* (Boston: Houghton Mifflin, 1914), pp. 23-24.

If there be those who would not save the Union unless they could at the same time destroy slavery, I do not agree with them. My paramount object in this struggle is to save the Union, and is not either to save or destroy slavery. If I could save the Union without freeing any slave I would do it, and if I could save it by freeing all the slaves, I would do it; and if I could save it by freeing some and leaving others alone I would also do that. What I do about slavery and the colored race, I do because I believe it helps to save the Union. . . .

The end of the Civil War on April 9, 1865, when the courtly Southern gentleman General Robert E. Lee surrendered his sword to the commander of the Union forces, General Ulysses S. Grant, was the beginning of a new era of social strife almost as violent as the previous four years had been.

Lincoln's assassination placed in the Presidency Andrew Johnson, a poor white from Tennessee who had fought his way to the top by overcoming opposition from upper-class whites. To Johnson, a member of the working class of whites, blacks were still an economic threat. When Congress passed a civil rights act in 1866 he vetoed it. Congress passed a second Civil Rights bill in 1867 over Johnson's veto. The act provided for negroes to be recognized as citizens of the United States and gave them the right to vote. The debate over the constitutionality of the act led to the framing of the Fourteenth Amendment to the Constitution, which passed both branches of Congress on June 13, 1866, and was ratified by two-thirds of the states by July 28, 1868.

This act had been passed in the first stage of the Reconstruction period, and it highlights the tensions between Congress and President Andrew Johnson.

Political reconstruction came in two stages. The first lasted from the end of the war until 1867. This was Presidential Reconstruction, carried out by the States, under Lincoln's and Johnson's supervision, with few conditions and not seriously interfered with by national agencies until the second stage approached. The second stage was Congressional Reconstruction, lasting from 1867 to 1876, carried on by the Republican politicians of the national legislature and forced on the unwilling South in detail by national agencies and national partisans.

From 1864 to early in 1867, under Presidential Reconstruction, the South was left free to resume fairly normal political activities. President Lincoln in a proclamation of December, 1863, set forth a plan for the rehabilitation of the seceded States. When ten per cent of the voting population of any State, "lately in rebellion," as determined by the election laws in force before the war, had taken an oath of allegiance, they might proceed to form a new State government, which, if republican in form, would be recognized and given protection under the Federal constitution.*

The South may have lost the war, but it was not going to surrender its traditions of white supremacy. In order to maintain some semblance of the old order, eight Southern states passed what became known as the "Black Codes." They required every black man to be in the service of some white,

* Paul Lewinson, *Race, Class and Party* (New York: Grosset and Dunlap), p. 18.

have both a lawful residence and a job, and carry an official certificate showing both. Vagrancy penalties were imposed on any person who could not
support himself and his dependents, who refused to work for "usual and
common" wages, and specifically on negroes found unlawfully assembling.
(The Union of South Africa was to adopt an identical system many years
later, and it became known as "apartheid.")

Furthermore, some of the states continued to resist the Fourteenth
Amendment.

Congressional exasperation with the paleolithic resistance of the Southern
states reached a boiling point in 1867, and in February, March, and April of
that year, the first series of Congressional reconstruction acts was passed.
They declared that no legal governments existed in the former Confederacy
and divided the region into five military districts under the command of
generals of the Army. They were to direct a registration of voters which
should include negroes and exclude ex-Confederates. These voters were to
elect conventions in the former slave areas, and the conventions, in turn,
were to adopt constitutions which, if acceptable to Congress, were to qualify
the states for readmission as soon as they had accepted the Fourteenth
Amendment. Congressional Reconstruction seemed designed to make the
ex-slaves citizens who could participate in the process of governing. The
shortcut to full equality was to be taken by means of the ballot boxes and
the election of public officials.

Unhappily, there was a welfare mentality in Washington, D.C., that was
a direct carryover from the white paternalism of slavery. This mentality
resulted in the establishment of the Freedmen's Bureau to assist ex-slaves
make the adjustment to their new status. The official title of the Bureau,
actually under the authority of the War Department, was The Bureau of
Refugees, Freedman and Abandoned Lands.

The Bureau was an early WPA for negroes. Its purpose was to administer
abandoned and confiscated plantations and act as a clearing house for the
return of ex-slaves to pardoned ex-Confederates; provide clothing, shelter,
medicine, and rations to the destitute, both blacks and whites. It is estimated by official sources that at that time the Bureau issued six million
rations to freed slaves and two million rations to whites. Some of the more
radical Republicans in Congress wanted the Freedmen's Bureau to redis-
tribute land to ex-slaves, but the South vigorously resisted this move and
the one commodity the blacks needed to achieve self-support—land—was
never acquired.

The next step in the program of Congressional Reconstruction was the
passage of the Fourteenth Amendment. This is generally believed to have
been passed to guarantee Negroes the right to vote, but it actually had a
larger purpose which is rarely recognized by historians. The Fourteenth
Amendment disqualified for Federal and state office any person who had
engaged in insurrections against the nation—i.e., the Confederates—and

made their amnesty conditional upon a two-thirds vote of Congress. In other words, Southern states first had to call new constitutional conventions to elect new governments which were to enfranchise all negroes over twenty-one years of age and disenfranchise whites who had fought against the Union.

The South was aghast. According to an estimate in the Senate, 672,000 Negroes had been enfranchised, as against a total possible white electorate of 925,000. But some hundred thousand of these whites had been disenfranchised, and 200,000 disqualified for office.*

It was open season on democracy.

Northern whites made their pilgrimage to the South to help the negroes establish these new governments. Many arrived with nothing but a carpet-bag containing all of their belongings, hence the word "carpetbagger," which meant a white Northerner who had come to impose black supremacy on Southern whites.

The constitutional conventions were held, and in all the Southern states, with the exception of South Carolina, whites were in the majority. By 1868, seven states had completed ratification of the Fourteenth Amendment to be readmitted to the Union, and by 1870, the last three, Virginia, Mississippi, and Texas, joined them. The stage was now set for the election of public officials on a combined Negro-Radical-Republican slate.

The first year black men were to be elected to the Congress of the United States was 1870. From 1870 to 1901, a total of twenty black Congressmen and two black Senators were to help make the laws of the land. In some states, black men were school superintendents, state treasurers, secretaries of state, lieutenant governors, and in Louisiana, an acting governor, P. B. S. Pinchback.

South Carolina was the blackest of all. Perhaps because it was the only state to have a majority of black delegates to the constitutional convention, South Carolina was also the only state to have a black associate justice of the state supreme court, Jonathan J. Wright. He was also the first negro to be admitted to the Pennsylvania bar. In one year, 1872, the entire delegation to the U.S. Congress was composed of black men—Robert C. DeLarge, Joseph S. Rainey, and Robert B. Elliott.

A reporter describing the first South Carolina legislature of the Reconstruction period wrote:

The Speaker is black, the Clerk is black, the doorkeepers are black, the little pages are black, the chairman of the Ways and Means is black and the Chaplain is coal black. At some of the desks sit colored men whose types it would be hard to find outside of the Congo. . . . It must be remembered also that these men, with not more than half a dozen exceptions, have been themselves slaves, and that their ancestors were slaves for generations.**

* Paul Lewinson, *Race, Class and Party*, p. 41.
** Quoted in Paul Lewinson, *Race, Class and Party*, p. 45.

This was the first manifestation of Black Power.

Black men were to play definitive roles during their brief sojourn in the political sun of democracy by helping to draw up budgets, passing laws that were the forerunners of much of our social-welfare legislation today, and administering governments.

The following men served in the House and the Senate between 1870 and 1901:

NAME	STATE	YEAR
U.S. Senate		
1. Hiram R. Revel	Mississippi	1870–71
2. Blanche K. Bruce	Mississippi	1875–81
U.S. House of Representatives		
1. Joseph H. Rainey	South Carolina	1870–79
2. Jefferson F. Long	Georgia	1870–71
3. Robert C. DeLarge	South Carolina	1871–73
4. Robert B. Elliott	South Carolina	1871–74
5. Josiah T. Wells	Florida	1871–76
6. Benjamin S. Turner	Alabama	1871–73
7. James T. Rapier	Alabama	1873–75
8. Alonzo J. Ransier	South Carolina	1873–75
9. Richard H. Cain	South Carolina	1873–75
		1877–79
10. John R. Lynch	Mississippi	1873–77
		1882–83
11. John A. Hyman	North Carolina	1875–77
12. Jeremiah Haralson	Alabama	1875–77
13. Robert Smalls	South Carolina	1875–79
		1882–83
		1885–87
14. Charles Nash	Louisiana	1875–77
15. James E. O'Hara	North Carolina	1883–87
16. Henry P. Cheatham	North Carolina	1889–93
17. John M. Langston	Virginia	1890–91
18. Thomas E. Miller	South Carolina	1890–91
19. George W. Murray	South Carolina	1893–97
20. George H. White	North Carolina	1897–1901

Of this group, two of the most outstanding were both from South Carolina, Robert Brown Elliott and Robert Smalls. An honor graduate of Eton, Elliott, who was born of West Indian parents in Boston, Mass., on August 11, 1842, was one of the most gifted and eloquent black politicians in American history. He held several political offices, being elected to the South Carolina legislative assembly at the age of twenty-six, to the Congress at twenty-eight; subsequently he became Speaker of the South Carolina legislature.

Elliott was a dark-skinned, heavy-set man who wore his hair in a bushy African style. During his service in Congress, he was one of that body's sharpest debaters, a fast thinker on his feet, and deeply committed to black equality. If some of the black Congressmen thought it best to maintain a discreet silence, Elliott did not. The Adam Clayton Powell of his day, he was quick to take on any display of bigotry on the House floor. Once, after a Southern Congressman had delivered a scurrilously racist attack, Elliott replied: "To the diatribe of the gentleman from Virginia, who spoke on yesterday, and who so far transcended the limits of decency and propriety as to announce upon this floor that his remarks were addressed to white men alone, I shall have no word of reply. Let him feel that a Negro was not only too magnanimous to smite him in his weakness, but was even charitable enough to grant him the mercy of his silence." This eloquent rejoinder brought applause from both the floor and the galleries.

Smalls, who served longer in Congress than any other negro Reconstruction Congressman, who born a slave in Beaufort, S.C., on April 5, 1839. On May 13, 1862, he distinguished himself during the Civil War by smuggling his wife and three children on board the *Planter*, a dispatch and transport steamer, assuming command of the vessel, and, with the Confederate flag flying to get him safely past Confederate lines, sailing the boat into the hands of the Union squadron blockading Charleston harbor. This daring exploit earned him a commission as a pilot in the Union Navy from Lincoln. He subsequently became a captain, the only negro to hold such a rank during the Civil War. Smalls was an outstanding Congressman who supported a wide variety of progressive legislation, such as a bill to provide equal accommodations for negroes in interstate travel and an amendment to safeguard the rights of children born of interracial marriages.

Another brilliant black politician was P. B. S. Pinchback, who held more political offices than any other black man, and who served in Louisiana as lieutenant governor, acting governor, Congressman-elect, and Senator-elect. He arrived in Washington, D.C., in January 1873, but the Senate refused to seat him. There were reports that the Senators' wives did not want to associate with Mrs. Pinchback. Pinchback was a strikingly handsome brown-skinned man with sharp Arabian features whom white women found attractive. After wrestling with his case for three years, the Senate rejected Pinchback's claim to the Senate seat, and he returned to Louisiana.

While black men were being elected to Congress, to high state posts, and to an occasional local elective office (in 1870, Robert H. Wood was elected mayor of Natchez, Miss.), white Southerners were organizing massive resistance campaigns. It was during these years that the Ku Klux Klan began an effort to intimidate negroes from voting and running for elective office. Not only were intimidation and force used against blacks, but business and social ostracism were used against whites who would not line up solidly against negroes in government. In Louisiana, the Democratic conservatives formed "White Leagues," ordered arms, and actually fought a pitched battle in New Orleans in which forty were killed and over a hundred were wounded. Had it not been for the presence of Federal troops, the government of Louisiana would have fallen to white racists.

This is the most important fact of the Reconstruction era which sent black men to Congress and to the various state assemblies: the tranquilizing presence of Federal troops. They kept law and order and protected the black man.

Then, in 1876, a man decided he wanted so desperately to be President that he was willing to scuttle democracy for it.

The Presidential contest between the Republican Ohio Governor Rutherford B. Hayes and the Democrat Samuel J. Tilden ended in a deadlock because of disputed elections in South Carolina, Louisiana, and Florida where mixed radical governments and all-white Conservative governments had both been elected and each claimed to be the legitimate government.

Because of the deadlock, the decision was to be resolved by the House of Representatives. Hayes claimed the disputed states of South Carolina, Louisiana, and Florida. But the representatives of those three states, acting in concert with other Southern representatives, were demanding a higher price for their votes than just the comfort of knowing they were responsible for the election of a President. They asked for a guarantee from Hayes that he would withdraw Federal troops from the South and uphold the principle of States Rights—i.e., that he would let the South handle the negro problem in its own way. Hayes's representatives in the negotiations agreed. An agreement was finally worked out on February 26, 1877, whereby Hayes's representatives handed the Southern representatives a note which read:

Gentlemen:
Referring to the conversation had with you yesterday in which Governor Hayes's policy as to the status of certain Southern states was discussed, we desire to say in reply that we can assure you in the strongest possible manner of our great desire to have adopted such a policy as will give to the people of the States of South Carolina and Louisiana the right to control their own affairs in their own way and to say further that we feel authorized, from an acquaintance with knowledge of Governor Hayes and his views on this question, to pledge ourselves to you that such will be his policy.

This paved the way for the Electoral Commission, composed of five Senators, five Supreme Court Justices, and five Congressmen, to vote on the disputed election, and they did—strictly along party lines, eight to seven. On March 2, 1877, Hayes had won by one electoral vote.

Not necessarily a racist, but a man of honor, Hayes kept his word and pulled the Federal troops out of the South. It was now "open season on niggers."

Southern states moved swiftly to wipe out all the political advances made by negroes. Several methods were devised to keep negroes from voting:

Polling places were set up at points remote from Negro communities. Ferries between black districts and political headquarters went "out of repair" at election time. . . . Without notice to the Negroes, the location of polling places might change, or the Negroes be told of a change which was then not carried out. The stuffing of ballot boxes and the manipulation of the count developed into fine arts.*

Backing up these various extralegal machinations were incredibly savage acts of white brutality against negroes attempting to vote or register as voters.

But Southern white leaders refused to concede publicly that they needed to rely on violence to preserve political white supremacy in the South. "It is on this, sir, that we rely in the South. Not the cowardly menace of mask or shotgun; but the peaceful majesty of intelligence and responsibility, massed and unified for the protection of its homes and the preservation of its liberties," declared Henry W. Grady, one of the South's foremost apologists for white racism, in a speech to the Boston Merchants Association in 1889.

This "peaceful majesty of intelligence" to accomplish black disenfranchisement was twisted into ingenious exercises in officially approved frauds. One of the most complicated was South Carolina's "eight-ballot-box" election law of 1882, which required a special ballot box in every voting place for each office to be filled. The boxes were properly labeled, and election workers would read the titles when requested, but no one was permitted to speak to the voter or insert his ballot for him. So, if a ballot went into the wrong box, it was not counted. This gimmick was aimed particularly at the large number of illiterate negroes, but thousands of illiterate whites were also disenfranchised.

Meanwhile, a poor whites' agrarian revolution was taking place in the South. Its greatest number of election victories took place in 1890. But the movement collapsed in 1896, and the issue of "political niggerism" was resurrected to reunite the divided South.

The one issue on which all white men could agree was disenfranchising the negro. The Southern states began to pass disenfranchising codes: poll taxes; the famed "grandfather clauses" (which ordained for the benefit of poor whites that permanent registrations were permitted for persons who had been able to vote prior to 1861 and for their descendants and for persons who had served in the Federal or Confederate armies or in the state militias and their descendants); and naked terriorism, by far the most successful of all devices. Those negroes who did manage to survive the gamut of white obstacles to registering and voting were threatened with reprisals, fired from their jobs, intimidated on the streets, beaten at night by Ku Klux Klan night-riders, lynched, murdered, their families abused, and their houses burned to the ground. For a black man living in the South to attempt to register to

* Lewinson, *Race, Class and Party*, p. 64.

vote was tantamount to a Jew living in Nazi Germany to try to live a normal life.

So successful was this organized conspiracy of massive Southern white power that within a few years, most negro voters were purged from the registration lists in all of the Southern states.

For the 1896 national election, the last before the disenfranchising code, there were registered in the State [of Louisiana] 130,344 Negroes; Negro registrants were in the majority in 26 parishes. For the 1900 national election, two years after the adoption of the new constitution, there were registered only 5320 Negroes, and no parishes showed a majority of Negro registrants.*

What happened in Louisiana was repeated throughout the Southern states, in some with more malice than in others. But all passed disenfranchising constitutions relegating the negro to the status of a noncitizen. A new era began, which Henry Lee Moon called "The Great Blackout." Negroes as voters, negroes as politicians were to become the political freaks of American society.

Black political power was to become nonexistent from 1890 to the 1940's. The vast majority of negroes lived in the South, and their effective disenfranchisement, for all intents and purposes, demolished any potential political power the negro might have had. In 1900, for example, about 90 per cent of America's negroes—7,922,969—lived in the South, while the other 10 per cent—911,025—were scattered throughout the North, Midwest, and West.

The only political power negroes were able to claim during these years was gratuitous Federal appointments in jobs reserved for negroes. One of the first such appointments occurred on April 16, 1869, when President Grant appointed Ebenezer Don Carlos Bassett as Minister Resident and Consul General to Haiti. He was the first negro to receive a diplomatic post. In 1877, Frederick Douglass was appointed a police commissioner by Grant, and, later in that year, Marshal of the District of Columbia by President Hayes. In 1880, former Mississippi Senator Bruce, the second negro to serve in the U.S. Senate, was appointed Register of the U.S. Treasury by President Garfield, and, in 1881, Garfield made Douglass Recorder of Deeds of the District of Columbia, a post that was to become almost the exclusive property of negroes. (It was a safe appointment. Negroes would be concerned with documents and archives and would have little time to be involved with the contemporary problems of their society.)

If, in 1967, the worst problem black people have is the overabundance of powerless national "negro leaders" who are regarded by white people as spokesmen (Whitney Young, Roy Wilkins, Bayard Rustin, etc.), this problem did not exist during and after the Civil War. There was a vacuum of negro leadership and an absence of black pride among negroes. Perhaps

* Lewinson, *Race, Class and Party*, p. 81.

the most effective, the most brilliant, and certainly one of the most militant black spokesmen negroes had was Frederick Douglass, the father of the protest movement. Douglass' eloquent oratory, moving prose, and his constant organized activity on behalf of the enslaved black man made him a national figure. "I supposed myself to have been born in February 1817," he wrote in his autobiography, *Narrative*, in Talbot County, near Easton, in Maryland. "I hardly became a thinking thing when I first learned to hate slavery."

Douglass' mother was a slave and his father a white man.

Self-educated, he was soon employed as an agent of the Massachusetts Anti-Slavery Society. He toured the country speaking publicly against slavery, and his booming voice and dynamic personality left an ineradicable impression on white audiences.

In an era when the safest approach was to be an "Uncle Tom" or even not to speak out at all, Douglass was an uncompromising fighter. In today's boiling racial cauldron, he more than likely would have been a member of the Student Nonviolent Coordinating Committee rather than the Urban League. His famous Fourth of July speech, made in Rochester in 1852, has been quoted many times.

What to the American slave is your 4th of July? I answer: a day that reveals to him, more than all other days in the year, the gross injustice and cruelty to which he is the constant victim. To him, your celebration is a sham; your boasted liberty, an unholy license; your national greatness, swelling vanity; your sounds of rejoicing are empty and heartless; your denunciation of tyrants, brass fronted impudence; your shouts of liberty and equality, hollow mockery; your prayers and hymns, your sermons and thanksgivings, with all your religious parade and solemnity, are to him, mere bombast, fraud, deception, impiety, and hypocrisy—a thin veil to cover up crimes which would disgrace a nation of savages.

. . . You shed tears over fallen Hungary, and make the sad story of her wrongs the theme of your poets, statesmen, and orators, till your gallant sons are ready to fly to arms to vindicate her cause against the oppressor; but in regard to the ten thousand wrongs of the American slave, you would enforce the strictest silence, and would hail him as an enemy of the nation who dares to make these wrongs the subject of public discourse.

The timidity of many of today's black leaders can best be measured by the fact that very few would dare utter such militant thoughts.

Although there were other negro leaders active in the black rebellions of those days—Sojourner Truth, Harriet Tubman, Nat Turner, Denmark Vesey, and Gabriel Prosser—none of them were politicians. None of them were elected officials controlling the apparatus of government. Even the few black men in Congress were not able to develop a national black consciousness or a posture of national leadership, if for no other reason than black people were not ready for a national black political leader. With exceptions such as Nat Turner, Harriet Tubman, Sojourner 'Truth, and Frederick Douglass, the negro leaders of their time were passive, meek, and exceedingly solicitous of the white man's approbation.

There was another revolution taking place in America at the same time the political pogrom to decertify black citizens was achieving its goals, the Industrial Revolution. It, however, was a revolution that was going to bring the good life to white, not black Americans. It was a revolution that would attract millions of immigrants from Europe to this country to develop wealth, security, and fame while black people stood still and marked time in the backyards of their segregated hovels.

As the table below indicates, European immigration slowly diminished the proportion of negroes in the population from 14.1 per cent in 1860 to 9.9 per cent in 1920. The waves of Irish, Italians, Poles, Russian Jews, Scandinavians, and Germans seeking the good life heavily increased the white population.

YEAR	U.S. POPULATION	NEGRO POPULATION	PERCENTAGE
1790	3,929,214	757,208	19.3
1800	5,308,483	1,002,037	18.9
1810	7,239,881	1,377,808	19.0
1820	9,638,453	1,771,656	18.4
1830	12,866,020	2,328,642	18.1
1840	17,069,453	2,874,000	16.8
1850	23,191,876	3,638,808	15.7
1860	31,443,790	4,441,830	14.1
1870	39,818,449	4,880,009	12.7
1880	50,155,783	6,580,793	13.1
1890	62,947,714	7,488,676	11.9
1900	75,994,575	8,833,994	11.6
1910	93,402,151	9,827,763	10.7
1920	105,710,620	10,463,131	9.9
1930	122,775,046	11,891,143	9.7
1940	131,669,275	12,865,518	9.8
1950	150,697,361	15,042,286	10.0
1960	179,323,175	18,171,831	10.5

As the South became industrialized, negroes found few employment opportunities. There was almost no work to be had in the textile mills, and work in the iron foundries and furniture factories was limited to the least desirable jobs. On the farms, they could either work for white planters for subsistence wages or engage in one of several forms of farm tenancy from which the year's labor yielded a bare existence.

Negroes slowly began the great migration northward in search of better opportunities at the same time as Europeans were immigrating to America for the same purpose. World War I accelerated the movement of negroes to Northern cities. Gunnar Myrdal states in *An American Dilemma* that to biggest job gains for negroes did not occur during the New Deal, as so many historians have written, but during this period. "This should be emphasized: large employment gains for Negroes in the North—except for the present war boom—occurred only during the short period from the First World War until the end of the 'twenties.'"*

As negroes crowded into the Northern cities—New York, Chicago, Detroit, Philadelphia—they acquired smatterings of political consciousness. There were occasional breakthroughs during these years for limited political power.

One of the most astute black politicians of all time came into power during the 1920's. He was Robert R. Church, a wealthy Memphis businessman who managed to maintain his place on Tennessee's Republican State Committee in the face of the "lily-white movement" of the Republican Party. Negroes credited Church with a series of appointments of negroes to Federal office, various acts of charity (he donated a public park in the middle of valuable urban property in Memphis), and, "perhaps most important of all, with invincible political cleverness." One of the vicious white racists of his time, Alabama Senator Heflin, paid unintended tribute to Church in the guise of an antinegro poem read during U.S. Senate investigations of patronage:

> Offices up a 'simmon tree,
> Bob Church on de ground;
> Bob Church said to de 'pointing power
> "Shake dem 'pointments down."**

Church understood the quid pro quo of politics and for years worked closely with Democratic boss Edward Crump by delivering the negro vote to Crump in exchange for patronage. Church was the black Frank Hague or Tom Pendergast of his day. There were others—Ferdinand Q. Morton of New York City, Oscar S. DePriest of Chicago (who as the sovereign of Chicago's black South Side was to be followed by William L. Dawson), and Texas' Norris Wright Cuney (who coined the phrase "lily-white").

It was sparse pickings for black politicians. Republicans were busy trying to divest black people of the independence that Lincoln had decreed for them. Naturally, most negroes voted Republican. From such political fidelity they expected a small amount of patronage that Republicans were not prepared to award to them. In the South, the Republican Party took steps to purge its negro state committeemen in an effort to keep pace with the Democrats, whose all-white credentials were above segregationist reproach.

By the time Woodrow Wilson was elected President in 1912, the negro was the nation's forgotten man. In the previous year, 1911, a national con-

* Gunnar Myrdal, An American Dilemma (New York: Harper & Brothers, 1944), p. 295.
** Lewinson, Race, Class and Party, p. 139.

vention of negro Democrats in Indianapolis "urged colored voters of the United States to note the conditions surrounding them, to cease following any one party to their detriment, and thus divide their votes." It was the hope of these negro Democrats that negro voters would begin to move away from the Republican Party, for it had begun to treat them as shabbily as the Democratic Party, which had never sought their electoral support. When Wilson won with a minority of the popular vote (Roosevelt, 4,216,-020; Taft, 3,483,922; and Wilson, 6,286,214), some negroes exulted in the thought that their votes had been of significance. They expected both an increase in Federal appointments and action at the executive level to end discrimination in some governmental departments. Their joy was short-lived. Wilson actually did less for negroes than some of his Republican predecessors. His was a racist administration.

The impoverishment of negro political power is best reflected by the national negro leadership of the early twentieth century. After Douglass, there seemed to be no national spokesman to whom whites could turn to find out what the negro was thinking. But in 1896, they found one who would gladden their hearts. In his famous "Atlanta Compromise" speech at the Atlanta Exposition that year, Booker T. Washington, an educator who had founded the Tuskegee Institute, called for negroes to "drop your buckets where you are," return to the soil, become skilled tradesmen, and lead lives separate and apart from white people. Washington was such a devout Uncle Tom that he even advocated "the protection of the ballot . . . for a while at least, either by an educational test, a property test, or by both combined."

Washington quickly became *the* national negro spokesman, and he said precisely what America's whites wanted to hear and believe. Washington's brand of head-scratching, shoe-shuffling accommodation to segregation angered the more militant negro leaders, such as W. E. B. Du Bois. It was to meet the challenge of Washington's political subservience that the Niagara Movement, which led to the founding of the NAACP, was born.

Negroes were becoming politically involved in some Northern cities. Negro candidates occasionally challenged white aldermen and white Congressmen in the heavily negro districts in St. Louis, New York City, Chicago, Philadelphia, and Cleveland. Most of them failed. One who succeeded was Oscar S. DePriest, a wily back-room manipulator with a fiery personality who played the game of politics as shrewdly as the white man. He was successively elected Chicago's first negro alderman and then first negro Congressman, in 1929. A Republican, DePriest was the first negro Congressman since 1901. He became an immediate national hero to negroes, but because of the taint of the corrupt "Big Bill" Thompson machine, which had elected DePriest, most white-controlled "respectable" negro leaders shied away from him. DePriest's notable achievement was ignored by the

NAACP, which awarded its Spingarn Medal that year to Mordecai W. Johnson, who was cited for his "successful administration of Howard University."

DePriest served in Congress for six years and then was defeated by a negro Democrat, Arthur W. Mitchell, who served for eight years.

The circumstances of the elections of other negro Congressmen are discussed in Chapters Ten and Twelve. A summary of their terms of service, as of 1967, follows:

NAME	STATE	YEARS
1. Oscar S. DePriest	Illinois	1929–35
2. Arthur W. Mitchell	Illinois	1935–43
3. William L. Dawson	Illinois	1943–66*
4. Adam Clayton Powell	New York	1945–66**
5. Charles C. Diggs, Jr.	Michigan	1955–66*
6. Robert N. C. Nix, Jr.	Pennsylvania	1959–66*
7. Augustus Hawkins	California	1961–66*
8. John Conyers, Jr.	Michigan	1965–66*

* Elected in 1966 to the Ninetieth Congress.
** Elected to the Ninetieth Congress, but excluded on March 1, 1967.

The election of negro Congressmen represented the only tangible evidence of black political power at the national level, and the small number constitutes an indictment of the black man's political acumen. Despite occasional negro Federal appointments, an occasional negro alderman or city councilman, a judge or a member of the board of education, negroes were never able to gain the kind of political power the Irish, the Italians, the Jews, and the Poles had acquired in a comparatively short time.

Meanwhile, the negro continued to make almost no economic or political progress. Lynchings in the South, racial segregation in public accommodations and the public schools, tacit "gentlemen's agreements" between Northern real-estate brokers created and maintained ghettos as severely restricted as any in South Africa.

In 1947, President Truman appointed a Committee on Civil Rights, and it issued a report called "To Secure These Rights." This was a documented account of the deprivations negroes suffered in housing, employment, and education. A rate of unemployment two and one-half times that of whites and total segregation in the public schools of the South were two of the factors the report listed as most detrimental to negro equality. Taking its cue from this report, in 1952 the NAACP filed suit in a Federal court to desegregate the public schools of the South. Few expected the U.S. Supreme Court to rule overwhelmingly in the NAACP's favor, but it did—unanimously—on May 17, 1954, declaring that "separate but equal" public schools were unconstitutional.

The first phase of the Negro Revolution, the litigative phase, was thus inadvertently launched. It was to be quickly followed by four successive stages: the sit-in phase beginning in Greensboro, N.C., on February 1, 1960; the massive demonstrations phase, beginning in April 1963 in Birmingham, Ala., and culminating in the August 1963 "March on Washington"; the insurrectionist or rebellion phase beginning in the summer of 1964 in Harlem and Bedford-Stuyvesant, N.Y., and spreading to Watts, Los Angeles, in the summer of 1965; and finally the black power phase, beginning in the summer of 1966 in Greenville, Miss.

During each phase, black political sensitivities were heightened and the rumblings of an aroused black political machine were heard in cities across the country.

CHAPTER FOUR

The Negro Vote:
Ceteris Paribus

Many wise men hold that the white vote of the South should divide, the color line be beaten down, and the Southern states ranged on economic or moral questions as interest or belief demands.

I am compelled to dissent from this view. The worst thing that could happen, in my opinion, is that the white people of the South should stand in opposing factions, with the vast mass of ignorant or purchasable Negro votes between.

Consider such a status. If the Negroes were skillfully led—and leaders would not be lacking—it would give them the balance of power.

—HENRY WOODFIN GRADY,
prominent Southern journalist
and orator, 1886

The historical paranoia of Southern whites about a black voting bloc rising like a Phoenix from the ashes of white oppression to become the decisive balance in all elections was a subconscious recognition that white brutality might one day ignite black retaliation.

The only reason blacks would be compelled to act or vote as an ethnic bloc would be to respond to a corresponding pattern of white behavior. It had never occurred to most whites—although a few did peer beneath the hypocrisy of their self-declared supremacy—that negroes would lose their sense of ethnocentricity only as they moved out of the maelstrom of slavery into the mainstream of democracy.

Instead the South, tormented by the constant threat of a black electoral juggernaut lurking in white backyards ready to crush white supremacy, chose to build a caste wall between the two races. The great irony of Southern history is that the black vote as a balance of power—with the one or two exceptions already noted—never became a serious threat to white unity and its attendant ethic of white supremacy. It was in the North that the black vote was to gain strength in electoral power politics.

While white Southern politicians fretted over the threat of the black vote as the difference between victory and defeat, Northern politicians joyfully realized it could be controlled. To the Northern political machines, the black vote was purchasable as a reliable and dependable guarantee of victory. It was to be sought after, cherished, and coddled. If treated properly, it would return its electoral affections with unthinking devotion. If carefully trained, it would not desert its masters in some whimsical exercise of political independence, but would allow itself to be trotted out on election day like a dog on a leash, vote as it was paid to vote, and then be hustled back to its comfortably furnished outhouse to await the next election. And the black vote followed this course with astonishing predictability.

Because of its controlled habits, the black vote can expect to be nothing more than an occasional and minimal influence in national, state, and local elections. For the negro vote to become a true balance of power, perpetually to be reckoned with, the element of *ceteris paribus*—all other things being equal—must be a precondition.

All other things being equal contains three factors:

1) Black political cohesion—a bloc vote.

2) A two-way split of the white vote—obviously, a preponderantly unified white vote will always defeat a preponderantly black vote, unless blacks are in the majority.

3) The political oscillation of fragile loyalties—the negro vote has to swing back and forth periodically between the two parties, shifting its loyalties with the same frequency as the white vote.

The third factor is the most important because once the negro vote is taken for granted—as it has been nationally since the New Deal—it loses its bargaining power. In politics, the predictable votes are never rewarded as abundantly as the uncontrollable groups who are ready to change their affiliation.

As I shall discuss in this chapter, owing to the absence of all three factors, *ceteris paribus*, in national, state, and local elections of the last twenty years, the negro vote has been considered more a loyal ally than a neutral balance of power by white party bosses. This is the principal reason that negro political power has not been accorded its share of the political spoils. The fact that blacks have not been able to translate their vaunted balance of power at the polls into jobs after an election seriously calls into question the loyal-ally concept.

Power is power only when it is exercised. Power does not exist in a vacuum, nor can it remain unrelated to political needs and aspirations. In world affairs, a nation that holds the balance of power is rewarded concretely with the protection of one or both of its neighboring enemies or with some form of technical, financial, economic, or military assistance. Power can be measured, and the effects of its application can be quantified.

Consequently, when the concept of the balance of power is applied to the black vote, an ancillary question must thus be raised: what have negroes gotten in political rewards for holding the balance of power? The answer is: virtually nothing, considering their proportion in the population and the crucial proportion their votes made between victory and defeat. It is, therefore, not completely accurate to conceptualize the negro vote as holding the balance of power—at least not in today's world of negro political weakness.

Black politicians and writers have understandably sought to aggrandize black electoral power.* Writers and politicians reasoned that if they could convince the white political bosses of the vote's size, its fragile political loyalties, and its capacity for retribution, the black community would be awarded more patronage and assigned a larger percentage of policy-making and job-dispensing positions.

Instead, just the opposite has been true of the black vote. It has always been: 1) smaller than the comparable proportion of the negro population as well as of the total vote; 2) unerringly loyal to one party; and 3) too unsophisticated to punish or defeat prechosen white carry-overs who have long ceased to serve black interests. Only when these political misfits were openly antagonistic to the black community has the vote addressed itself to their retirement.

The black vote as a national balance of power was first comprehensively described by Henry Lee Moon, in his book *Balance of Power: The Negro Vote*, published in 1948, just before that year's Presidential election.** In this penetrating and scholarly analysis of the negro vote as a newly matured political force, Moon traces the vote's emergence from its chained nonexistence in the post-Reconstruction period to its curried omnipresence in the 1948 Presidential election. Because Moon was the first political writer to set down with precision the historical and political factors responsible for the negro vote as a balance of power in national elections, both his theory and its supporting array of facts deserve a separate critique.

According to Moon, the "maximum negro voting strength" as of 1948 was 7,250,000 negroes—all negroes over twenty-one years of age as counted by the U.S. Census. With a total U.S. population of 91,600,000 citizens

---

* During his editorship of negro newspapers in Chicago, New York City, and Washington, D.C., this author was equally guilty.
** Garden City, N.Y., Doubleday & Co.

over twenty-one years of age, negroes comprised a maximum potential of only 7 per cent of a projected national vote.

The number of potential voters, however, is usually smaller than the number of registered voters or of those who finally vote on election day. In 1940, as Moon indicates, there was a total vote turnout of only 49,815,000, or 54 per cent of Americans eligible to vote. In 1942, an off year, the percentage dropped to 32 per cent, or 29,441,000 votes. In 1944, a Presidential-election year, the size rose sharply to 52 per cent, then dropped again in 1946 to 38 per cent, or 35,000,000 votes.

As of 1948, two-thirds of the potential negro voters still lived in the South. By Moon's count, there were 750,000 qualified negro voters in the Southern states. He anticipated that more than one million negroes would be qualified to vote, indicating a possible total of 3,500,000 negro voters in 1948.

In contrast to their Southern brothers, black people were able to register in the major Northern cities with little difficulty. They slowly became serious repositories of political strength in the states of New York, Pennsylvania, New Jersey, Ohio, Indiana, Michigan, Illinois, and Missouri. This apparently explains why Moon hailed the importance of the negro vote in the 1944 elections:

. . . without it, Franklin D. Roosevelt could hardly have been elected—it can, with wise and independent leadership, be even more important in the 1948 elections.

. . . This vote is more decisive in presidential elections than that of the Solid South. In sixteen states with a total of 278 votes in the electoral college, the Negro, in a close election, may hold the balance of power; *that is, in an election in which the non-Negro vote is about evenly divided.*[*]

Moon then explains why he believes Roosevelt's 1944 victory was primarily the result of the negro's balance-of-power vote:

In the 1944 elections there were twenty-eight states in which a shift of 5 per cent or less of the popular vote would have reversed the electoral votes cast by these states. In twelve of these, with a total of 228 electoral college votes, the potential Negro vote exceeds the number required to shift the states from one column to the other. Two of these marginal states—Ohio with 25 votes and Indiana with 13—went Republican. The ten remaining states—New York, New Jersey, Pennsylvania, Illinois, Michigan, Missouri, Delaware, Maryland, West Virginia and Kentucky—gave to Mr. Roosevelt 190 electoral college votes essential to his victory. The closeness of the popular vote in the marginal states accented the decisive potential of the Negro's ballot.[**]

Concerning the role of the black vote in Congressional elections, Moon believed that "an alert, well-organized Negro electorate can be an effective

[*] Moon, p. 10.
[**] Moon, p.198.

factor in at least seventy-five congressional districts in eighteen northern and border states."

Although there is a paucity of specific examples supported by actual voting statistics in negro precincts to fully authenticate the balance-of-power theory, Moon nevertheless is on solid ground in his contention, if for no other reason than that both Roosevelt and his closest political advisers were convinced the negro vote would be a key factor in his re-election. Accordingly, the black political community was wooed and caressed in 1944. The CIO-PAC which played a leading role in organizing the labor, negro, and urban vote devoted special attention to negro precincts.

According to Moon, their efforts were rewarded by a loyal Democratic negro vote. Although the statistics Moon uses are not so conclusive as some that he uses to validate his balance-of-power theory in other elections, his analysis does merit consideration:

A post-election analysis by Herbert Brownell, Jr., chairman of the Republican National Committee, claimed that "a shift of 303,414 votes in fifteen states outside of the South would have enabled Governor Thomas E. Dewey to capture 175 additional electoral votes and to win the presidency with an eight electoral-vote margin." In at least eight of the fifteen states listed by Brownell, the Negro vote exceeded the number needed to shift in order to place them in the Republican column. In Maryland the 50,000 votes which Negro citizens in Baltimore alone cast for F.D.R. were more than double his 22,500 state plurality. Negro voters of five New Jersey cities gave the President a total of 28,780 votes to assure him a winning margin of 26,540. Michigan, which Roosevelt lost in 1940 by the narrow margin of 6,926, was carried by 22,500 with the colored citizens of Detroit casting 41,740 votes for him. Negro voters in Kansas City and St. Louis accounted for 34,900 of the President's margin of 46,180 in Missouri. In Chicago, 121,650 voters in predominantly Negro districts contributed to the 140,165 margin by which the President carried the state of Illinois. The black belts of New York City and Buffalo accounted for 188,760 Roosevelt votes or more than half of his state plurality of 316,000. The combined American Labor and Liberal party tickets for which many Negroes voted gave the President a total of 825,640, enough to overcome the Republican lead over the Democratic slate and hold New York's 47 electoral votes. The President carried Pennsylvania by 105,425 votes, to which Negro votes in Pittsburgh and Philadelphia contributed no less than 52,000. These seven states account for 168 votes in the electoral college and were essential to the Roosevelt victory. In addition, Negro votes contributed substantially to the Roosevelt lead in West Virginia, Kentucky and Delaware.*

It should be noted that Moon uses the word "contributed" in discussing the role of the black vote in this analysis. To be an effective balance of power in any election, a vote does not contribute to the outcome, it *decides* the outcome. This, Moon is unable to substantiate by use of the above figures.

The one critical omission Moon makes in this analysis of the negro vote as the balance of power in Roosevelt's 1944 victory is the failure to compare

* Moon, pp. 35-36.

the proportion of the white vote with that of the negro vote that went to Roosevelt. For example, unless the white vote was split almost evenly and the negro vote was fairly solid (70 to 80 per cent) for Roosevelt, the negro vote cannot be viewed as a balance of power. It does little good to cite the number of negro votes in a city or state for Roosevelt unless the total number of negro votes is also cited, determining what percentage of the negro vote Roosevelt won to guarantee him victory. Thus, if the figures cited by Moon represent a heavy majority of the negro vote, then that vote can indeed be accorded a significant share of credit for Roosevelt's victory.

It must always be remembered, however, that the white vote must *first* split if the negro vote is to be considered a balance of power. This did not happen in 1948. It did in 1960. Truman defeated Dewey, 24,179,345 to 21,991,291, while J. Strom Thurmond, the States Rights candidate, polled 1,176,125 votes and Henry A. Wallace, the Progressive Party candidate, polled 1,157,326 votes. But in 1960, Kennedy, as will be shown later in this chapter, defeated Nixon by only 112,827 votes. The white vote was split almost equally in 1960. It was not in 1948.

Republicans can count just as well as Democrats. It is significant that Brownell did not attribute Dewey's loss to the Republicans' failure to win the negro vote in 1948, but Thruston Morton, the Republican National Committee Chairman in 1960, did.

Moon does cite one off-year Congressional election in which the negro vote was measurably decisive. In 1946, the Kansas City Pendergast machine decided to retire Fifth Congressional District Representative Roger C. Slaughter for his unshakable conservatism and opposition to President Truman's liberal legislation. As a key member of the House Rules Committee, the "traffic cop" of House legislation, Slaughter had arrogantly boasted: "I sure as hell opposed the bill for a Fair Employment Practices Commission, and I'm proud of the fact that my vote [in the Rules Committee] was what killed it."*

Although black people comprised 15 per cent of the potential total electorate in Slaughter's district, he apparently did not believe that they were in any way responsible for his 5193-vote margin in the 1944 elections. Moon describes what happened in the 1946 Democratic primary:

In the next election he was defeated by a margin of 2783, with 7000 Negro votes cast against him. His vote in the thirty predominantly Negro precincts was negligible. In two of these precincts he received not a single vote, and the highest was 35. This solid Negro vote was the decisive factor in the defeat of Slaughter.**

A similar classic example of the negro vote as a balance of power in a

* Moon, p. 51.
** Moon, p. 51.

local election occurred in Atlanta's 1961 mayoralty race. A racial moderate, businessman Ivan Allen, Jr., defeated staunch segregationist Lester Maddox by a vote of 64,000 to 36,000. The white vote divided almost equally, with segregationist Maddox garnering a slight majority of Atlanta's white votes. An estimated 36,000 white votes were won by Maddox compared to Allen's estimated 33,000 white votes.

The black vote proved to be decisive for Allen's victory. Of the estimated 31,000 votes cast by negroes, according to an analysis of the negro weekly newspaper, *The Atlanta Inquirer*, only 179 negro votes were cast for Maddox.

Ceteris paribus, the negro vote in Atlanta in 1961 was the balance of power in deciding the outcome in favor of Mr. Allen—a passionately united negro vote and a schizophrenically divided white vote.

The 1960 and 1964 Presidential Elections

Just as it was possible to measure fairly accurately the black vote's major role in defeating Kansas City Congressman Slaughter in 1946 and Atlanta's apostle of apartheid, Maddox, in 1961, the 1960 Presidential election offered the first unchallengeable evidence of the black vote's decisive effectiveness as the balance of power in a national election. On the other hand, the 1964 Presidential election proved how totally ineffective the black vote as a balance of power could be when the element of *ceteris paribus* is missing.

In 1960, after John Fitzgerald Kennedy announced his candidacy for the Presidency, there were some uneasy feelings in the negro community. For one thing, the young Massachusetts Senator was an unknown quantity with regard to civil rights. He was no bigot, but he was no advertised friend of racial equality. For another, he had breakfasted with Alabama Governor Patterson in what appeared to be open courtship of the white Southern vote.

As a result, the Kennedy campaign failed to excite any real enthusiasm among black people. Furthermore, negro voters had begun to augment a political shift that took place in 1952. In that year, when 57 per cent of the white electorate voted for the Republican, Eisenhower, only 21 per cent of the black electorate did.

But by 1956 the negro electorate, unquestionably influenced by the U.S. Supreme Court's unanimous 1954 decision outlawing racial segregation in public schools and by the belief that the Eisenhower-appointed Chief Justice, Earl Warren, had played a decisive role in the decision, deepened its affection for the Republican Party. The estimated 1956 negro vote for the Republicans was 39 per cent, the highest for a Republican Presidential candidate in twenty years.

In 1960, there was no reason for black people to be suspicious of Nixon as an anti-civil-rights candidate. In fact, Nixon's backers spread the word that he had been one of the civil-rights proponents in the Eisenhower administration. If the country seemed unable to make up its mind as the campaign progressed, negroes were equally irresolute until Kennedy made one of the most famous and critically decisive telephone calls in political history. On Wednesday, October 26, 1960, he called Mrs. Martin Luther King, Jr., to express his deep concern about a four-month prison sentence meted out to her husband in Georgia on a technical charge of not possessing a driver's license. No other important political figure had publicly expressed any dismay at this latest miscarriage of white Southern justice, and Kennedy's call to Mrs. King electrified the black community.

Word of the telephone call swept the Negro community. King's father, the Reverend Martin Luther King, Sr., who had earlier endorsed Nixon—some suspected because of an entrenched Southern Baptist lack of affection for Catholicism—quickly changed political horses. "Because this man was willing to wipe the tears from my daughter's eye, I've got a suitcase of votes and I'm going to take them to Mr. Kennedy and dump them in his lap," he declared. Kennedy's phone call broke the ice. He was now the negro's friend. Other Baptist ministers followed the Reverend King's endorsement, and the negro vote was no longer in doubt.

While Kennedy's wafer-thin margin of victory over Nixon was attributed to many factors, few political observers could disagree that the 112,827-vote margin out of a total 68,770,294 votes was due to the negro vote.

Estimates of Kennedy's share of the national negro vote range from the Gallup Poll's estimated 68 per cent to this author's estimated 77 per cent to that of several political experts whose calculations went as high as 80 per cent.

Because of this wide discrepancy, it might be instructive to re-examine the negro vote in several of the nation's largest cities. According to a more detailed analysis of specific negro precincts reported in a November 21, 1960, issue of *U.S. News & World Report*, this is a cross-section of the Negro vote for Kennedy:

CITY	BASE	PER CENT OF VOTE
Chicago	4 wards	77.7
Cleveland	10 wards	77.5
Detroit	4 wards	89.9
Gary	36 precincts	81.9
Los Angeles	5 precincts	86.6
New York City	4 districts	76.3
Philadelphia	20 divisions	77.1

Using those very same figures in conjunction with a more comprehensive analysis, the *New York Times* concluded that "Nationwide . . . close to 80 per cent of the Negro voters cast their ballots for [Kennedy]."

When one remembers that New York City, Los Angeles, Chicago, Philadelphia, Detroit, and Cleveland are respectively the country's first, second, third, fourth, fifth, and eleventh largest cities and that they had a total 1960 black population of 3,671,500, or one-fifth of the nation's negroes, then the voting percentages for Kennedy in those cities are far more persuasive than Mr. Gallup's ubiquitous polls.

Whatever the exact percentage of the negro vote for Kennedy in 1960, it was his insurance of victory. Rarely mentioned by any of the postelection analysts was the fact that Nixon actually won the white vote while Kennedy won the black vote and the Presidency of the United States. Theodore H. White, in his comprehensive *The Making of the President 1960*, assigned significant credit to the relationship between the Kennedy telephone call to Mrs. King and the negro vote's responsibility for Kennedy's victory.

One cannot identify in the narrowness of American voting in 1960 any one particular episode or decision as being more important than any other in the final tallies: yet when one reflects that Illinois was carried by only 9,000 votes and that 250,000 Negroes are estimated to have voted for Kennedy; that Michigan was carried by 67,000 votes and that an estimated 250,000 Negroes voted for Kennedy, that South Carolina was carried by 10,000 votes and that an estimated 40,000 Negroes there voted for Kennedy, the candidate's instinctive decision must be ranked among the crucial of the last few weeks.*

The electoral college votes of those three states—Illinois, twenty-seven; Michigan, twenty; and South Carolina, eight—totaled fifty-five. Subtracting those fifty-five votes from Kennedy's electoral-college vote total of 303 and adding them to Nixon's 219 reverses the outcome in favor of Nixon, 274 to 248. A small shift in the negro vote to Nixon in those three states alone would have given Nixon the Presidency with five more than the required 269 electoral college votes. What White does not point out, however, is that the negro vote was larger than the total Democratic majority not only in those three states, but also in the four states of Mississippi (eight electoral-college votes), New Jersey (sixteen), Pennsylania (thirty-two), and Texas (twenty-four). For example, Kennedy won Texas, where an estimated 100,-000 black people voted for him, by only 46,233 votes.

The day after the 1960 election, Thruston Morton, Republican Senator from Kentucky and Chairman of the Republican National Committee at that time, said in a television interview that it was obvious that the Re-

* Theodore H. White, *The Making of the President 1960* (New York: Atheneum, 1961), p. 323.

publicans' loss of the negro vote played a major role in Nixon's defeat.

In 1960, the element of *ceteris paribus* was operative in the negro vote's decisive role as the balance of power. Black political cohesion was reflected by the more than 70 per cent of the national negro vote for Kennedy. The equal split of the white vote was indicated by the difference between the winning and losing percentages of 49.7 and 49.5. The possibility that the negro vote might complete its defection to the Republican Party, already underway in the 1956 Presidential election, was neutralized by Kennedy's accelerated aggressive campaigning for negro votes and Nixon's failure to do so. The political oscillation of fragile loyalties oscillated no longer after the Kennedy call to Mrs. King.

In the 1964 Presidential election, the political situation was completely reversed. Openly expressing opposition to the 1964 Civil Rights Act, the Republican Presidential candidate, Senator Barry Goldwater, frightened the black community with his campaign's latent racial hostility. His speeches were directed solely to the white community, and neither Goldwater nor his aides made any attempt to mask their contempt for the negro vote. But if negroes were dismayed by his lack of compassion for the Civil Rights Act, the white electorate was stunned by his Charge-of-the-Light-Brigade foreign-policy proposals. Whether he intended to or not, Goldwater gave the impression that his election as President would mean a quick escalation of the war in Vietnam. His conservative pronouncements on domestic affairs offended many prominent Republican businessmen who would ordinarily be expected to support the Republican candidate.

It was soon evident that a massive swing to the Democratic incumbent, Lyndon B. Johnson, was in the making. Equally obvious was the fact that Johnson would receive an overwhelming majority of the white vote, and that he would not have to rely on the black vote for his victory. He conducted his campaign accordingly. Preaching his peculiar brand of consensus politics, Johnson egomaniacally pursued the broadest spectrum of electorate support. He had been reared in the tradition of Southern politics that was founded on an old axiom: "If you get the white folks on your side, you don't need the niggers."

Besides, the black vote had nowhere else to go. The Republican candidate did not seek it, and Johnson became for many negroes the lesser evil. Whereas Kennedy had several black people in key campaign positions in various cities and as members of his personal campaign team, Johnson had none. Johnson even kept his favorite "house negro," loyal and devoted Hobart Taylor of Detroit, under wraps after he realized he had secured the negro vote.

On November 3, 1964, Johnson had racked up an electoral-college total of 486 to Goldwater's fifty-two. Out of a total popular vote of 70,643,526,

Johnson's plurality was 15,951,083—the highest ever. His winning percent-age of 61.1 over Goldwater's 38.5 also broke an election record, exceeding the former record of 60.8 held by Roosevelt in the 1936 election. Negroes had given Johnson 94 per cent of their vote.*

His victory was so overpowering that he could have lost all five Northern states whose black votes gave Kennedy his margin of victory—and still have won. Furthermore, Johnson could have conceded the four Southern states whose black vote totals were greater than his margin of victory—and still have defeated Goldwater.

Of the seven states—Illinois, Michigan, Mississippi, New Jersey, Pennsyl-vania, South Carolina, and Texas—whose 1960 black vote totals were greater than Kennedy's margin of victory in those states, two—Mississippi and South Carolina—shifted their fifteen electoral-college votes to Goldwater in 1964.

If the 119 electoral-college votes of the other five states are also sub-tracted from Johnson's winning total of 486 and shifted to Goldwater, Johnson would have still defeated Goldwater, 367 to 171. In those five states, Johnson's percentage of the total vote rendered the black vote harm-less as a balance of power:

STATE	JOHNSON	GOLDWATER	ELECTORAL VOTE
Illinois	59.5	40.5	27
Michigan	66.7	33.1	20
New Jersey	65.6	33.9	16
Pennsylvania	64.9	34.7	32
Texas	63.3	36.5	24
			119

Because of the 1964 Civil Rights Act, political observers carefully scruti-nized the 1964 election results to determine whether the Act's passage had any substantial impact on the ability of Southern negroes to register as voters and thereby contributed to Johnson's victory.

Perhaps their overzealous analyses led them to their effusive conclusions about the Southern black vote. Expert after expert seemed to discover some hidden meaning in these facts: 1) Arkansas, Florida, Tennessee, and

* In Harlem's four assembly districts, the Eleventh, Twelfth, Thirteenth, and Four-teenth, Johnson received 122,194 votes to Goldwater's 7928, or 94 per cent. In Chicago's predominantly Negro Second, Third, Fourth, Sixth, Seventeenth, Twentieth, and Twenty-Fourth Wards, Goldwater only squeezed out 7372 votes from a total of 217,438, or 3 per cent. In the Twenty-Fourth Ward, there were 296 Goldwater votes, or 1 per cent of the total of 22,194. Asked to explain Goldwater's ability to win so many votes in Harlem despite his anti-civil-rights stand, Adam Clayton Powell replied: "We got our kooks in Harlem, too."

Virginia would not have gone Democratic without the black vote; and 2) the five Southern states that did swing their electoral-college votes to Goldwater—Alabama, Georgia, Louisiana, Mississippi, and South Carolina— might have gone Democratic if black voters had been permitted to register in numbers approximating their proportion of the population. Neither fact was significant for Johnson's 1964 election. If the forty-three electoral-college votes represented by the four Southern states of Arkansas, Florida, Tennessee, and Virginia are added to the 119 electoral-college votes represented by the seven states of Illinois, Michigan, Mississippi, New Jersey, Pennsylvania, South Carolina, and Texas (states whose Negro votes gave Kennedy victory in 1960) and then subtracted from Johnson's final electoral-college tally of 486, he *still* would have defeated Goldwater, 324 to 214.* Only one salient fact emerges from this analysis: Johnson simply did not need black people to win in 1964.

As for the five Southern states that went Republican because of official resistance within these states to increased black voter registration, Johnson had already lost them. The probable fact that an increased black registration in those five Southern states would have switched those states to Johnson would have resulted in his gaining what the late E. E. Schattsneider, distinguished professor of political science at Wesleyan University, once labeled "the unearned increment of politics"—unnecessary additional votes for victory.**

If there is one political fact a candidate for public office knows as well as he knows his name, it is who was responsible for his election. In 1960, Kennedy, his advisers, and most political observers knew the black vote had been responsible for his election to the Presidency. The immediate civil-rights thrust of his administration, with its historic negro appointments, established this fact. In 1964, Johnson likewise knew that the black vote had played no significant part in his election. Furthermore, the Republicans had written off the black vote by their nomination of Goldwater, who, in

---

* The four Southern states whose 1964 negro votes exceeded the Democratic margin of victory were:

STATE	NEGRO VOTE	MARGIN OF VICTORY
Arkansas	67,600	65,400
Florida	211,800	37,800
Tennessee	165,200	126,000
Virginia	166,600	76,704

** As of 1964, the percentage of eligible negro voters registered in these five states was as follows: Alabama, 19.2 per cent; Georgia, 27.4 per cent; Louisiana, 32 per cent; Mississippi, 6.7 per cent; and South Carolina, 37.3 per cent. (These figures were compiled by the U.S. Civil Rights Commission and published in March 1965. The Commission noted that official Southern registration data "vary widely in accuracy," and that unofficial figures "are subject to even greater inaccuracies."

the words of one Democratic leader, had "shot Lincoln in the head as surely as John Wilkes Booth."*

That Johnson introduced and supported less legislation and fewer programs favorable to negroes than Kennedy is a result of their electoral base as well as their personal and political attitudes toward civil rights. Kennedy's victory in 1960 proved that the black vote could be a balance of power in deciding election outcomes if—and only if—the condition of *ceteris paribus* —all other things being equal—is controlling. Similarly, as 1964 proved, the black vote as a balance of power is inconsequential and politically impotent where the condition of *ceteris paribus* is inoperative.

The 1932, 1936, 1952, and 1956 Presidential Elections

Like situations also occurred in the 1932, 1936, 1952, and 1956 Presidential elections. In all four elections, negroes exerted no influence on the final outcome because of their emotional attachment to the political party which the rest of the country was retiring.

The firm devotion of Negroes to the Republican Party for their manumission was highlighted in 1932, when the Democratic candidate, Roosevelt, swept forty-two of forty-eight states for 472 electoral-college votes to Herbert Hoover's fifty-nine. While white voters were displaying a massive disenchantment with Hoover's "Mr. Magoo" ineptitude, black voters nestled snugly in the Republicans' bed as visions of emancipated slaves danced in their heads. The Democrats did manage to crack through this stubborn fidelity in New York City, Kansas City, Detroit, and Pittsburgh. But in New York City and Kansas City, two of the country's most efficient and corrupt political machines, Tammany Hall and the Pendergast machine, were responsible for the negro shift to the Democrats. In Chicago, where, in 1967, the negro vote is the exclusive property of the Democratic Party, Roosevelt received a paltry 23 per cent of the negro vote. In Cleveland's negro wards, only 24 per cent of the vote went Republican. This pattern was repeated in Baltimore, Columbus, and Philadelphia.

By 1936, negroes, economically benefited by the employment and welfare policies of the New Deal, began to shift their votes to the Democrats, but still at a slower pace than the rest of the country. This time, the negro vote came as close to splitting as it ever has in a Presidential election. This split rendered it ineffective. Furthermore, Roosevelt's percentage increase of the white vote negated any potential impact of the negro vote on his re-election.

Gunnar Myrdal's analysis in *An American Dilemma* of fifteen negro

* Quoted by Paul Duke in his article "Southern Politics and the Negroes," *The Reporter*, December 17, 1964.

wards in nine cities indicates that the Republicans were still able to hold the negro vote in six of those fifteen wards.* Not until 1940 was the negro vote to complete its spiritual transformation as a unified Democratic ally.

In the 1952 and 1956 Presidential elections, the national negro vote, already welded together as a bloc vote by big-city Democratic machines, was estimated by the Gallup Poll as 79 per cent Democratic in 1952 and 61 per cent Democratic in 1956. In those two elections, the white vote was estimated by the Gallup Poll to be 57 per cent Republican in 1952 and 59 per cent Republican in 1956. Because the Republicans were able to win both Presidential elections without the support of the black voters, it was politically understandable why there was no sense of urgency within the party for a more aggressive posture on civil rights. Had there been a greater shift of the negro vote in 1956 to the Republican Party, there likewise might have been a more rapid liberalization in the national Republican policy on civil rights.**

Moon Revisited

Political hindsight always enables the critic to look better than the exponent, for at least the critic has not made predictions that were struck down by unforeseen events. Moon, in an otherwise excellent political analysis of the negro vote and its growth to a power of national significance, has nonetheless occasionally permitted his ideological bent to shape his

* Per Cent of Major Party Vote for Roosevelt, 1932, 1936, 1940, in Each Ward Having More Than Half Its Population Negro, Selected Cities

	BALTIMORE			CHICAGO			COLUMBUS	
Ward	5	14	17	2	3		6	7
1932	46.4	49.2	43.0	25.4	20.7		27.9	23.2
1936	64.2	54.6	46.9	47.9	50.1		47.7	46.6
1940	72.1	60.7	59.6	51.2	54.2		50.7	57.1

	DETROIT			KANSAS CITY, KANSAS	KANSAS CITY, MISSOURI	NEW HAVEN	PITTS-BURGH	WILMING-TON
Ward	3	5	7	2	4	19	5	6
1932	46.0	50.2	53.9	41.5	70.8	38.9	53.3	28.3
1936	71.4	75.0	79.0	61.3	79.4	61.0	76.6	40.1
1940	75.3	79.2	80.0	59.6	66.5	58.7	77.1	41.5

The cities selected are all those with over 100,000 population, containing wards having 50 per cent or more of their population Negro, where Negroes were allowed to vote unhampered or almost unhampered, and where ward lines were not changed over the period 1932-1940. The only exception is Philadelphia, which refused to supply information. The data in this table were collected for this study by Shirley Star.

** President Eisenhower, in a moment of exasperation while discussing the negro community's failure to support him or the Republican Party more heavily in 1956, is reported to have remarked: "What does it take to get these people to support you?"

final conclusions and value judgments. For example, he writes that "unlike the southern vote, the negro vote is tied to no political power. It cannot be counted in advance."*

By 1948, when his book was published and when Truman unexpectedly beat Dewey, the negro vote had matured so much into a bloc vote for the Democratic Party that it was unable to shake its unthinking loyalty and join the country's political shift in 1952. If, as Moon indicated, the negro vote could not be counted in advance, somebody forgot to inform the Democratic machine bosses of all the major cities in 1952 and 1956.**

Naturally, a party does not reward loyalists in its hip pocket with the same amount of political patronage as it does its uncertain or more casual supporters. Once married, the husband is not the ardent wooer of the housewife as he was of the capricious maiden. It would, therefore, be to the political advantage of the negro politician or writer to merchandise the impression that the negro electorate is more than a dancing puppet in order to entice both parties to compete in the expenditure of political attention and favors. This possibility explains Moon's judgment that "the vote of negro citizens in 1948 will certainly not be a bloc vote. It will probably not go overwhelmingly to either party unless one of the parties chooses completely unacceptable candidates."***

The 1948 Republican Presidential nominee, New York Governor Thomas E. Dewey, was certainly not an "unacceptable candidate" to negroes, in view of his record as the first state governor to get a Federal Employment Practices Commission passed. Yet negroes voted as a bloc for Truman in 1948, giving him an estimated 69 per cent of their votes. Truman's margin of victory over Dewey in three crucial states—Illinois, 33,612; California, 17,865; and Ohio, 7107—was due to the negro bloc vote. Moon's conclusions must be seriously challenged when he states: "The negro vote is in the vest pocket of no party. It is certainly as independent as the vote of any considerable segment of the American electorate."****

Were it not for Moon's respectable credentials as both a civil-rights and political analyst, such a statement would be ridiculed by the very facts he has assembled to reach his conclusion. The negro vote was held by the Democratic Party in 1944 and has remained there snugly oblivious to the world.

To be an enduring "balance of power" in elections, any interest group

---

* Moon, p. 11.

** When Harlem Congressman Adam Clayton Powell unexpectedly switched his public support from Stevenson to Eisenhower in 1956, his charisma, which had made him one of the most powerful and nationally beloved negro politicians, did not shake the devotion of Harlem voters for the Democratic Party. They still gave Stevenson over 70 per cent of their vote.

*** Moon, p. 213.

**** Moon, p. 213.

must enjoy a certain amount of independence and capacity for political oscillation. Above all, it must receive its proportionate share of public offices and appointments. This the negro has not been able to do as of 1967. Until black people operate as do other ethnic groups, with the same critical appreciation of the element of *ceteris paribus* in national elections and the demand that they get their 10, 20, or 30 per cent of the jobs and elective offices, their political power as a major factor in future Presidential races will be circumscribed by their shortsighted single-party loyalty.

Until the black vote learns that the political oscillation of fragile loyalties is the only ultimate insurance of secured participation in the policy-making councils of both parties, Democrats will continue to treat it like a stepchild and Republicans will deny it was ever a member of the family.

Finally, and of greatest importance, the black vote cannot be accurately classified as a true balance of power until the decisive role it has played in specific elections results in a proportionate acquisition of top-level jobs and appointments, just as in the cases of the Irish, the Italians, the Jews, and the Poles. These four ethnic groups, as will be demonstrated later, have been a true balance of power in many elections. They, in turn, have managed to garner their proportionate share of the political spoils.

Power is power only when it is applied. The black vote did this in two elections in 1967—the election of mayors in Cleveland and Gary. In both elections, the overwhelming solidity of black voters was necessary for victory. If anything, the white vote in both cities was the balance of power, and both newly elected black mayors recognized this fact by appointing whites to key jobs in their administrations.

Eventually, the black vote will become a true balance of power by securing a proportionate share of the elective offices and top-level appointments that the black percentage in the population deserves. Until that day comes, the black vote as a balance of power resembles a conceptual toy for political scientists and writers.

CHAPTER FIVE

Measuring Black Political Power

In general, we understand by "power," the chance of a man or of a number of men to realize their own will in a communal action against the resistance of others who are participating in the action.

—MAX WEBER

In the American political system, organizations and interest groups wield power, individuals don't. Individuals can affect power outside organizations only if they possess charisma, that undefinable quality of body and spirit reserved for a few "world historical individuals." Such charismatic leaders must still, however, rely on followers, and eventually these followers become institutionalized into some form of organizational structure.

If organizations are the true power brokers in society, then political parties represent summit political power. Their power is measurable by the number of elections they win, the number of public officials they elect, and the amount of control they can exercise over the administration of government. Because the state is the supreme power in any society, that organization which controls the government controls the state. Political parties control governments. The power of political parties is measured by the degree of sovereignty they exercise over the heads of government, its appointees, its domestic and foreign policies, and its dispensation of patronage.

The measurement of the political power of an ethnic group, an economic class, or another interest group is far more difficult. Such a group's claims of political achievements are usually exaggerated and extravagantly publicized. On occasion, they have been able to establish a direct connection between the defeat or election of a candidate inimical or responsive to their wishes. But this group's ability to deliver the vote of its members is not always subject to scientific verification. Their leaders may fervently endorse a particular candidate or policy. But the group's members, by their decision at the polls, will vote diametrically opposite to the official position of the interest group. For example, in the Gary mayoralty election of November 1967, the labor union leaders in Gary publicly endorsed the Democratic candidate, a negro. In a political race governed by strong racial overtones, white steel workers from the Gary steel mills ignored the official posture of their labor leaders and instead gave 89 per cent of their vote to the white Republican candidate.

This is a classic example of the social variables that impinge on the consciousness of individuals, forcing them to structure a priority of loyalties and then decide which loyalty will determine their political decisions. As the distinguished Lebanese philosopher and statesman Charles Malik has written: ". . . man has other loyalties than his loyalty to the state. He has his loyalty to his family, to his religion, to his profession; he has his loyalty to science and to truth. These loyalties are equally exacting as the loyalty to the state."*

Thus, a white Roman Catholic living in an integrated city neighborhood whose children attend integrated schools is not likely to respond as antagonistically to his church's call for more integrated schools as is a white Roman Catholic living in a wealthy suburb where no negroes live or attend school. Nor are union members of an industrial union with a large percentage of negroes likely to be as determined to bar union participation of negroes as the racially exclusive crafts unions.

Throughout the history of American politics, various interest groups have tended to follow rather than reject the advice of their leaders in tacit fealty to the pragmatic doctrine that to do otherwise would dilute the group's credibility and power. Interest groups have sought political power through five methods:

1) Political oscillation—threatening to take their votes to another candidate or party.

2) Proportionate control of policy-making jobs in government—placing its members in sensitive positions in order to influence public policy favorably toward their interests.

3) Retribution—punishing politicians through a "backlash vote" for opposing the group's interests.

4) Educational propaganda—influencing other members of the electorate to a sympathetic adoption of the group's point of view through the use of pamphlets, meetings, and public statements.

5) Lobbying in Congress and state legislatures for legislation which promotes the group's interest or against legislation which threatens the group's survival and political power.

Of these five methods, the first and second have tended to dominate the

* Extracts from the Proceedings of the United Nations Commission on Human Rights, 1947.

activities of most interest groups. The possibility of other groups determining the outcome of an election as the result of a "backlash" and the confluence of other groups also lobbying with equal effectiveness for a piece of legislation decrease one group's ability to claim sole credit for such accomplishments. With very infrequent exceptions, negroes have been unsuccessful in all five methods.

Occasionally, they have managed to rally friends to their cause—the passage of civil-rights laws, the creation of the open society—but their success has stemmed more from their activities outside politics (demonstrations, marches, sit-ins) rather than within the framework of the political system. One of the greatest tragedies of the civil-rights movement has been its inability—or maybe its lack of understanding—to transmit the fervor of civil-rights activities into political activity.

Civil-rights demonstrators make good marchers, but poor politicians.

Civil-rights leaders can get up a good boycott, but they can never get out a good vote.

Civil-rights laws provide for equality of opportunity, but do not ensure equality of results.

Equality of results is what the science of politics is concerned with.

Because they have never concerned themselves with real power in society, civil-rights leaders have danced on the fringes of the political and economic apparatuses that control society.

As already stated, they have feared that any diligent seeking of real political power, resulting in the possible displacement of sympathetic politicians, might in turn alienate those politicians. But politicians are not primarily concerned with any ethnic group's rights as much as they are concerned with their own right to survive.

In one of the most perceptive columns ever written about this paradox, Mike Royko, a white columnist for the *Chicago Daily News*, commented in his April 5, 1967, column the day after a Chicago primary:

. . . black power was available in sizable quantities in Chicago Tuesday. And a person didn't have to march, sing, riot or boycott to get it.

It was inside the voting machine. By pulling a lever or using a pencil, the Negro could have thrown a scare into City Hall.

Instead Chicago Negroes went out and gave something like 80 to 85% of their vote to Mayor Richard J. Daley; about 10% to John Waner and just a dib and a dab to Dick Gregory. And Daley didn't even campaign in the Negro areas.

I'm not saying they shouldn't have voted for Mayor Daley. If he is their man —fine. But is he their man? If so, they show it in strange ways.

They should remember that the city was in an uproar most of last summer because the civil rights wing of the Negro population was marching to protest the way the Negro was being treated by the mayor's administration.

It was the mayor's house that was being picketed for the last couple of summers. It was the administration's school system that they boycotted and raged against.

It was the mayor's police department that was accused of being unkind to Negroes. The mayor's firemen were the ones shot at and stoned. And it was his fire department that was accused of being segregated.

. . . The inconsistency mounts when you consider that the poorest Negro areas—the most riot-inclined areas—were where Daley got his best support. He didn't do much better in his own neighborhood than he did in some West Side wards. . . .

And finally, if there is a leader of Chicago's Negroes, he is Richard J. Daley, that rosy-cheeked Irishman from the Back of the Yards. . . .

So this summer, don't sing me that old refrain of "black power." The voting machine was listening Tuesday, but he couldn't hear you even humming.

While Royko's analysis defines the peculiarity of the Chicago political machine with its tyrannical control over the electorate because of the crime syndicate's enforcement powers, it is a fact that the black vote has not always predictably followed its best civil-rights interests.* Black voters have invariably been more slavishly loyal to a political machine with its built-in hostility to their best interests than other ethnic groups. Nevertheless, the classical myth—and fear—of the black vote as a balance of power in close elections has persisted.

In some quarters, recognition has been given to the appointment of negroes to high office for the first time (member of a Federal agency, the Cabinet, the U.S. Supreme Court, etc.) as an example of the potency of the black vote.

High-level negro appointments are still rare, and, because they are, they must be categorized as symbolic appointments. Symbolic negro appointments do not control power. Usually, they are more honorific than substantial and are extremely impressive to black people. The appointment of a negro does not guarantee any improvement in the economic, educational, or political conditions of the black masses, however. Not a single additional negro receives an increase in his wages because one negro is appointed to the Supreme Court.

Worse still, the symbolic negro appointment is ofttimes a promotion to a higher position. In such an instance, the promotion is valueless because negroes have gained no new political power.

When Carl Rowan was promoted from Ambassador to Finland to the directorship of the United States Information Agency, a negro was not appointed Ambassador to succeed him. Negroes thus lost that appointment. They gained no power. This has occurred repeatedly in government, particularly under the Johnson administration. The appointment of Thurgood Marshall to Solicitor General and then to the U.S. Supreme Court does not mean an accretion of political power because one negro has simply been rotated between jobs.

The only way in which black people can develop political power in gov-

* See Chapter Eight for a detailed analysis.

ernment is to be able to control the hiring processes. This they have never been able to do. When negroes have been placed in top-level positions, they have usually refused to hire other negroes.

As other ethnic groups have achieved political power, they have expanded their power base by bringing members of their own group into the bureaucratic mainstream of government. Certain departments, certain job classifications have become the exclusive province of certain ethnic groups. In certain agencies, an Irish Catholic has been expected to head that department, just as certain specialties have been reserved for Jews. The success of an ethnic group in maintaining exclusive dominion over certain policy-making jobs as well as reserving an unspecified percentage of jobs for their group is the true exercise of ethnic political power.

Once they have been appointed to high positions, negroes have shied away from hiring other negroes in the belief that a quick and perceived upswing in the number of negro employees would tend to increase the possibilities for resegregation. The civil-rights movement's philosophical emphasis on integration has taken its psychic toll of negro office-holders.

Moreover, negro office-holders have usually been appointed either to positions that control little patronage or with an understanding that their hiring policies would be governed by other ethnic and political considerations.

There is also the elation many black people have felt in being a "first" or even an only negro within a department. For them to encourage the employment of other negroes within their departments or the appointment of negroes to similarly high positions would be to diminish the honorific distinction of their achievement.

Given the paucity, then, of black appointments to high office, analyses of negro political power have been confined to measuring the black vote. Because of their high visibility and physical confinement to ghettos, negro voting strength has been more easily measured than that of other ethnic groups.

The vast majority of black people in any city live in definable areas—in New York City, Harlem; in Chicago, the South Side and the West Side; in Philadelphia, the North Side; in Los Angeles, Watts. To rely on the vote as the sole standard of measurement of negro political power is sterile. The electoral process is merely one step in the acquisition of power, and votes do more than simply elect officials. Votes guarantee a favorable disposition of an ethnic group's aspiration and demands. Votes should ensure that the members of a particular group will be appointed in significant numbers in the policy-making councils of government. Votes are promissory notes on the dispensation of jobs. Votes are judgeships, commissionerships, governorships, mayorships, Congressional seats, aldermanships, superintendencies, political party chairmanships, government contracts, Federal aid, construction projects, and political contributions. Consequently, discussion of any group's voting strength as the sole measurement of its political power neglects the realities of politics and misunderstands the relationship of government to pressure groups.

Proportional Political Patronage

The most important indices of a group's political power are its numerical percentage of the population and its percentage of the vote during an election. For example, an ethnic group might comprise 20 per cent of the population in a city but regularly deliver, on the average, only 10 per cent of the vote. Somewhere between these two percentages should lie the accommodation by the party organization and its control of the government to the demands of the particular ethnic group.

Nationally, black people comprise approximately 12 per cent of the population. In America's thirty largest cities, the proportion of negroes in the population ranged from a low of 4 per cent in Minneapolis, Minn., and 5 per cent in Phoenix, Ariz., to a high of 66 per cent in Washington, D.C., and 47 per cent in Newark, N.J.*

Proportion of Negroes in Each of the 30 Largest Cities,*
1960 and 1965 Estimated

CITY	1960	1965	CITY	1960	1965
New York, N.Y.	14	18	Pittsburgh, Pa.	17	21
Chicago, Ill.	23	28	San Antonio, Texas	7	8
Los Angeles, Calif.	14	17	San Diego, Calif.	6	7
Philadelphia, Pa.	26	31	Seattle, Wash.	5	7
Detroit, Mich.	29	34	Buffalo, N. Y.	13	17
Baltimore, Md.	35	38	Cincinnati, Ohio	22	24
Houston, Texas	23	23	Memphis, Tenn.	37	44
Cleveland, Ohio	29	34	Denver, Colorado	6	9
Washington, D.C.	54	66	Atlanta, Ga.	38	44
St. Louis, Mo.	29	36	Minneapolis, Minn.	2	4
Milwaukee, Wis.	8	11	Indianapolis, Ind.	21	23
San Francisco, Calif.	10	12	Kansas City, Mo.	18	22
Boston, Mass.	9	13	Columbus, Ohio	16	18
Dallas, Texas	19	21	Phoenix, Ariz.	5	5
New Orleans, La.	37	41	Newark, N.J.	34	47

* As of 1967, the six black U.S. Congressmen (including Adam Clayton Powell, who was excluded from the Ninetieth Congress on March 10, 1967) came from the five largest cities, New York City (Powell), Chicago (William L. Dawson), Los Angeles, Calif. (Augustus Hawkins), Philadelphia (Robert N.C. Nix), and Detroit (Charles C. Diggs, Jr., and John Conyers). All six are Democrats.

* Although these figures are from a joint report prepared by the Bureau of the Census and the Bureau of Labor Statistics in October 1967, titled "Social and Economic Conditions of Negroes in the United States," they are for the year 1965. Newark officials and various city agencies concerned directly with urban renewal and race relations agree that in 1967 Newark had a majority of negroes in its population—52 per cent for 1967.

Two unanswered questions about black political power are: 1) What are the political circumstances that in 1965 enabled New York City, with an 18 per cent black proportion, and Los Angeles, with 17 per cent, to have one black Congressman each among its Congressional delegation, while twelve other cities, all with proportionally larger black populations, have none? (Baltimore, 38 per cent; Cincinnati, 24 per cent; Cleveland, 34 per cent; Dallas, 21 per cent; Houston, 23 per cent; Indianapolis, 23 per cent; Kansas City, 22 per cent; Memphis, 44 per cent; Newark, 47 per cent; New Orleans, 41 per cent; Pittsburgh, 21 per cent; and St. Louis, 36 per cent.)

2) What combination of racial cohesion and political organization enabled the Detroit black electorate to elect *two* black Congressmen in 1964 with a black proportion of 34 per cent, while five cities with larger black proportions were unable to elect even one?

Part of the explanation for the absence of black Congressmen from Memphis, New Orleans, St. Louis, Baltimore and Kansas City are the Southern traditions and orientations of these cities. Black voters have yet to exhibit the fierce independence and black pride that would unleash a black leader who could whip ambition together into a phalanx of bloc voting in exchange for black spoils—i.e., a Congressional seat.

But the election of black Congressmen is only one facet of black political power in a city. Black state senators and representatives, black city councilmen or aldermen, black city and state judges, black heads of city departments (commissioners, etc.), black members of boards of education, black key figures in the state and city political organizations, and other honorary appointments that recognize the individual power and importance of black community leaders comprise a more accurate measurement of the ethnic group's political power.

The first law for measuring the political power of an ethnic group is that there must be a direct relationship between the proportion of its vote in an election or its proportion of the population—whichever is higher—and its proportion of all political jobs and elective offices.

This is the theory of proportional equality, and, as will be demonstrated in the chapter "The Irish, the Italians, the Jews, and the Poles," practically every other ethnic group in America has been able to develop political power at the national, state, and local levels commensurate with its proportion of the population.

Stone's Index of Proportional Equality

Political power can be quantified and measured by the proportion of elective offices and jobs in specific areas. Stone's Index of Proportional Equality establishes minimum standards for measuring the political power of an ethnic group. There are six factors, which include the proportion of the ethnic group within a city in the following areas of political activity: 1) U.S. Congressmen; 2) city councilmen and aldermen; 3) state representatives; 4) heads of municipal departments; 5) judges (at the city, state, and national levels); and 6) members of the board of education.

Again, as will be proved in the chapter on the four ethnic groups, the Irish, the Italians, the Jews, and the Poles have all developed political control in several cities where they are numerically strong by dominating in all six areas. A political canon of the Irish when they first became active in politics was: "It is better to know the judge than the law."

The reason all city departments are included in this standard of measurement is the tendency for black appointments of department heads to be concentrated in the weaker, or "human relations" and "welfare," departments. Black people are rarely appointed as heads of the departments that control finance, real estate, construction, city contracts, public works, buildings, and taxes. Instead they saturate the departments of welfare, human relations, and education. There is little political power in these departments.

Thus, if black people constitute 10 per cent of the vote or 10 per cent of the population and are given 10 per cent of the jobs and elective offices in a city and state administration, and if this 10 per cent is concentrated in the lower-paying positions or unimportant elective offices, then black people in that situation do not have political power.

As of 1967, negro political power at the Federal level was insignificant, with the exception of two appointments, Housing and Urban Development Secretary Robert C. Weaver, one of the twelve members of the President's Cabinet, and U.S. Supreme Court Justice Thurgood Marshall, one of nine Associate Justices.

But using the black national proportion of 12 per cent for 1966 as a base index, the relationship of this proportion to negroes' total political participation in the Federal legislative, executive, and judiciary branches of government can be assessed. It is important to keep in mind the national proportion of 11 per cent in any kind of analysis of black political activity.

U.S. Congress, 1966

Of 435 U.S. Representatives elected to the 89th Congress in 1966, only six, or 1.3 per cent, were black. (Compare this proportion, for example, to the number of Jewish Congressmen. In 1966, Jews comprised 3 per cent of the population—5,600,000 out of 200,000,000—and also constituted 3 per cent (15 Jewish Congressmen) of the Congress.

Of one hundred Senators, one, or 1 per cent, was black (the first to be elected since 1881).

Thus, nationally, it is mournfully obvious that negroes can exert very little influence as legislators in the U. S. Congress. Rather, they must rely on a tenuous alliance with committed white liberals or white Congressmen with significant black constituencies to secure the passage of legislation designed to elevate the economic and educational standards of black people.

White Congressmen with substantial black constituencies are not going to be influenced unless their districts are politically unstable and tend to swing back and forth between the two parties. Only in such instances, if the negro vote cohesively acted as a balance of power to guarantee the election of a Congressman, and if he, in turn, recognized this fact, would he be responsive to negro demands.

But, of the ninety-six Congressmen who have a 20 per cent or greater black constituency, sixty-five are Southerners. Because of a traditional pattern of massive racial intimidation and oppression through murders, bombings, and economic reprisals, negroes still have not registered or voted in numbers approximating their proportion. Even where they have voted, they still have tended to simplistically (lazily) accept the lesser of two white evils rather than cut the umbilical cord of white subordination by voting for a strong black challenger. This happened in the Memphis, Tenn., October 5, 1967, primary. In a seven-man race for mayor, one of the candidates was black state representative A. W. Willis. Although the registered black vote was exactly one-third of the total number of Memphis votes (80,033 out of 235,303), a united vote behind one negro candidate could have placed him in the final run-off, assuming a split white vote among the other six candidates. Memphis negroes instead voted for the incumbent white mayor, and even gave a substantial proportion of their votes to a former white mayor. Willis ran a poor fourth. He subsequently charged that Memphis negroes had been brainwashed all their lives. During his campaign, he declared that the campaign was raising for the first time "the real problems of racial inferiority. The Negro has been taught to be inferior. He thinks the white man's ice is colder, his sugar is sweeter, his medicine is better."

In most Southern communities, black people will also support a racist Congressman who, despite his consistent antinegro votes in Congress, looks after his black constituents with the same benevolent paternalism of the old plantation owner. Negroes in South Carolina's Sixth Congressional District have continued to vote for Representative John L. McMillan, even though he was known as one of the staunchest opponents of home rule for the District of Columbia because of its black majority. In Tampa, Fla., not one negro publicly criticized Tampa's Representative Sam M. Gibbons for leading the move to strip Representative Adam Clayton Powell of his powers as Chairman of the Education and Labor Committee in September 1966.

If Congress is a microcosm of the white racism that continues to dominate the United States, Congressional staffs show the same loving affection for this pattern. Of the five black Congressmen, four have negro women as administrative assistants. Representative John Conyers has a white administrative assistant, as does Senator Edward W. Brooke. Until his exclusion from the Congress, Adam Clayton Powell was the only man in either the House or the Senate to have a black man as an administrative assistant. He had two. His first was Livingston Wingate, who later became executive director of Harlem's antipoverty program HARYOU-ACT. The second was myself. Powell was also the only Congressman to employ black people in several capacities as professional staff members. Not only was his special assistant a black, but the chief clerk of the committee, Miss Louise Maxienne Dargans, and the education chief, Dr. Eunice Matthews, were black.

None of the other 535 Representatives and Senators has black legislative assistants. One Indiana Congressman assigned such a title to one aide, but on closer investigation, it was revealed that the aide was, in fact, a very intelligent office boy who performed routine office chores instead of drafting bills and doing legislative research.

There is a plethora of negro secretaries on Capitol Hill, but only because there is a shortage of secretaries. Although the average Congressman is a racial bigot, he is also a pragmatist. So, negro secretaries are hired, if for no other reason than to keep the office running.

Of the sixteen Senate committees and the twenty House committees, only one committee in the House, as of 1967, had a professional negro staff member. She is Mrs. Christine Ray Davis, staff director of the House Government Operations Committee, whose chairman is William L. Dawson. Mrs. Davis was the first negro to become a staff director of a Congressional committee. She has served as the top staff member of that committee since 1949, when Dawson became its chairman and she was appointed chief clerk. During 1952-53, when the Republicans were in control of the House, she was a minority staff consultant, and in 1954, when Democrats resumed control of the House, she was appointed staff director.

The unwritten law against black pages in the House and Senate was broken in the first half of the Eighty-ninth Congress, in 1965, when Lawrence W. Bradford, Jr., of New York City, became the first black page in the Senate and Frank V. Mitchell, Jr., of Detroit, Mich., became the first black page in the House. Oddly enough, both boys were sponsored by Republicans, who secured their appointments.

U.S. Congress, 1968

For the Ninety-first Congress beginning in January 1969, there will be a new high of eight black Congressmen and possibly nine, depending upon what happens in the Third Congressional District in Chicago, where a white Congressman is being seriously challenged for the first time by a black man.

Adam Clayton Powell has announced his intention to run again and, barring a most cataclysmic unforeseen event, will be re-elected, as will the other five black Congressmen. Two new black Congressmen will come from Cleveland's newly formed Twenty-first Congressional District, and Brooklyn's newly formed Twelfth Congressional District representing that community's black ghetto, Bedford-Stuyvesant.

The Democratic candidate for Cleveland's new Congressional District is Louis Stokes, brother of that city's black mayor, Carl B. Stokes. While the Democratic candidate for Brooklyn's Twelfth Congressional District had not been nominated as of this writing, that race portends excitement with the entry of former C.O.R.E. executive director, James Farmer, who has been endorsed by both the Liberal and Republican Parties. Although not a Brooklyn resident, Farmer is expected to wage a strong race because of his famed civil rights role.

U.S. Executive

Of the many public exercises that have seemed to delight the Southern heart of President Lyndon Baines Johnson, none has been carried off with more P. T. Barnum fanfare than the announcement of a "first negro appointment." So much carnival hoopla has attended these sessions that the impression has been gained that this President, who, as a Congressman, vigorously fought against civil rights for negroes, "has done more for the cause of civil rights" than any other President "in our history."[*]

The spectacular appointments of the first negro Cabinet member, Robert C. Weaver, as Secretary of the Department of Housing and Urban Development on January 18, 1967, Andrew F. Brimmer as the first black Governor of the Federal Reserve Board, Thurgood Marshall as the first black Solicitor General in the Department of Justice and the first black Supreme Court Justice, and Mrs. Patricia Harris as the first black woman ambassador (to Luxembourg) have created the external appearance of a government where black people are taking giant steps forward in helping to run their country.[**]

---

[*] From the brochure "This President . . . Is Doing More," published in 1967 by the Democratic National Committee.

[**] The author had lunch with Louis Martin, Deputy Chairman of the Democratic National Committee, a few days after Secretary of Defense Robert S. McNamara's appointment to the presidency of the World Bank had been announced. Martin said that he received a telephone call from a very prominent Southern white politician, who growled into the phone, half-jokingly but with just enough rancor to indicate his belief in the possibility: "What nigger have you got lined up for the Secretary of Defense job now?"

In the history of American politics, no greater charade has been played by any President. The fact is that these showcase appointments have not substantially changed the administrative and policy-making patterns of government.

Again, bearing in mind that blacks comprise 11 per cent of the national population, the progress of negro employment in the higher councils of the Federal government can be measured. In the Executive Office of the President, the following is the breakdown of black positions, as of 1967, among the top positions listed in the Congressional Directory of the Nine-tieth Congress, First Session, but revised for subsequent changes in the latter part of the year:

OFFICE	NUMBER OF TOP POSITIONS	NUMBER OF NEGROES
White House Office	25	0
Bureau of the Budget	26	0
Council of Economic Advisers	4	0
National Security Office	7	0
Central Intelligence Agency	5	0
National Aeronautics and Space Agency	6	0
Office of Economic Opportunity	16	1
Office of Emergency Planning	16	0
Office of Science and Technology	5	0
Office of Special Representative for Trade Negotiations	15	0
TOTAL	125	1 (1 per cent)

Were it not for the one black executive in the Office of Economic Opportunity, the eleven offices within the Executive Office of the President would be lily-white.

Of the forty-four largest Federal independent agencies, only one—the Equal Employment Opportunity Commission—is headed by a "Negro," Clifford Alexander, Jr., a colorless and mediocre lawyer who was previously a Deputy Special Counsel to the President with no precise administrative responsibilities. Typical of the excessively cautious Federal civil servant, Alexander climbed slowly through the ranks by becoming a faceless negro who neither made controversial comments nor militantly condemned the injustices against negroes in American society.

Of the 183 Commissioners, members of the boards and the executive directors or administrators of these forty-four independent agencies, only seven, or 3 per cent, were negroes: Mrs. Frankie Muse Freeman, of the U.S. Commission on Civil Rights; Clifford L. Alexander, Jr., Chairman, and Samuel C. Jackson, member, of the Equal Employment Opportunity Commission; Dr. G. Franklin Edwards, member of the National Capital Planning Commission; Howard Jenkins, Jr., member of the National Labor Relations Board; Dr. Kenneth W. Clement, member of the National Selective Service Appeal Board; and Dr. Andrew F. Brimmer, governor of the Federal Reserve Board. No independent agency in the Federal government is headed by a black staff member.

A third index of the exclusion of negroes from the policy-making and executive positions of government is indicated by the number of negro assistant secretaries and deputy assistant secretaries. This is the administrative level at which Cabinet departments are compartmentalized into operational units of responsibility.

Of the 220 assistant secretaries and deputy assistant secretaries in the twelve Cabinet departments and the Army, Navy and Air Force, only five, or 2 per cent, are negroes. These five negroes are concentrated in only four departments: State, Labor, Health, Education and Welfare, and Agriculture: Samuel Z. Westerfield, Jr., Deputy Assistant Secretary of State for African Affairs; Mrs. Charlotte M. Hubbard, Deputy Assistant Secretary of State for Public Affairs; George L. P. Weaver, Assistant Secretary for International Affairs in the Department of Labor; Shelton B. Granger, Deputy Assistant Secretary of HEW for Education, International Affairs; and Alfred L. Edwards, Deputy Assistant Secretary of Agriculture for Rural Development and Conservation.

Thus, there is not a single negro among the 130 Assistant or Deputy Assistant Secretaries in the Departments of the Treasury, Defense, Army, Navy, Air Force, Justice, Post Office, Interior, Commerce, Housing and Urban Development, and Transportation.

Two of the Federal government's most powerful negroes who do not have Assistant Secretary or Deputy Assistant Secretary status are Miss Barbara Watson, Acting Administrator of the State Department's Bureau of Security and Consular Affairs, and Edward C. Sylvester, Jr., Director of the Labor Department's Office of Federal Contract Compliance. Both make critical decisions which respectively shape America's foreign and domestic policies. Miss Watson has been the target of intensive lobbying by white industrialists with heavy investments in Africa and Mr. Sylvester has been the constant target of the various construction trades unions which have resented his rulings requiring nondiscriminatory union practices in order to work on Federal projects.

This pattern of "white-out" for negroes, however, is far more entrenched than the obvious executive levels would indicate.

Within the twelve Cabinet departments, there are no black staff executives or appointees in the eleven top positions of the U.S. Mission to the United Nations, the twenty-six top positions in the Agency for International Development, the twenty-three top positions in the Peace Corps, the eleven top positions in the Internal Revenue Service, the eleven top positions in the Bureau of Customs, the fifteen top positions of the Office of the Comptroller of the Currency, and the seven top positions of the Secret Service.

In the twelve Cabinet Departments, there are *no negroes* in any of the policy-making or responsible administrative positions in the Coast Guard, Office of Merchant Marine Safety, Director of Defense Research and Engineering, the Joint Chiefs of Staff, Defense Atomic Support Agency, Defense Communications Center, Defense Contract Audit Agency, Defense Intelligence Agency, Defense Supply Agency, Office of Civil Defense, the Army Staff, the Navy Administrative Staff, Naval Office of Civilian Manpower, Naval Office of the Comptroller, Naval Office of Information, Office of Naval Research, Naval Office of Program Appraisal, Office of the Judge Advocate of the Navy, Navy Appellate Review Activity, the U.S. Marine Corps, Naval Bureau of Medicine and Surgery, National Naval Medical Center, Office of the Chief of Naval Operations, Bureau of Naval Personnel, Naval Air Systems Command, Naval Ordnance Systems Command, Naval Ship Systems Command, Naval Electronic Systems Command, Naval Supply Systems Command, Naval Facilities Engineering Command, U.S. Naval Station, Air Force Office of Information, the Air Staff, Comptroller of the Air Force, Deputy Chief of Staff for Personnel, Deputy Chief of Staff for Plans and Operations, Deputy Chief of Staff for Programs and Resources, Deputy Chief of Staff for Systems and Logistics, Deputy Chief of Staff for Research and Development, the Immigration and Naturalization Service, Bureau of Prisons, Board of Parole, the Federal Prison Industries, Inc., the Post Office's Bureau of Personnel *(despite the fact that negroes comprise an estimated 40 per cent of Post Office employees)*, the Post Office's Office of General Counsel, Bureau of the Chief Postal Inspector, Bureau of Research and Engineering, the *Interior Department's* Fish and Wildlife Service, Geological Survey, Bureau of Indian Affairs, Bureau of Land Management, Bureau of Mines, National Park Service, Bureau of Reclamation, Office of Territories, Bureau of Outdoor Recreation, Federal Water Pollution Control Administration, the *Agricultural* Stabilization and Conservation Service, Commodity Credit Corporation, Federal Extension Service, Foreign Agricultural Service, International Agricultural Development Service, Consumer and Marketing Services, Commodity Exchange Authority, Rural Development and Farmers Home Administration, Forest Service, Rural Electrification Administration, Soil Conservation Service, Economic Research Service, Statistical Reporting Service, Office of Budget and Finance, Office of Information, Office of Management Services, Office of Personnel, Office of Plant and Operations, Office of the General Counsel, Office of the Inspector General, *Commerce Department's* Office of Business Economics, Bureau of International Commerce, Office of Foreign Commerce Activities, Business and Defense Services Administration, Bureau of the Census, Maritime Administration, National Bureau of Standards, Patent Office, Bureau of Public Roads, National Highway Safety Agency, *Labor Department's* Labor-Management Services Administration, Office of the Solicitor, the Wage and Labor Standards' Bureaus and Divisions, the Food and Drug Administration, Vocational Rehabilitation Administration, the Public Health Service, Bureau of Disease Prevention and Environmental Control, Bureau of Health Manpower, Bureau of Health Services, National Institutes of Health, National Institutes of Mental Health, Social Security Administration, Welfare Administration (this is a particularly ironic form of racial discrimination since such a large proportion of Negroes are on public welfare), the Housing and Urban Development's Federal National Mortgage Association, and the HUD Regional Offices.

The appointment of a black assistant secretary, or Cabinet official, or member of a commission makes front-page news. The nonappointment of black people as administrators, assistant administrators, deputies, office managers, and to the thousands of administrative categories that make policy for the U.S. government is not news. And the exclusion pattern of black people from the apparatus of policy-making and responsible positions in the Federal government, with the exceptions already listed, is as rigid and as racially determined as ever. Racial bigotry in America begins at the White House.

The Federal Courts

There are 480 Federal judgeships.* These include the nine in the U.S. Supreme Court, eighty-eight in the eleven Judicial Circuits of the U.S. Court of Appeals, 342 in the U.S. District Courts, and forty-one in the five Special Courts (U.S. Court of Claims, U.S. Court of Customs and Patent Appeals, U.S. Customs Court, Tax Court of the United States, and the U.S. Court of Military Appeals).

Of these 480 Federal judgeships, eleven, or 2 per cent, are held by black people:

U.S. Supreme Court	Thurgood Marshall
U. S. Court of Appeals	
District of Columbia Circuit	Spottswood W. Robinson, III
Third Judicial Circuit	William Henry Hastie
Sixth Judicial Circuit	Wade Hampton McCree, Jr.
U.S. District Courts	
District of Columbia	William B. Bryant
Illinois (Northern)	James B. Parsons
New York (Northern)	Mrs. Constance Baker Motley
Pennsylvania (Eastern)	Leon Higginbotham
Virgin Islands	Walter A. Gordon
U. S. Customs Court	
	Scovel Richardson
	James L. Watson

* Administrative Office of the United States Court, Washington, D.C.

Judge Hastie was the first negro in the history of the United States to be appointed to a Federal court. President Roosevelt appointed him in 1937. Judge Parsons became the first negro in 1961 to be appointed to a Federal District Court. President Kennedy made the appointment.

The generally conservative orientation of the Federal courts, compounded by the dual standards of justice for blacks and whites of Southern judges, has been one of the factors most acutely inhibiting the negro's quest for racial equality. Invariably, the burden of proof of discrimination, intimidation, denial of Constitutional rights, or simple denial of the most elementary exercise of his rights rested on the negro.

In making Federal appointments, Presidents, as a matter of political courtesy or to minimize the risk of disapproval, clear their prospective choices with Senators, Congressmen, or state officials in a region, depending upon which wields the most power. Naturally, Southern officials will seek to influence the appointments of Southerners. And 99 per cent of all white Southerners, even in 1967, are hard-core racists.

The historical pattern of justice dispensed firmly, but unequally, for negroes in the South can be traced to the racial orientations of the judges appointed. Only with rare exceptions have Southern judges been able to break through their Southern backgrounds and render decisions which guarantee the Constitutional rights of negroes. One such rare exception, which electrified the black community, was the ruling by a South Carolina U.S. District Judge, J. Waites Waring, on July 12, 1947, that South Carolina's exclusion of negroes from Democratic primaries was a de facto denial of the right to vote. Judge Waite's decision was upheld by the U.S. Circuit Court of Appeals, and the lily-white primaries of South Carolina's Democratic Party were dead forever. After his ruling, Judge Waring was acclaimed as one of the negro community's new heroes and was honored and feted by a variety of negro and interracial organizations throughout America.

The Revolving-Door Negro

The thesis can be advanced, of course, that negroes have made phenomenal progress in government and politics in the Kennedy and Johnson administrations, compared to previous gains. There is a persuasiveness to the argument that negro political power measured at 3 per cent is a three-hundredfold increase over 1 per cent. Yet, a close examination of many Federal appointments reveals that frequently the same negro has been appointed to two or even three history-making positions during the course of his career. While the historical value of the racial breakthroughs has been acclaimed for their favorable impact on the state of race relations, the rotation of two or three appointments within the career of one negro means that negroes have not acquired any additional political power, nor has there been an accretion of policy-making positions for black people in government.

Those negroes who have been appointed to a series of high-level Federal appointments by a President are what are known as "revolving-door negroes." They are used by the President to initiate a racial breakthrough in several areas. After they have been appointed to their new position, a negro is never appointed to their previous position. The "revolving-door negroes" do not add more negroes to the policy-making positions in government. Instead, they add more status to the individual achievements of that particular negro appointee. His personal pride is increased, not the political power of his race.

This is not an indictment of the negro accepting a series of such appointments or even an indictment of the negro's personal ambitions. Rather, the inability of a President to find an additional black man for a high-level Federal appointment is the harshest indictment of that President's limited approach to the solution of the racial problem. It is the President who makes the decision that he has sufficient respect for only one or two negroes to fill the various positions to which they are appointed. The "revolving-door negro" is simply another manifestation of the racism inherent in the office of the President of the United States. While the "revolving-door negro" is utilized most successfully and exploited with the greatest fanfare by one President, it is nonetheless possible for two or three Presidents to appoint the same negro to a variety of prestigious positions because this particular "negro leader" has established impeccable credentials to national leadership or personal achievement.

Historically, a "revolving-door negro" could be a militant, or he could be one who was forthright and uncompromising in his fight for equality. More often than not, however, he was usually the safest the Congressional traffic could bear without provoking a united opposition to the appointment. In the Johnson administration, the "revolving-door negro" has either been an "Uncle Tom" or one who could be counted upon not to cause any serious emotional dislocation of the body politic. Still a Southerner by temperament and in his relations with negroes, President Johnson has gravitated toward those negroes who did not make him feel personally uncomfortable and who could assure him that everything he was doing in the area of race relations was right, good, and proper. Thus, one of Johnson's favorite negroes, to whom he often turned for advice, was the moderate-conservative executive secretary of the NAACP, Roy Wilkins.

Probably the first "revolving-door negro" in the Federal appointive process was that brilliant and legendary "father of the protest movement" and the intellectual forerunner of the Black Power philosophy, Frederick Douglass. Douglass was appointed first by President Grant in 1871 to be the secretary of the Santo Domingo Commission. In 1877, President Hayes appointed Douglass as Federal Marshal for the District of Columbia, and in 1881, President Garfield appointed him Recorder of Deeds for the District of Columbia. In 1889, President Harrison named him Minister Resident and Consul General to Haiti. In Douglass' case, not only were his appointments well deserved, but there was a paucity of men of his incredible intellect and personal charisma. There were other negroes on the national scene who could have held these jobs and administered them with the same degree of competence as Douglass. But Douglass was unquestionably one of the most distinguished black men of his day, and his appointments were a justifiable recognition by the Federal government of his contributions to progress. What the series of Douglass appointments did do, however, was to lay a kind of prior claim by negroes to that office and to endow the office with new respectability and remove it from the category of "for whites only."

The second nationally prominent revolving-door negro was William H. Hastie, a scholarly lawyer and former dean of Howard University Law School. In 1940, President Roosevelt appointed him a civilian aide and race-relations adviser to Secretary of the Army Henry Stimson. In 1943, Hastie did something that very few negro Federal appointees have ever had the courage to do—he resigned in protest against an Army decision to establish a segregated technical training school at Jefferson Barracks, Mo. His unusual display of personal courage apparently did not injure his promising career, and in 1946 Hastie was named Governor of the Virgin Islands by President Truman. In 1949, President Truman nominated Hastie to be the first black member of the U.S. Circuit Court of Appeals, where he now serves with distinction.

While President Kennedy was the first President to make many historic appointments for negroes within one administration, he appointed few "revolving-door negroes" because of his determination to avail himself of a quantity of competent negro appointees.

On the other hand, President Johnson has shown a propensity for keeping the black revolving door whirling constantly. Of the twenty-eight major appointments during the first four years of his administration (including the first negro to the U.S. Supreme Court, the first negro member of the Federal Reserve Board of Governors, the first negro director of the U.S. Information Agency, the first negro Cabinet member, and the first negro woman ambassador), six were "revolving-door negroes," Thurgood Marshall, Robert C. Weaver, Carl T. Rowan, Clifford L. Alexander, Andrew F. Brimmer and Hobart Taylor.

The "revolving-door negro" process may knock down racial barriers, but it does not build up racial political power. Thus, the proportion of negroes in policy-making positions in government is increased at an agonizingly sluggish pace. Had black people recognized earlier the built-in element of

political retardation in the "revolving-door negro" process and complained
about its efficiency in delaying a true accretion of black political power, they
might have been able to move rapidly into the higher councils of Federal
power.

The States

Negro political power as reflected by state representatives, elected and
appointed state officials, and judicial appointees varies with individual states.
For the most part, however, negroes have not been successful at the state
level in striking any remote balance between the proportion of negro elective offices or appointments and their proportion in the population.

As of the November 1967 elections, thirty states had black state legislators
in either the lower house or the senate.

As of 1967, only Connecticut had an elected official among the five top
state offices of governor, lieutenant governor, secretary, treasurer or controller, and attorney general. He is Gerald A. Lamb of Waterbury, the state
treasurer, who was nominated in 1962 on the Democratic ticket after the
Republicans had already nominated a negro attorney from Hartford, William Graham. Lamb defeated Graham in a Democratic sweep and was subsequently re-elected for a second term in 1966.

As of 1967, only three states had negroes in the state cabinet—New York,
California, and Ohio. At the time of these appointments, all three states
had Republican governors (Nelson A. Rockefeller, New York; Ronald
Reagan, California; and James A. Rhodes, Ohio).

As the following table indicates, negro membership in thirty state legislatures was 127 out of a total of 657 or 4.4 per cent in 1967. Illinois led with
the largest number of negro state legislators (thirteen) in the lower house,
but Missouri negroes should be regarded as possessing more political power
in the state legislature since their twelve negro members constituted 11.1 per
cent of the total in the lower house, compared to Illinois's negro legislators,
who constituted only 7.3 per cent. When these two percentages are related
to the percentage of the two states' negro population—Missouri, 9.0 per cent
and Illinois, 10.3 per cent—we see that the legislative power of Missouri
negroes is appreciably greater.

As the electoral patterns in the loyalties of negroes in the last twenty years
have indicated, the overwhelming majority of elective offices have been held
by Democrats.

Progress in the short span of seven years in the state legislatures has kept
pace with the strident urgency of the civil-rights movement. As of 1960,
there were only an estimated thirty state representatives and six state
senators.

Extent of Negro Representation in State
Legislative Bodies in U.S. (1966-67)*

| | IN STATE LOWER HOUSES | | | IN STATE SENATES | | | |
State	Total Members	Negro Members	Negro Per Cent of Total	Total Members	Negro Members	Negro Per Cent of Total	Negro Per Cent of Total Population
Michigan	110	9	8.1	34	3	8.8	9.2
Illinois	177	13	7.3	58	4	6.8	10.3
Missouri	163	12	7.3	34	1	2.9	9.0
Ohio	127	9	6.5	33	2	6.0	8.1
California	80	5	6.2	40	2	5.0	5.6
Tennessee	99	6	6.0	----	--	----	16.5
Georgia	205	12	5.8	54	2	3.7	28.5
Delaware	35	2	5.7	17	1	5.8	13.6
Maryland	123	7	5.6	29	2	6.9	16.7
New York	150	8	5.3	58	3	5.1	8.4
Pennsylvania	210	10	4.7	50	1	2.0	7.5
Indiana	100	4	4.0	40	1	2.5	5.8
New Jersey	50	3	6.0	21	1	4.7	8.5
Colorado	65	2	3.0	35	1	2.8	2.3
Nevada	37	1	2.7	----	--	----	
Oklahoma	119	3	2.5	44	1	2.2	6.6
Arizona	80	1	2.5	----	1	----	3.3
Nebraska	43	1	2.3	Unicameral Body			
Kentucky	100	2	2.0	----	--	----	7.1
Iowa	108	2	1.8	----	--	----	0.9
Connecticut	294	4	1.3	36	1	2.7	4.2
Texas	150	2	1.3	31	1	3.2	
Massachusetts	240	3	1.2	----	--	----	2.2
West Virginia	100	1	1.0	----	--	----	4.8
Washington	99	1	1.0	----	--	----	1.7
Wisconsin	100	1	1.0	----	--	----	1.9
Kansas	125	1	0.8	40	3	7.5	4.2
TOTALS	3281	126	3.8	657	31	4.4	

* Statistics were compiled by Ernest Calloway and published in the November 25, 1966, issue of the *Missouri Teamster*. It is one of the most comprehensive studies ever undertaken of negro state representation. As has been already indicated earlier, three Deep South states—Virginia, Louisiana, and Mississippi—elected negroes to state legislatures in 1967, thus bringing the total of the states that have negro state representatives to 30.

There is still a political blackout of negro state legislators in the Southern states of Alabama, Arkansas, Florida, and South Carolina, even though negroes are respectively 30 per cent, 22 per cent, 18 per cent, and 35 per cent of the population. As of 1967, the Bureau of the Census estimated that 55 per cent of the country's black people still lived in the South.

As is true for the Federal judiciary, the judiciary of most states have traditionally barred negroes from their higher courts. As of 1967, there were no negroes in any of the state supreme courts or highest courts. The negro judge occupying the highest state judicial position is Harold A. Stevens, a

Justice of the Appellate Division of the Supreme Court of New York State. (The highest court in New York State is the Court of Appeals, which hears cases from the Appellate Division of the Supreme Court.)

According to a study made by California State Senator Mervyn M. Dymally in 1967, published in the *Christian Science Monitor* on November 4, 1967, there were eight negroes serving on state college governing boards.

In summary, the pattern of negro political power in the state executive, legislative, and judicial branches is one of weakness. The greatest power is exhibited in the legislatures and there is a near absence of any negro representation in the state courts. As will be demonstrated in the case studies of the cities, negro political power has been most successfully orchestrated in the cities. Here, the black vote, as a balance of power and as a cohesive bloc to elect black officials, has realized its fullest expression.

Rarely, however, has the negro vote been organized by negro politicians or been responsive to their leadership as a punitive force. Blindly loyal and as affectionately faithful as an overgrown sheep dog, the black vote has lain at its white master's feet, lapping up the small bones of patronage tossed its way. When the master has commanded the vote to exhibit its fidelity, it has stirred itself from the fireplace of its second-class status, risen slowly, and lumbered to the polls to vote without question or discrimination. After the vote, it has returned to its preferred place by the smoldering coals of contentment and lazily waited for a few more tiny bones of patronage to keep it amused as a substitute for the large delights enjoyed by other ethnic groups.

There are two classic examples of the black vote defying the expected pattern of behavior. In one instance, it successfully switched parties to elect a mayor. In another instance, it supported a negro candidate at the risk of causing the defeat of a liberal white candidate, but did so deliberately to teach the white politician a lesson.

The first instance, one of the very few remarkable displays of outright Machiavellian maneuvering by a negro politician, occurred in 1928 in Memphis, Tenn., under the astute and shrewd generalship of Robert R. Church, one of America's most brilliant black politicians.

The incumbent Democratic mayor, Rowlett Paine, had been elected in 1923 with the help of negro votes by promising certain improvements in the black community and a cessation of police brutality against negroes. Subsequently, these promises were not fulfilled to the satisfaction of negroes. Compounding their disappointment was the construction of a garbage incinerator only a few hundred yards away from a negro high school and a negro amusement park, despite their organized protests. Negroes angrily struck back. Church threw the full weight of his organization and political skills to the support of Watkins Overton, the Democratic nominee for mayor, against the Republican nominee supported by Paine. Church led a voter-registration drive among negroes and it was this expanded vote that was credited with the election of the Democratic candidate, Overton.*

The political ingredients of this particular election are a fascinating study in power politics. A powerful Republican negro politician turned his back on the nominee of his own party in a Southern city, crossed over to the Democratic Party to support its nominee, organized a vote drive, and brought the black vote with him to defeat the nominee of his own party! That is a classic example of black political power in the most splendid exercise of its retributive energies to make a point.

A second instance of black political power operating for a different purpose—the recognition of demands in an election or the deliberate scuttling by negroes of an entire slate to cause its defeat—occurred in Houston in 1956. Samuel Lubell describes what happened:

> In Houston, Texas . . . a loose sort of understanding existed under which Negroes joined with labor unions and other "progressive" groups in supporting "liberal" candidates. When the 1956 campaign for the school board started, the liberal leaders wanted to avoid the segregation issue, believing that raising it meant certain defeat. When this view was presented to Carter Wesley, who published a string of Negro newspapers in the Houston area, he insisted the segregation question be met head on. Declaring "it's time to stand up and be counted," Wesley demanded the coalition run a Negro as one of its candidates. When the coalition refused, a Negro entered the race independently. He was defeated, along with the entire liberal slate.
>
> "We knew he couldn't win without liberal support," explained Wesley, "but we showed them they could not win without us either.**

That commitment to "us" among black politicians has been as much a political rarity as attendance by Alabama's George Wallace at a meeting of the Student Nonviolent Coordinating Committee.

Black voters have not yet developed the political sophistication of retribution to the extent other ethnic groups have. A politician voting against the state of Israel will lose 95 per cent of the Jewish vote. A legislator voting to sever diplomatic relations with Italy would lose 95 per cent of the Italian vote. A politician who is an uncompromising advocate of birth control would be treated just as uncompromisingly at the polls by Irish Catholic voters. Yet, at the 1964 Democratic National Convention in Atlantic City, very few black delegates protested when the segregated Mississippi delegation was seated and the Mississippi Freedom Democratic Party's predominantly negro delegation was rejected. Despite the tense emotionalism of this issue and the fact that the MFDP voted unanimously to reject the so-called compromise plan offered by the Credentials Subcommittee, there was

---

* Paul Lewinson, *Race, Class and Party*, p. 141.
** Samuel Lubell, *Black and White* (New York: Harper & Row, 1964), p. 70.

little black delegate support for the Mississippi negroes. Racial loyalties were overcome by political chains.

An almost shocking example of the black voters' lack of ability to discern loyalty to the cause of advancing the interests of his ethnic group occurred in the April 1964 Democratic primary in Chicago.

Running for re-election in the Sixth Congressional District was Representative Thomas J. O'Brien, an elderly fourteen-term Congressman. Ill for several months prior to the primary, O'Brien had been unable to campaign in the predominantly black district on the West Side. Running against him was a young black woman who had long been active in civic and civil-rights programs. On primary day, Congressman O'Brien died. But that did not matter to the black voters in his district. They went out anyway and voted for a dead white man over a live colored woman, re-electing O'Brien.

Loyalty, whether it derives from a religious or a racial background, is the most important element in building a powerful bloc vote. After loyalty, the ability to punish enemies is next. The four most important elements in building a powerful voting bloc are: 1) ethnic loyalty at any cost; 2) the ability to promise punishment and make good on the promise; 3) the capacity to switch political loyalties at any given time on any issue; and 4) the ability to secure jobs and important policy-making appointments for members of that voting bloc.

Political switching involves ticket-splitting, a habit that not only has eluded black voters, but has evaded the intelligence of most white voters. Thus, while it was logical for negroes to vote for Kennedy in 1960, it was not equally consistent for them to vote for Democratic Southern racists. Had the black vote, critical in Texas, South Carolina, and Illinois, which provided the margin of victory in those three states and thus Kennedy's election, voted for the local or state Republicans who were not so antagonistic to black ambitions as their Democratic opponents, the white political bosses would have acquired a new respect for—and fear of—black voters.

The last element, the ability to secure jobs for its members, has been the area of greatest weakness among negroes. This is because black voters have been brainwashed with the sterile value of their vote as a balance of power.

The voting process must relate to the governmental process. Unless the black vote has been able to guarantee a significant increase in jobs, better housing, high-level appointments, and more modern educational facilities, then the vote is useless as a force for negro progress.

Although the black vote in the South has increased from a 1940 low of approximately 85,000 to a 1966 comparative high of 2,700,000, there has been no comparable increase in black political strength in the legislatures, the courts, and the state policy-making positions. With the exception of Georgia and Texas (and in 1967, Virginia, Louisiana, and Mississippi, which each elected the first negro to their state legislatures since Reconstruction),

Southern negroes have been unable to make the political impact of their vote felt at the state level. Thus, the mere announcement of a dramatic increase in negro voter registrations is meaningless unless it is juxtaposed with a comparable increase of black judicial and executive appointments and elective offices.

Nor is there evidence to date that this increase in the Southern black vote has influenced the Southern white vote toward a more liberal posture on equal rights for negroes. Thus, in 1966, the two most segregationist candidates in the race for governor of Georgia, Republican Howard H. Callaway and Democrat Lester G. Maddox, polled the largest number of votes in their respective primaries. Any candidate for office in the Deep South who has dared to take a remotely liberal position on the race question has been defeated and will continue to be defeated unless there is a sufficiently large black voting bloc that can ensure his victory in combination with a small number of liberal white votes. This has happened in Atlanta, where the liberal Democrat Charles Weltner was elected to the House of Representatives in 1962 with nearly solid support of Atlanta's black voters, who comprised 38 per cent of the electorate.

Until black voters begin to demand more jobs and appointments for their support, politicians will continue to seek the black vote only as a necessary balance of power to guarantee the margin of victory. Until black voters develop the kind of sophistication that the Memphis negroes exhibited in 1928, when they switched political parties to punish an official who had reneged on his promises, white political bosses will have no respect for the black vote. Until black voters are secure enough and militant enough to demand that white politicians take a strong liberal stand on the racial issue, even at the risk of defeat, the white politicians will continue to compromise and postpone the inevitable day of full black participation in the administration of American democracy.

CHAPTER SIX

The Two Parties: Political Spoils and Racial Progress

*Opposing President Roosevelt that year
[1940] was Wendell Willkie, the big corporation lawyer and businessman. . . . Immediately following the nomination, he
told reporters from the Negro press: "I
want your support. I need it. But irrespec-
tive of whether Negroes go down the line
with me or not, they can expect every consideration. They will get their fair proportion of appointments, their fair representation on policy-making bodies."*

—HENRY LEE MOON, *Balance of Power:
The Negro Vote*, pp. 31-32

One of the most persistently troublesome problems confronting social scientists and historians has been the establishment of indices to measure negro
progress. What is racial progress? A decrease in the number of lynchings?
A decrease in violence between the white and black races? A decline in the
number of negro-committed crimes? A decline in the proportion of black
people on welfare? A proportionately greater drop in black than white unemployment? A proportionately higher increase of negro median family in-
comes vis-à-vis that of whites? An upsurge in interracial marriages? Bigger
budgets for the NAACP, the Urban League, and the National Conference
of Christians and Jews? The proliferation of integrated housing? The increase of integrated schools? A higher proportion of negro jobs in the
Federal government? An increase in the number of negroes holding high-
level positions in government?

Independently, any one of the above groups can be submitted as a persuasive index of advancement and racial progress in the mainstream of white America. Concomitantly, statistics from any one of the same group can be used to contradict another as a measurement of such progress.

While the number of lynchings in the South during the last fifty years has declined, the number of segregated public schools in the North has increased. While the median family income of negroes has continuously increased, it still has remained half that of whites. While the budgets of the NAACP, the Urban League, and the National Conference of Christians and Jews have high-jumped all out of proportion to their value and worth to American society, black violence in American cities has escalated just as rapidly.

Relations between the white and black races have deteriorated and are at their lowest ebb in decades.

While integrated private housing has increased, segregated public housing has also proliferated. While negroes have been appointed to a larger number of policy-making positions in the Federal government, they have been virtually excluded from such positions in state governments.

Progress, of course, shows more clearly when taken in the perspective of a century. The progress of the negro in America is quickly evident from his emancipation from the debauchery of slavery in 1863 to the election in 1967 of negro mayors in two of the country's largest and most important cities; the Presidential appointment of a negro mayor of the nation's capital; and the existence of sixteen negro-owned banks, thirty-nine negro-owned insurance companies, forty-six negro-owned Federal savings and loan associations, 170 negro-owned newspapers, scores of negro-owned businesses and small enterprises, and—keeping faith with the American dream—even a few black millionaires.

Granted that all these achievements, compared with those of whites, represent the most wretched example of tokenism, they nevertheless must be recognized as a form of progress, no matter how limited. Whether black people will be able to sustain such economic and political progress in the future instead of reverting to the familiar historical fate of organized repression that characterized the post-Reconstruction era cannot be predicted.

Whatever happens will depend on the Federal government. More accurately, it will be the responsibility of the political parties.

The progress of a people, of a country, of a nation is the progress orchestrated by its government. Governments fight wars, create depressions, prevent plagues, and keep criminal activity within manageable limits. Governments set monetary policies, raise taxes, control employment, and establish new boundaries of Federal concern for the welfare of the people.

In a democracy, the government is controlled by political parties. Political parties chart the course and determine the domestic policies a government will pursue. The party leaders decide who shall run the government and then turn over the reins of power to the winners of the elections. At that point, the political party takes a back seat.

A political party's sole purpose is to win elections. It is not an apparatus of social engineering. It leaves that process to the elected officials and their appointees. But a political party can win elections only so long as it is responsive to the largest proportion of the electorate and can most successfully reconcile its divergent and conflicting interests. People don't count, only voters.

A political party must be able to point to a series of accomplishments and outstanding achievements that have "made this country great" or returned it to "normalcy," given the people a New Deal or promised to end the war in Korea. Whatever promises are made must be fulfilled, or the party will not be able to convince the people to return the government to office. At all times, the electorate must experience a sense of progress and a feeling of continuing change for the better.

Parochialism of Black Expectations

For negroes, the government, particularly the Federal government, has assumed a greater dimension of importance because of their powerlessness. The negro's lack of mobility, his abject poverty, and his brutal oppression by local and state authorities acting under the cloak of legality have forced negroes as a group to turn to the Federal government for relief.

Although the Federal government has been slow to respond to their needs and demands—and, in many instances, has even been hostile—black people have still solicited its intercession for only one reason. They have had no choice, no other place to go.

As a result, national political parties have had to decide every four years, in convention platforms, in the kind of candidate they nominate, and in their posture to the entire white electorate, just how many concessions can and should be made to negroes without alienating whites. But platforms are merely signposts along the road of political progress. They only tell where a party is likely to go, not what it actually intends to do.

Again, the government, controlled by the ideology of the political party responsible for its existence, makes the crucial decisions about the specifics of intended policy.

The history of the negro in America conclusively demonstrates that no one political party, no one government, no single President, can claim sole credit or even a major share of the responsibility for the negro's economic, educational, and political progress. Rather, each party, each government has tended to improve, sometimes more slightly than massively, upon the policies of the previous government, even when it had inaugurated a series of spectacular gains.

If the negro's first measurable economic gains were made during World War I, then it is equally logical to assign credit for black progress to war and not to the Democratic Party. (Unless, of course, the Democratic Party wished to accept political responsibility as the "war party.")

But, as Table I indicates, the growth of negro median family income has

TABLE I

Median Money Income of Families in Current Dollars,
By Color of Head: 1947-64

YEAR	WHITE	NONWHITE
1947	$3,157	$1,614
1949	3,230	1,650
1950	3,445	1,869
1951	3,859	2,032
1952	4,114	2,338
1953	4,392	2,461
1954	4,339	2,410
1955	4,605	2,549
1956	4,993	2,628
1957	5,166	2,764
1958	5,300	2,711
1959	5,643	2,917
1960	5,835	3,233
1961	5,981	3,191
1962	6,237	3,330
1963	6,548	3,465
1964	6,858	3,839

Statistical Abstract of the United States, 1966, p. 340

been steadily upward through the governments of both political parties. Neither political party has been able to engineer any dramatic elevation of the negro's economic condition. Instead, the collectivity of local and state discriminatory practices, racist oppressions, depressions, wars, inflations, and Federal policies toward racial discrimination have conjointly regulated the pace of negro economic progress.

There are, however, two major periods of economic change in the economic condition of the negro. The first was his emancipation in 1863 and subsequent receipt of American citizenship. The other was his participation in the New Deal of the 1930's.

Not only did the New Deal provide jobs for hitherto unemployed black people as well as succor them on relief rolls, but the Roosevelt administration appointed fifty-five Negroes to minor policy-making jobs in its early years and, by 1940, increased that number to one hundred. None of these jobs could be compared to the top-level appointments of the Kennedy administration, but they did represent the first time that negroes had been employed in significant numbers in the Federal government to do something besides hold the traditional honorary negro jobs.

Henry Lee Moon describes the economic progress of negroes under the Roosevelt administration thus:

The gains made under Roosevelt were tangible and lasting: the 66,850 new low-rent dwellings made available for low-income Negro families who formerly were compelled to live in slums; the hospitals, schools and recreational centers built with federal aid, the training of thousands of young Negroes in the programs of the National Youth Administration and the Civilian Conservation Corps, the aid to more than half a million Negro farmers, the opening up of new employment opportunities in government and in private industry, the stimulation of a progressive non-discriminating labor movement, the breaking down of some of the barriers in the armed services and in the merchant marine, the elimination of Jim Crow in most important cafeterias and bureaus, and perhaps most important, the appointment of a liberal Supreme Court which vindicated the Negro's right and by banning the white primary, opened the way to mass Negro voting in the South."*

That last statement by Moon was, of course, both wishful thinking and literary exaggeration. There was no "mass negro voting in the South," or even registration, until the passage of the Voting Rights Act in 1965. The South was simply a most proficient evader of the law and constantly discovered new techniques and methods to prevent negroes from registering and voting.

Samuel Lubell shares Moon's enthusiasm for the impact of the New Deal on the negro's economic status, but he draws a precise relationship between the negro's economic improvement and his switch from Republican to Democrat during the Roosevelt years. According to Lubell, "In the nation as a whole the really big Negro political break came in 1936. . . . At the time observers credited this astonishing political conversion to work relief provided by the creation of WPA." Lubell offers the following table of statistics as substantiation of this position:**

	PER CENT OF NEGROES UNEMPLOYED	PER CENT OF REPUBLICAN VOTE FOR PRESIDENT IN NEGRO WARDS	
	1932	1932	1936
Chicago	30	77	51
Cleveland	33	76	38
Philadelphia	28	73	34
Pittsburgh	25	48	17
Detroit	37	50	25
New York City	24	41	19

* Moon, pp. 36-37.
** Samuel Lubell, *White and Black: Test of a Nation* (New York: Harper & Row, 1964), p. 53.

Continuing his assessment of the economic impact of the New Deal on the negro's voting habits, Lubell writes:

Nearly every aspect of Negro life was touched—and transformed.

WPA itself, for example, really served as an economic floor for the whole Negro community. As long as a Negro could go on WPA he was not forced to accept work at any wage that might be offered him. Rarely has any single government action so suddenly lifted the economic bargaining power of a whole race.

The CCC camps drew something like 200,000 Negroes off the city streets, 30,000 of them living in integrated camps. PWA funds were allocated to build housing, schools and hospitals for Negroes. The swelling rosters of government employees included a record number of Negro appointees.

More significant perhaps than the increase in the number of Negro appointees was the change in the quality of this patronage. Under Republican Presidents a handful of federal posts had been reserved by tradition for Negroes. Invariably these positions—the recorder of deeds in Washington, D.C. and the register of the Treasury, or as envoys to Haiti, to Liberia and other parts of Africa—were far removed from any concern with domestic Negro problems.*

Lubell, of course, ignores the fact that the Republicans nevertheless initiated the breakthroughs on Federal appointments, even though they were "far removed" from Negro problems. A pattern was established. Once it was, the Democrats were forced to improve upon such appointments, and they did.

Had there been no Republican-appointed recorder of deeds, Federal marshal of the District of Columbia, register of the Treasury, or envoys to Haiti and Liberia, there would have been no Democratic-appointed "Black Cabinet." The existence of this informal Black Cabinet irritated white Southerners and delighted black people. The idea that an informal group of black men and women were actually determining Federal policy, no matter how limited or restricted, was a source of sheer ecstasy to negroes. The titular head of the Black Cabinet was Mrs. Mary McLeod Bethune. Because of her close friendship with Mrs. Eleanor Roosevelt, Mrs. Bethune had access to the White House, and, many alleged, the President's ear.**

Mrs. Bethune was first asked by Roosevelt to serve on the Advisory Committee of the National Youth Administration. At a meeting in 1935, she made a moving speech about the wretched conditions of America's black youth. Impressed with her eloquence, the President subsequently set up an office of Minority Affairs within NYA and appointed her as Administrator,

---

* Lubell, pp. 54-55.
** One of the many wonderful stories told about Mrs. Bethune and her enormous dignity and pride in her black skin concerns one of her frequent trips to the White House. One day, she was trudging up the pathway to the White House to see the President, and a Southern white gardener watched this stout black woman walking with the air of a prominent statesman. "Hey, there, Auntie, where y'all think you goin'?" he said. Mrs. Bethune stopped, walked quietly over to the gardener, peered intently at him, and said: "For a moment, I didn't recognize you. Which one of my sister's children are you?"

the highest Federal post to be held by a negro woman as of that year. Later, the title and the division were changed, and Mrs. Bethune became Director of the Division of Negro Affairs. Her influence as head of the Black Cabinet was pervasive and intensive.

Other members of the Black Cabinet included William H. Hastie, the brilliant lawyer who was to later become a Federal judge; Robert C. Weaver, who began in the Interior Department as a race-relations adviser under Harold Ickes and later served in the Federal Housing Administration, where he acquired the basis of his expertise, later evident in his appointment as Secretary of Housing and Urban Affairs; and Walter White, the shrewd, easy-going executive secretary of the NAACP. There were others, but this small group wielded the most influence and was able to affect Federal policy to the limited extent that it could be favorably directed toward negroes. Their collective efforts resembled a mole hill more than a mountain, and, as the late Louis Lautier, Washington correspondent for the National Negro Publishers Association and the first black reporter to be admitted to membership in the House press gallery, once observed sarcastically: "In actual practice, race relations advisers perform very little, if any, useful service to the agency in which they are employed or to the people whose special interests they are supposed to serve."

But, with the built-in limitations of the Roosevelt administration, still dominated by a Southern-controlled, racist-oriented Congress and a civil service hostile to improving the plight of negroes, progress was made.

As was true of the Lincoln administration, the Roosevelt administration benefited the Negro incidentally, and almost inadvertently. Neither Lincoln nor Roosevelt initiated his policies intentionally to lift the negro from his second-class citizenship. Both Presidents were racial conservatives who constructed their policies to save the nation and help the country. If negroes benefited, well and good. But negroes were not intended as the prime targets of Federal good will.*

Recognizing the Tweedledee and Tweedledum efforts of the Democratic and Republican parties to alter their impoverishment, and the lack of any permanent moral commitment to racial equality, negroes concentrated on acquiring the outer and more visible trappings of full citizenship: civil rights —the right to vote instead of the guarantee of the right to vote; the right to

---

* If negroes were not quite convinced that Roosevelt had become their great Economic Savior, whites certainly were. Harry Golden, in *Mr. Kennedy and the Negroes*, p. 73, describes a typical Southern white reaction to Roosevelt's widely imputed commitment to economic improvement for negroes:

"Not long after I came to Charlotte in 1941, I shared a taxicab with a Negro passenger. His destination was first and he gave the driver a five-dollar bill. He got his change and as we drove off, the cab-driver said: 'God-damn that Roosevelt.'

" 'Why?' I asked.

" 'When the hell did a nigger ever have a five-dollar bill?' he answered."

use public accommodations instead of the guarantee of an income which would ensure utilization of that right; and the right to an equal education instead of the guarantee of an excellent education.

Unlike ethnic groups and minorities which had previously meshed into the American way of life, negroes chose the most narrow and least productive approach to equality. Undoubtedly, the blackness of their skin was the one factor that set them apart. In a culture that prided itself on the nobility of its whiteness, there was a certain security with which any white person was endowed, no matter how low his station in life. Black people suffered from historical timidity.

As a result, negroes devoted themselves to acquiring those peripheral social manifestations which would dilute the harshness of their inferiority. Theirs was a concern more for symbols than for substance. Symbols are cheap, and negroes learned to think cheap. The parochialism of black expectations ensured a paucity of bold achievements. Because symbols were important, symbolic achievements were accepted as substitutes for racial progress. White liberals, alleged friends of the negro, encouraged him to believe that a symbolic black appointment would somehow filter down through the iron curtain of race hate and uplift hundreds of thousands of black people from poverty.

But the symbolic negro appointment was also part of the phony veneer of American democracy. Not only negroes but women have traditionally been excluded from the decision-making process in American politics. The first woman to be appointed to a high-level position in local, state, or Federal government or the first woman to win an elective office has always been the cause for much editorial congratulation.

But all the "negro firsts" have still not raised black people to an economic, political, or educational level with whites.

As of 1960, according to a report of the House Education and Labor Committee, only 18.6 per cent of all white families earned less than $3000 a year, compared with 49.4 per cent of all negro families. This pattern of black poverty—approximately two and one-half times less income than that of whites—has persisted since 1935, one of the first years when negro median family incomes were measured separately from whites'. Black unemployment has also stabilized at two and one-half times the rate for whites. (See Table II.)

As an additional index of racial discrimination and the lack of significant negro economic advancement, negroes have been concentrated in the unskilled and lower-paying jobs.

Even as the unemployment rate for whites has dropped, Negro unemployment has continued to rise. An article in the *Washington Post* on September 5, 1967, headlined this dismal fact of life: "More Negroes Jobless Than Ever as Employment Peaks." According to the article,

This summer, more Americans held jobs than at any·time in the Nation's history and the unemployment rate for the country as a whole was less than 4 per cent.

But this summer too, more American Negroes were unemployed than ever before. The rate of Negro unemployment in nine major cities checked by the Department of Labor was an official 9.5 per cent—more than twice the over-all rate. If "under employment" figures are included, however, an astounding 33.9 per cent of the cities' Negroes either had no jobs, worked only part-time or were so ill-paid they still were poverty cases.

TABLE II

1967 Department of Labor Survey on Negro Unemployment

CITY	TOTAL UNEMPLOYMENT RATE	WHITE RATE	NEGRO RATE
St. Louis	4.7%	3.1%	12.7%
Detroit	4.5	3.2	10.7
Newark	4.7	3.8	10.5
San Francisco-Oakland	5.8	5.0	10.2
Cleveland	3.8	2.7	9.5
Baltimore	3.8	2.3	8.3
Chicago	3.2	2.3	8.2
Philadelphia	3.7	2.8	8.0
Los Angeles-Long Beach	5.5	5.3	7.6

In a September 11, 1966, article, the *New York Times* headlined the question: "Negro Jobless Up—Why?" Finally, in a report released by the Department of Labor on December 13, 1967, it was revealed that a third of the country's unemployed and nearly 40 per cent of all jobless negroes are concentrated in the nation's fifteen largest metropolitan areas. W. Willard Wirtz, the Secretary of Labor, whose department is completely controlled by the AFL-CIO, was quick to issue a simultaneous denial that the study showed any correlation between high negro unemployment (partially fostered by unyielding bars in labor unions) and severe racial unrest. Wirtz was blandly able to make this denial despite the fact that Detroit and Newark, which ranked second and third respectively in negro unemployment, had had two of the nation's worst racial rebellions in the summer of 1967.

The seat of American democracy, the capital of the United States, Washington, D.C., provides an object lesson on the depth and extent of racial discrimination against negroes in labor unions. Despite the publicized good intentions of both Democrats and Republicans, neither political party has been willing or able to break down the racial barriers in D.C. unions. In fact, President Johnson accorded such discrimination a kind of Presidential blessing when he appointed J. C. Turner, secretary of the Central Labor Council of Greater Washington, to the City Council as one of nine councilmen. No one man has been more responsible for the racial exclusion of negroes from the D. C. unions than Turner. But it took a Presidential appointment to honor him for his reluctance.

According to a June 18, 1967, report by the D.C. Apprenticeship Council, there were no black journeyman glaziers, lathers, plumbers, pipefitters, sheet-metal workers, tile and terrazzo workers, machinists, photoengravers, or non-construction painters. Out of 2081 apprentices undergoing training as of that date in the District, only 384, or 13 per cent, were negroes. This pattern of racial exclusion not only was an abominable contradiction of democracy in the nation's capital, but was further accentuated by the fact that negroes constitute 66 per cent of the District's population!

As proficient in making surveys as the other Cabinet departments, the Department of Labor is a determined practitioner of racial discrimination in its hiring policies. While the other Cabinet departments are headed by men who are either personally antinegro or simply too lazy to worry about the lack of integration within their agencies, the Department of Labor's policy is strongly influenced by the bigotry of the AFL-CIO. Under the leadership of George Meany, a cigar-chomping, bald-headed machinist who worked his way up from the gutters of the union and never permitted the dirt of racism to be washed from his mind, the AFL-CIO has called the shots in the appointments of officials within the Labor Department. Any negro who has shown the slightest aggressiveness or independence has been vetoed by Meany or his lieutenants. Wirtz, a well-intentioned lawyer who has tried to move forthrightly on the lack of integration within his department as well as on the inefficacy of the various manpower training programs which have been scuttled by labor, has nonetheless been tied in political knots by the person-to-person maneuvering of Meany to President Johnson.

The statistics in the following table, published by the U.S. Civil Service Commission in "Study of Minority Group Employment in the Federal Government 1966," show the comparative lack of advancement of negroes in the Federal government, particularly at the policy levels, where jobs are created, decisions are made to hire personnel, and programs are implemented to hire large numbers of hard-core unemployed. But such statistics fail to tell the whole story, because of the dishonest method of reporting and the deliberate misrepresentation practiced by the Civil Service Commission. The reason the categories GS 12 through 18 are combined is to disguise the failure of the Federal government to encourage the appointment of more negroes at a faster rate in "super-grade" jobs (GS 16 to 18). Naturally, a greater increase would be expected in the lower grades, GS 12 to 15. By lumping the super-grade jobs with the lower grades, an impression of rapid advancement is created.

TABLE III

Federal Service Negro Employment Summary, All Agencies, June 1966

| PAY CATEGORY | Identified Employment* (91.8 Per Cent of Total Employment) | | |
| | TOTAL EMPLOYMENT | NEGRO EMPLOYMENT | |
		NUMBER	PER CENT
TOTAL, all pay plans	2,303,906	320,136	13.9
Total, class, act, etc.	1,126,985	109,658	9.7
GS 1 to 4	352,514	65,548	18.6
GS 5 to 8	309,754	31,205	10.1
GS 9 to 11	254,635	9,642	3.8
GS 12 to 18	210,082	3,263	1.6
Total, Wage Board	537,681	110,590	20.6
Up to $4499	78,587	33,886	43.1
$4500 to 6499	233,096	58,943	25.3
$6500 to 7999	172,490	16,223	9.4
$8000 and over	53,508	1,538	2.9
Total, Postal Field Service	594,220	94,449	15.9
PFS 1 to 4**	507,602	87,686	17.3
PFS 5 to 8	69,225	6,410	9.3
PFS 9 to 11	13,514	296	2.2
PFS 12 to 20	3,879	57	1.5
Total, other pay plans	45,020	5,439	12.1
Up to $4499	11,927	3,997	33.5
$4500 to 6499	9,843	899	9.1
$6500 to 7999	4,176	146	3.5
$8000 and over	1,074	397	2.1

 * Of 2,511,052 employees, 207,146 (8.2 percent) are unidentified.
 ** Includes fourth class postmasters and rural carriers.

It must be noted, however, that negroes are concentrated in the lower pay plans. Thus, when the question of the extent of racial progress is raised, the percentage of negroes in the lower grades, GS 1 to 4, increased from 18.1 per cent in 1962 to 18.6 per cent in 1966. The increase of negroes in GS 12 to 18 from .8 per cent in 1962 to 1.3 per cent in 1966 was achieved more easily because: 1) There is a smaller total of employees in those grades compared with the lower grades; and 2) the doubling of the comparatively small number of negro employees in the higher grades appears to be more dramatic than the evidence would warrant.

With the 18.6 per cent concentration of negroes in the lower grades, it was an easy exercise in administrative braggadocio for President Johnson to claim on March 17, 1966, that, "As of June 1965, the Government had about 375,000 members of minority groups on its rolls, of which 308,657 were Negroes. Negroes accounted for 13.5 per cent of the Federal work force, while they actually made up approximately 10 per cent of our over-all population."

But the over-all pattern of black employment within the Federal government is one of severe racial discrimination. While President Johnson can boast of his "Negro 13 per cent," other Cabinet departments do not begin to approach this percentage. The Department of Justice, which is responsible for administering equal treatment of the races, had only 5.9 per cent negro employees; Interior, 4.4 per cent; and Agriculture, 5.1 per cent.

In three departments, negroes comprise nearly 50 per cent of all personnel in the four lowest grades: State, 45.7 per cent; Post Office, 49 per cent; and Labor, 42.7 per cent.

One of the most rigidly segregated departments in the government is the Government Printing Office. It is permitted this immoral luxury because it is beholden only to the Congress of the United States, itself a determined perpetrator of racial segregation in its employment policies. Of all employees of the Government Printing Office, 41.7 per cent are negro, and 59 per cent of all employees in the four lowest grades are black. And yet, as of June 1966, there was not a single negro in any of the top six grades, GS 12 to 18.

The inability of the Federal government to practice fair employment in allocating its higher positions was never more sharply reflected than in its hiring policies during the establishment of the Equal Employment Opportunity Commission. As a story in the June 20, 1965 issue of the *Evening Star* pointed out, 'The new Equal Employment Opportunity Commission is wrestling with an embarrassing problem: it has recruited no negroes for top staff jobs."

It took pressure by the House Education and Labor Committee Chairman, Representative Adam Clayton Powell, in an exchange of personal and friendly letters with EEOC Chairman, Franklin D. Roosevelt, Jr., to subsequently get two negroes appointed to the positions of general counsel (Charles T. Duncan) and director of contract compliance (George Holland). That was a successful exercise of power.

The Defense Department, also one of the more racially segregated Cabinet departments, has dragged its administrative heels at home while prosecuting a very integrated war in Vietnam. Despite persistent complaints about black servicemen's inability to rent or buy homes in the restricted suburbs of Washington, D.C., the Defense Department waited until December 26, 1967, to issue an order placing all segregated apartment houses within a three-mile radius of the Pentagon off-limits to military families moving in after January 15, 1968. While the order can be expected to have a salutary influence on the ability of black servicemen and their families to rent apartments, it will still pose difficulties, since the Defense Department order excluded private-home rentals.

The depth of racial discrimination in the Northern Virginia area surrounding the Pentagon is evidenced by the overwhelming number of white families living in that area compared to the trickle of black military families.

On the 11,894 military families living in Northern Virginia apartments, only 93, or .8 per cent, were black. Of the 14,194 military families living in apartments in both the Maryland and Virginia suburbs, 933, or 6.5 per cent, were black.

The issuance of the order, which civil-rights leaders argue should have been a matter of Defense Department policy years ago, when black men were dying in the Korean War, was interpreted to be Defense Secretary Robert S. McNamara's last administrative gasp for acceptance as a believer in racial equality. McNamara's appointment as President of the World Bank had been announced several weeks before the issuance of his off-limits order on apartment rentals. But he has been as stubborn in maintaining racial discrimination and segregation in the hiring and promotional policies of the Defense Department as any of the Cabinet secretaries. His refusal to insist on a vigorous enforcement of nondiscrimination in the hiring policies of Defense contractors and his failure to support the Defense Office of Contract Compliance in this area says more about his attitudes on race than the order placing apartments off limits.

But if negroes have been busy treading water in both Federal and private job markets, they have been drowning in the public-school systems.

According to a report issued on February 9, 1967, by the U.S. Commission on Civil Rights, the overwhelming majority of students attend segregated schools. The report, "Racial Isolation in the Public Schools," stated that:

Sixty-five per cent of all first grade Negro pupils surveyed attended schools that have an enrollment 90 per cent or more Negro, while almost 80 per cent of all first grade white students surveyed attend schools that are 90 per cent or more white. A substantially greater proportion of Negro students attend schools that are 50 per cent or more Negro. Approximately 87 per cent of all Negro first graders are in such schools—72 per cent in the urban North; 97 per cent in the urban South.

. . . The Commission's investigation found that in the Nation's metropolitan areas—where two-thirds of both the Nation's Negro and white population now live—school segregation is more severe than the national figures suggest. And it is growing.

Racial concentration also is severe within the central cities.

The Negro Revolution notwithstanding, the economic and educational plight of the negro has still failed to show any dramatic improvement.

It is possibly for such reasons that both the press (white and black) and the Federal government have tended to extol the glamorous virtues of new negro appointments to high positions in government with hyperbolic pretensions of racial progress. But there is still an emptiness in the bottom of the well of these appointments as outlined in the chapter "Measuring Black Political Power."

As Table IV suggests, both political parties have made unusual strides in

TABLE IV

*The Most Significant Black Appointments and Political Breakthroughs
in the Administrations of the Two Major Political Parties*

Republicans	*Democrats*
1863, January 1	
Emancipation Proclamation.	
1865, February 1	
John S. Rock, first negro admitted to practice before the U.S. Supreme Court.	
1866	
First two black men elected to any legislative body in U.S.: Charles L. Mitchell.	Edwin G. Walker.
1867, January 8	
Bill giving black people in D.C. right to vote, passed over Johnson's veto.	
1867	
First Reconstruction Act passed.	
1868, June 13	
Oscar J. Dunn, ex-slave, formally installed as Lt. Governor of Louisiana, highest elective office held by a negro.	
1869, April 16	
Ebenezer Don Carlos Bassett, first negro to receive an appointment in diplomatic service, Minister to Haiti.	
1870, February 25	
First black man to be sworn into Congress, Hiram Rhoades Revel as U.S. Senator from Mississippi.	
1870, December 12	
First negro to be sworn in the U.S. House of Representatives, Joseph H. Rainey of South Carolina.	
1870	
Jefferson Franklin Long elected to U.S. Congress, only negro to serve from Georgia.	
Robert H. Wood elected mayor of Natchez, Miss.	
1872	
P. B. S. Pinchback Acting Governor of Louisiana.	

Republicans   *Democrats*

1875, March 1
Civil-rights law prohibiting discrimination in hotels, theaters, and
on public carriers signed by President Grant.
1877
Frederick Douglass appointed police commissioner by President
Grant and then later in year as
Marshal of D.C. by President
Hayes.
1880
Blanche K. Bruce appointed Register of U.S. Treasury by President
Garfield. Frederick Douglass appointed Recorder of Deeds by
Garfield.
1884, June 3
John Roy Lynch, former Congress-   James M. Trotter appointed Regis-
man from Mississippi, elected tem-   ter of U.S. Treasury by President
porary chairman of Republican   Cleveland, first Democratic Presi-
Convention—first negro to pre-   dent since Civil War.
side over the deliberations of a
national political party.
1901
Booker T. Washington dines at
White House with President Theodore Roosevelt, causing violent
editorial reaction in South and on
floor of Congress.
1929
Oscar S. DePriest elected to House
of Representatives in Chicago, Ill.,
first negro in Congress since 1901.

                                        1934
                                        Arthur Mitchell, first negro to be
                                        elected to Congress as a Democrat,
                                        in Chicago, Ill.
                                        1937
                                        First black Federal Judge, William
                                        H. Hastie, appointed by President
                                        Roosevelt as U.S. District Court
                                        judge in Virgin Islands.

1939
First black woman in U.S., Jane
M. Bolin, to be appointed judge
of City Court of Domestic Relations by Mayor LaGuardia.

Republicans

Democrats

1940
First black general in U.S. history, Benjamin O. Davis, appointed by Roosevelt.

1941
Roosevelt issues Executive Order 8802, establishing FEPC to prohibit racial discrimination in defense work.

1943
Hastie resigns as Civilian Aide to Secretary of War in protest against army policy of segregation.

1944
Adam Clayton Powell, first black Congressman from East, elected.
Irvin C. Mollison becomes first black U.S. Customs Court judge.

1945
First state Federal Employment Practices Commission; law passed, in New York under Governor Dewey.

1946
Hastie named first negro Governor of Virgin Islands.

1947
President Truman's Committee on Civil Rights condemns racial injustice in report, "To Secure These Rights."

1948
First black ambassador, Edward R. Dudley, named, to Liberia. Truman issues Executive Order 9981 ending segregation in U.S. armed forces.

1949
First black to become chairman of Congressional committee, Rep. William L. Dawson of Chicago, chairman of Government Operations Committee. William H. Hastie, first black to U.S. Court of Appeals, named by Truman.

1950
First black alternate delegate to U.N., Edith Sampson of Chicago, named.

1953
First black Manhattan Borough President elected, Hulan E. Jack; highest elective office held by a negro in U.S.

Republicans

Democrats

1954

J. Ernest Wilkins named Assistant Secretary of Labor by President Eisenhower; first negro to be appointed to a subcabinet post; first black general in Air Force, B. O. Davis, Jr., appointed by Eisenhower; first black Permanent Member of U.N. Delegation, Charles H. Mahoney of Detroit, appointed.

Charles C. Diggs, Jr., elected as Michigan's first negro Congressman.

1955

First black White House staff member, E. Frederick Morrow, named.

1957

First black chairman of President's Committee on Government Employment Policy, Archibald Carey of Chicago, named; Civil Rights Act of 1957 signed by Eisenhower —first since 1875.

1958

First black envoy to a European country, Clifton R. Wharton, Sr., named Minister to Romania.

First black Congressman for Pennsylvania, Robert N. C. Nix of Philadelphia, elected.

1960

Eisenhower signs Civil Rights Act of 1960.

Andrew T. Hatcher named White House associate press secretary to President Kennedy.

1961

Rep. Adam Clayton Powell named Chairman of Education and Labor Committee in Congress. Robert C. Weaver appointed by Kennedy as Administrator of Housing and Home Finance Agency, first negro to head a Federal agency and highest position in government ever held by a black man.

1961

Clifton R. Wharton appointed by Kennedy as ambassador to Norway, first black ambassador to Western European country. James B. Parsons appointed to U.S. District Court—first negro to be appointed to U.S. District Court in continental U.S. Thurgood Marshall to U.S. Court of Appeals.

Republicans

Democrats

1962

First black attorney general of a state elected, Edward W. Brooke of Mass.

First black Congressman from California, Augustus F. Hawkins of Los Angeles.

1963

First black man to serve as a member of a Federal regulatory agency, A. Leon Higginbotham, appointed to Federal Trade Commission by Kennedy.

1964

Civil Rights Act of 1964 signed by President Johnson on July 2; Act considered strongest in U.S. history. John Conyers elected to Congress from Detroit; city is first in U.S. to have two negro Congressmen. First black Director of U.S. Information Agency, Carl T. Rowen, named.

1965

First two black pages named to House and Senate by Republicans in a Democratic-controlled Congress: Lawrence W. Bradford, Jr., to Senate and Frank V. Mitchell to House.

First black Solicitor General, Thurgood Marshall, by Johnson. First black woman ambassador, Patricia Roberts Harris, named to Luxembourg. First black ambassador to U.N. Security Council, James M. Nabrit, Jr., named.

Voting Rights Act of 1965 signed by Johnson, providing that Federal examiners in South register negro voters turned away by state officials.

1966

First black elected to U.S. Senate since 1881, Edward W. Brooke of Mass.

First black Cabinet member, Robert C. Weaver, named Secretary of Housing and Urban Development. First black woman Federal judge, Constance Baker Motley, appointed to U.S. District Court by Johnson. First black member of the Federal Reserve Board of Governors, Andrew F. Brimmer, appointed by Johnson.

1967

First black man named to U.S. Supreme Court, Thurgood Marshall.

advancing the political cause of blacks. In the latter years, however, the Democrats have made more noteworthy negro appointments. In their brief fling in the White House for eight years, from 1953 to 1961, the Republicans were still able to pave the way for similar dramatic appointments. Two good examples were the Eisenhower appointments of the first black assistant secretary of a Cabinet department, J. Ernest Wilkins, in the Department of Labor in 1954, and the first Negro White House aide, E. Frederic Morrow, in 1955.

Both of these anteceded the Kennedy appointments of George L. P. Weaver as the first black Assistant Secretary of Labor in 1961 and of Andrew T. Hatcher as associate White House press secretary in 1961, the first black man to hold such a high position in the White House.

It is also interesting to note in Table IV that in the years of the great negro gains under Democratic administrations, Republicans were still able to make some of the most important gains nationally for negroes, even though such gains were made at the state and local levels—the appointment of the first negro woman judge in the history of America, Jane M. Bolin in 1939; the election of the first negro as state attorney general, Edward W. Brooke in 1962; and his subsequent 1966 election as the first negro to be elected to the U.S. Senate since 1881.

No one political party or any one President or administration has had a monopoly on black progress. The interrelationship between the events of the past and the requirements of the present has been too formidable to ignore. As Victor Hugo observed, "There is one thing stronger than all the armies in the world: and that is an idea whose time has come."

The idea of emancipating the slaves came in 1863. The idea of *Plessy* v. *Ferguson*, the decision upholding the "separate but equal" doctrine, prevailed in 1896, but the idea that it was unconstitutional came in 1954. The idea of a new civil-rights law—inadequate, weak, and almost useless—nevertheless was necessary in 1957, and that idea arrived and was implemented.

The Republicans Pushed and the Democrats Moved

Although the ebb and flow of high-level black appointments or election victories in various administrations have been heavily influenced by the events of previous administrations, there have been occasions when a crucial nomination or election by one party forced the other party to follow suit and the reluctant party subsequently won the election and received credit for a "negro first."

On two separate occasions, Republicans nominated a negro for an important office, and the Democrats, in both instances, indicated they were not going to follow suit, later reversed themselves, and then nominated a negro. In both instances, the black Democrat was elected.

This first occurred in 1953 in New York City. On July 23, 1953, the Republicans nominated Elmer Carter for Manhattan Borough President. Carter, a negro, was one of the five Commissioners of the State Commission Against Discrimination. Immediately, several Harlem Democratic leaders called for the Democratic Party to follow suit and warned that the party would lose negro votes unless it did. Several prominent negroes were mentioned as possible candidates: Representative Adam Clayton Powell, City Councilman Earl Brown, and Lieutenant Colonel Chauncey M. Hooper.

However, the Jews felt that this nomination should go to a Jew, and they refused to knuckle under to pressures for a negro nominee on the Democratic ticket. So, on July 27, Assemblyman Herman E. Katz of the Tenth District was nominated for Manhattan Borough President. Four negro Democratic District leaders, Joseph Pinckney of the Eleventh, Herbert L. Bruce of the Twelfth, Hulan E. Jack of the Fourteenth, and Lucius Butts of the Thirteenth, repeated their demands that the nomination go to a negro.

On July 31, Mayor Vincent Impelliteri, who was running for re-election as an Independent Democrat after the party bosses (Carmine DeSapio of Manhattan and Ed Flynn of the Bronx) refused to endorse him, chose Lieutenant Colonel Hooper as his running mate, for the office of Manhattan Borough President. That now made two negroes in the race for office. Then, on August 14, both Katz and Arthur Braun (the Liberal Party candidate for the Manhattan Borough Presidency) withdrew from the race. Three days later, the Liberal Party executive committee voted to accept the Reverend James H. Robinson, a distinguished negro clergyman, as the party's candidate for Borough President.

Tammany was still dragging its feet and finally gave some indication it might be shifting toward nominating a negro. The New York Times reported on August 18 that the choice would be either Fourteenth District Assemblyman Hulan E. Jack or City Councilman Earl Brown.

The next day Jack was nominated. Thus, all candidates for the Manhattan Borough Presidency were negro.

In November, the Democratic organization, functioning with its customary efficiency, was able to elect its entire ticket—including Mayor Robert F. Wagner and, of course, Hulan E. Jack. The Democrats were credited with another "negro breakthrough," but they had had to be shoved, pushed, cajoled, and threatened by black party leaders to take the step. It was the Republicans who had moved first. The Democrats followed, but afterward, they were credited with an historical first.

This election displayed an almost perfectly balanced ethnic ticket for the Democrats. The elected mayor, Wagner, was half Irish; the president of the

City Council, Abe Stark, was a Jew; Comptroller Lawrence Gerosa was an Italian; and Manhattan Borough President Hulan E. Jack was a negro. It represented the first time a negro was included as a member of the balanced ticket. And for black people, the Manhattan Borough Presidency was to become the negro office. They had gotten their toe in the door and were not going to let the party shut it in their faces.

In Connecticut, a similar political exercise was to occur in 1962, nine years later. On February 27, Attorney William D. Graham, a bright and hard-working negro member of the Republican faithful, announced his candidacy for the nomination for lieutenant governor.

After some horse-trading and political quid pro quos to fulfill promises to other ethnic groups, Graham was nominated for the position of state treasurer on June 6, at the Republican state convention. He was the first negro in the state's history to be nominated for any state office by either major party. After Graham's nomination, several top Democratic leaders were quoted publicly as saying they had "no intention" of placing a negro on their ticket at the Democratic convention in Hartford, July 13 and 14. What they instead proposed was the nomination of negroes from Hartford and New Haven for the state senate.

A week later, Democratic Party leaders began publicly discussing the possibility of a negro on the ticket. Gerald Lamb, a black dental technician and alderman in Waterbury, was mentioned most frequently as the candidate. On July 14, at the Democratic state convention, Lamb was nominated for state treasurer, thus guaranteeing the election of a negro to this post.

In November, the Democrats swept all the state offices, and Lamb was elected, the first negro in Connecticut to hold a statewide elective office. Once again, the Republicans had taken the first giant step. The Democrats were dragged along by the scruff of the neck. But in the end, the Democrats were credited with another historic first for negroes in politics.

The U.S. Supreme Court

Americans love to indulge themselves with the political opiate that the U.S. Supreme Court is above politics. It is not, and is, in fact, one of the most political institutions in the country. Judicial objectivity only exists when it depends on who is calling the political shots. During its history, the Supreme Court has been as political in its attitude and rulings on the negro's legal struggle to obtain full American citizenship as the other Federal branches. It has swung from outright support of white racism to advocacy of the negro's equal rights.

One can only imagine what progress the negro would have made if the

Supreme Court had read the same U.S. Constitution in the 1896 *Plessy* v. *Ferguson* case, when it upheld the doctrine of separate but equal, that it did in 1954, when it struck the doctrine down in *Brown* v. *Board of Education*.

There have been seven major U.S. Supreme Court decisions affecting the negro's political progress in America:

1857

The Dred Scott decision upheld the Fugitive Slave law, opened Federal territory to slavery, and denied citizenship rights to American negroes.

1883

The Civil Rights Act of 1875, one of the most far-reaching ever passed, was declared unconstitutional.

1896

The *Plessy* v. *Ferguson* case upheld the doctrine of separate but equal.

1915

Guinn v. *United States* held that the Southern states' "grandfather clause" was unconstitutional. Specifically this case dealt with the clause in the Oklahoma constitution.

1927

Nixon v. *Herndon* declared unconstitutional a Texas law which barred negroes from voting in the "white" primary. This was one of the important breakthroughs for negroes in political activity in the South.

1948

Shelly v. *Kramer* declared that the Federal and state courts could not enforce restrictive covenants designed to prevent negroes from buying property.

1954

Brown v. *Board of Education* declared public-school segregation unconstitutional and stated that the separate-but-equal doctrine could not be enforced any more.

Summary

In his uphill battle for his share of the political spoils and control of the political machinery of government, black people have been favored by both major political parties at certain periods in history, depending not upon that party's commitment to equal rights, but upon the political events of the time.

In 1865, Republicans were the negro's friend. Today, it is the Democrats. There are signs that under Lyndon B. Johnson the Democrats are beginning to tire of this role. More than likely, the next few years will witness a hastening of the departure of negroes from the Democratic Party toward a more sophisticated posture. They will ask only one question each time they vote: "What have you done for me lately?"

CHAPTER SEVEN

The Irish, the Italians, the Jews, and the Poles

In New York City, the Irish run it, the Jews own it, the Italians clean it up, and the Negroes enjoy it.

—Popular saying in Harlem

Men have made careers and politicians have won office by being (or claiming to be) experts on the Polish vote, the Jewish vote, the Irish vote, the Negro vote, the Scandinavian vote, the Italian vote and what the rights, expectations, offices and dignities of each of those blocs are.

—WHITE: *The Making of the President 1960*, p. 223

Let each man honor and love the land of his birth and the race from which he springs and keep their memory green. It is a pious and honorable duty. But let us have done with British-Americans and Irish-Americans and German-Americans, and so on, and all be Americans. . . . If a man is going to be an American at all let him be so without any qualifying adjectives, and if he is going to be something else, let him drop the word American from his personal description.

—HENRY CABOT LODGE, December 21, 1888

This nation has a curiously obstinate capacity for self-fulfilling prophecies. The mystique of nationhood—its legends, heroes, history, and exaggerations —are all bundled up into an ethic we call nationality. This sense of nationality, this national self-concept, is the emotional matrix political leaders use to perpetuate an ethos of unity that is their power base and insurance for survival.

The younger a nation is, the more zealous its search for a fierce identity. It popularizes the most favorable notions about itself and glorifies its external symbols. To know who you are is to develop a pride in your knowledge of self. America knew who and what it was when it was founded. It was to become less certain seventy-five years later, when the Irish, Italians, Poles, Germans, and mid-European Slavic groups were to flood its shores.

The democratic ethic, which had never made any pretense of including negroes, nevertheless sought a logical justification for the incorporation of European immigrants. How could the United States weave the ethnic threads into the fabric of American society when they clung so stubbornly to their own traditions? How could pride in America be fostered when pride in one's nationality, religion, or mother tongue competed for a prior and higher affection?

The unifying force, of course, was to be the English language. "We have room for but one language here and this is the English language, for we intend to see that the crucible turns our people out as Americans and not as dwellers in a polyglot boarding house," defiantly declared Theodore Roosevelt on January 5, 1919. Maybe some of the immigrants were less assimilable than others. Some indeed refused to surrender certain ingrained living habits, culinary practices, and methods of illegal political activities. But they all possessed a common denominator: a white skin. Once they mastered the English language sufficiently to communicate, their white skin could open doors which had been shut for a century to native black Americans. They could find jobs and housing and move about. White skin was at least an immediate guarantee of horizontal mobility. Above all, this white skin was to guarantee the continuing viability of the "New World" society. "America is God's Crucible, the great Melting Pot where all the races of Europe are melting and reforming," triumphantly proclaimed Israel Zangwill in his 1920 book, *The Melting Pot*. The white skin and the English language were the ore and the Bessemer process that forged a new steel of American nationality. A new self-concept was born, and it was a magnificent myth.

Various nationalities and religions did not "melt" or disappear. They maintained little cultural islands which found expression in business activity and politics. In the security of ethnic enclaves, they built organizations of economic and political power. As fast as one succeeded, he reached back into the ghetto he had just left and brought his relatives and friends along. The Irish took care of the Irish. The Jews looked after the Jews. Italians protected the Italians. The Poles advanced the Poles. And everybody pretended they were Americans first.

They all paid lip service to Henry Cabot Lodge's injunction to drop their ethnic hyphenation, but in the sanctuaries of their political clubs, associations, synagogues, restaurants, and neighborhood clubs, they adhered to the emotionalism of their ethnic backgrounds. Still, the myth of the melting pot was lovingly fostered by writers and historians, pompously extolled by self-seeking politicians, and nourished in the fertilizer of white journalism by jingoistic editors.

There was never any melting pot; there was only an "emulsion bowl." The ethnic diversities remained separate in their loyalties. To have believed and asserted this sociological truth would have been tantamount to a betrayal of the political ethic of democracy, so Americans dwelt comfortably in the temple of hypocrisy erected to the myth of the melting pot. It was a time of growth and excitement. Everybody could "hear America singing." Everybody but black people.

But this was irrelevant. The melting pot was supposed to be able to absorb the slag of black skins after it had supposedly melted the other white skins into the new unity of Americanism. It did not, however.

The contradiction was soon recognized, and sociologists started comparing the emergence of the black man from slavery with the arrival of the white immigrant from Europe. This resulted in one of the great conceptual stupidities of all time: The conclusion that the assimilation problems of European immigrants and native-born black Americans were identical. Ignored were the negro's previous condition of slavery, the absence of a parent culture with which he could identify, and his major distinguishing characteristic, his black skin, which encased him in a persecuted subculture. The negro was expected to "lift himself by his bootstraps" as had other ethnic groups, despite white America's refusal to let him wear boots. The black man spoke English fluently, but every time the white man looked at his black skin, he was unable to hear the black man's voice or understand his words. The black American has been talking for almost two hundred years now, and the white American still has not heard him.

Within the pluralism of the mythical melting pot, certain ethnic groups managed to achieve their rightful share of political power. The Irish Catholics became big city bosses of corrupt but efficient political machines. Ofttimes they were unable to elect one of their own to a top political position, yet were powerful enough to determine the candidate.

Jews made isolated breakthroughs into the power structures of certain states and cities where their numerical proportion assured their entry. In a few instances, their control of segments of the labor movement gave them national power and influence. Italians, concentrated in a few Northeastern states and cities, were slow to develop political power, but in recent years have begun to displace the Irish as both the political bosses and the political representatives. They have also been helped by their control of organized crime through the Mafia. Poles, like Italians, have tended to settle only in certain cities and states. The preponderance of Poles has been in the Mid-western urban areas.

Each of these four groups exerts enormous political power within its respective ethnic enclave, and they are the final arbiters of a political slate's composition. For the Irish, this power is still concentrated in New York State and City, Boston, and Chicago. For Jews, it's New York State, New York City, and Baltimore. For Italians, it's Massachusetts, Connecticut, New York City and Newark, N.J. For the Poles, it's Chicago and Milwaukee.

Each of these areas will be analyzed for the ethnic political power wielded and why such power has survived or is growing. For an ethnic group to be a controlling force or a balance of power in the decision-making processes of government, it must be a significant proportion of the electorate, cohesive, uncompromising in its demands for leadership roles, and fragile in its political loyalties—i.e., it must occasionally oscillate.

The most difficult aspect of measuring ethnic political power is taking an accurate census of the ethnic group. Negroes live in fairly rigid and ecologically defined ghettos. Skin color is an easily identifiable characteristic. The compilation of statistics on white ethnic groups who are dispersed complicates the process of determining how an ethnic group votes. Finally, the most difficult problem of all remains: What standards are used in counting, for example, Irish, Italians, and Poles? For how many generations do members of an ethnic group remain hyphenated?

Counting Ethnic Noses

The problem of counting ethnic noses accurately has long concerned the U.S. Bureau of Census. Intermarriage between members of various ethnic groups has tended to blur the definable characteristics that determine membership. And as various nationalities have married out of their ethnic group, they have either "joined" another ethnic group, thus augmenting its population, or simply merged into the integrated mainstream of American society.

The term "foreign stock" is used by the U.S. Census Bureau to cover "both the foreign-born population and the native population (i.e., born in America) of foreign or mixed parentage. The foreign-born population comprises all persons residing in the United States who are not natives. The native population includes all persons born in the United States, the Commonwealth of Puerto Rico or a possession of the United States. . . . The category 'native of foreign or mixed parentage' comprises native persons, one or both of whose parents are foreign born." This guideline for counting ethnic noses could be labeled the two-generation test—either persons born in another country or the native-born progeny of such persons.

Using these indices, the U.S. Census Bureau determined in its 1960 Census the following totals for three ethnic groups from their respective countries:

COUNTRY	NUMBER	PER CENT OF TOTAL U.S. POPULATION
Ireland	1,773,312	.006
Italy	4,543,935	3
Poland	2,780,026	1

(According to the Jewish Statistical Bureau, there were an estimated 5,721,000 Jews in 1967 in the United States.)

The gross inadequacy of the Census Bureau's two-generation method for counting ethnic noses and using those figures to account for political power is immediately apparent when the political power of the three ethnic groups of foreign stock is assessed. Obviously, the political power of these three ethnic groups—their control of the electoral and governmental processes—far outweighs their proportion in the population. This discrepancy raises the question of whether additional factors must be considered in measuring ethnic political power.

The first factor, of course, would be extending the generation test to three and maybe four generations of foreign stock. President Kennedy was a second-generation Irish-American. But there were third- and fourth-generation Irish-Americans whose support of Kennedy was decided by the overriding emotional pull of ancestry and religion. Because there are third- and fourth-generation members of ethnic groups whose national or religious identification is the dominant factor in political decisions, the Census Bureau would provide more insight into many sociological problems by extending its generation test. Certainly the fact of religion is a major, if not the most important, social characteristic of Jews and Catholics, and conversely of Protestants.

This raises a new dimension in the analysis of ethnic political power—the element of ethnic identity. The disparity between a census-taker's count and the self-conception of the member of an ethnic group varies with the intensity of the control that ethnic self-conception has over that group. For the leaders of these groups, it is important to perpetuate this group-oriented force in order to stay in power. Their bargaining power for patronage is proportionately increased by the identifiable cohesion of the groups they represent. Consequently, it is difficult to get a precise reading of an ethnic group's national political power. At the local and state levels, the statistical refinement of data on ethnic groups makes it possible to determine more accurately their proportion of the population, their common identity, and the proportion of the decision-making jobs in government they control.

Irish Political Power

Irish political power came into being on April 24, 1817. That evening, a group of some two hundred Irish laborers and tradesmen were meeting in Dooley's Long Room in New York City, discussing the black-out on Irish politicians by the Society of St. Tammany, which controlled New York City politics. It was time, they agreed, for Tammany to nominate some prominent Irish leader, such as Thomas Emmet, for Congress. Up until that time, Tammany had rigorously excluded Irishmen from its political slates. Angrily concluding Tammany was guilty of discrimination against the Irish, the group, two hundred strong, marched on Tammany Hall and interrupted a caucus of party leaders to present their demands. Their request was refused. Having failed in this exercise in nonviolence, the Irishmen began to break up the furniture and a fight ensued between the sons of Ireland and the sons of St. Tammany. Only after reinforcements from a nearby tavern arrived were the Tammany leaders able to disperse the Irishmen.

The group which had met at Dooley's tables did not change any minds that evening, but the urgency of their demands could not be ignored. Although Tammany continued its strong "nativist" outlook by slating only "native-born Americans," it did begin to realize the importance of the cohesive Irish vote.

In 1846, Tammany nominated a prominent Irish leader, Michael Walsh, for the state assembly, and in 1850, Walsh became the first Irish Catholic from New York State to be elected to the U.S. House of Representatives.

Within a few years, the Irish had grabbed complete control of Tammany Hall, the Democratic Party leadership in New York City. The process had started with William Marcy "Boss" Tweed's quiet takeover in 1865, and fifteen years later, in 1880, New York City's first Irish Catholic mayor, William R. Grace, a millionaire shipping magnate, was elected. He was the first in a long line of Irish Catholic mayors of New York City.

The success of the Irish was due to their numbers, their organizational loyalties (undoubtedly a carry-over from their strict fidelity to the efficient organization of the Catholic Church), and, more than anything else, their determination to be in control. Once they became part of an organization, they took it over for the benefit of their group first and the good of their country second. At all times, the Irish came first—first in terms of the control and distribution of political power. This is how Irish Catholics were able to assume command of political machines in cities where they were in a numerical minority. As organizers and manipulators of corrupt politicians or public officials, they were without peer.

But the real key to their success was due to their rapid numerical increase in the population. The Irish migration to America began in the 1820's, when 150,000 arrived. In successive decades, Irish immigrants flooded American shores—"1.7 million in the 1840's, 2.8 million in the 1870's, 5.2 million in the 1880's, 8.8 million in the first decade of the twentieth century. ... By 1850, after the potato famine, they had replaced England as the chief source of new settlers, making up 44 per cent of the foreign-born in the United States."*

As Irish immigration increased, so did native American resistance to these people who spoke English with a thick brogue and practiced a "foreign religion" with dedicated passion. The proud clannishness of the Irish confused and angered many Americans. As a result, the American Party was formed in the 1850's to curtail immigration, promote the election of "native Americans" to political office, advance more stringent naturalization legislation, and curb the influence of the Roman Catholic Church. The party was quickly labeled "Know-Nothing" because members would reply, as instructed, "I know nothing," when asked about the party's activities.

At the height of their political power, the "Know-Nothings" were able to elect to the Thirty-fourth Congress in 1855 five Senators, forty-three Representatives, and approximately seventy other prominent public officials who admitted accepting public direction from the party. But the "Know-Nothings" did not reckon on the unflinching determination of the Irish to become assimilated into American society. The activities of the party only served to strengthen the ties that bound the Irish together and solidify their aspirations for public office. A less hardy group of people might have backed down before such a massive confrontation of political opposition. The Irish never wavered, and many a brawl between Irish and Know-Nothings flared in New York City, Philadelphia and other major cities.

Few ethnic groups could match the Irish for the ferocity of pride in themselves. A combination of deep religious convictions and strong ties to the authoritarianism of the Catholic Church and an intensity of affection for Irish culture provided the matrix for ethnic unity and consequent political progress. It was the kind of pride that impelled Boston Mayor John F. "Honey Fitz" Fitzgerald to stand up at a 1906 banquet in honor of a new Catholic archbishop, William O'Connell, and declare unashamedly: "The high reputation of the government of this Catholic city, compared with places like Cincinnati and Philadelphia, proves the mass of the Catholic people to be upright and clean in their political relations."**

Mayor Fitzgerald obviously was not thinking of William Marcy Tweed. A three-hundred-pound, six-foot mastiff of a man, Tweed took over the

* John F. Kennedy, A Nation of Immigrants (New York: Harper & Row, 1964), p. 17.
** William V. Shannon, The American Irish (New York: Macmillan, 1963), p. 182.

political reins of Tammany Hall in 1865, when he was forty-two years old, after Tammany's candidate won the election for mayor in a three-way contest. He then settled down to consolidating his power over the city, and for the next six years Tweed ran New York as if it were his personal fiefdom. He controlled the Board of Aldermen, hand-picked the city administrators, and packed the courts. It was during his rule that the phrase "It is better to know the judge than to know the law" became popular.

In six years, Boss Tweed, whose huge nose made him a favorite target and delight of cartoonists, managed to plunder the city treasury of thirty million dollars. Today, the political machine of Chicago's mayor, Richard Daley, the last of the all-powerful Irish Catholic big-city bosses, permits its cronies to make fortunes at the expense of the city. But there is a difference. Daley believes in good government. And if politicians are still murdered, restaurants blown up, and undercover gang warfare carried on, the citizenry is not nearly so aroused because Daley is paving the streets, collecting the garbage, and building new housing projects.

Tweed did not believe in "good government" nor did he understand the function of government. As Shannon, an Irish American writer, points out· "The Tweed group simply did not know what to do with the machinery of government once it was theirs except to steal openly whatever was not nailed down."*

This view of the Irish-American's political shortsightedness is echoed by Daniel P. Moynihan, a political scientist and, like Shannon, an Irishman: "In a sense, the Irish did not know what to do with power once they got it. . . . They never thought of politics as an instrument of social change—their kind of politics involved the processes of a society that was not changing."**

There were exceptions to this generalization, however. One was Alfred E. Smith, governor of New York State and unsuccessful candidate for President in 1928. Al Smith was the New Yorker's New Yorker. Witty, a shrewd, self-educated man, he rose through the ranks in politics to become successively Speaker of the House in 1913 (the same year James Michael Curley was elected mayor of Boston), Sheriff of New York County (he saved $105,000 in two years for his share of the fees collected as Sheriff), president of the Board of Aldermen, governor for four terms, and finally the Democratic candidate for President.

Al Smith tried to run an efficient, honest, and tight ship as governor of New York. Although he played the game according to the political rules, he did not allow patronage to interfere with sound administration.

Smith's overwhelming defeat in his bid to become the first Roman Catholic President of America was blamed on his religion. But a more

---

* Shannon, p. 70.
** Glazer and Moynihan, *Beyond the Melting Pot* (Cambridge, Mass.: M.I.T. Press, 1963), p. 229.

careful assessment of Hoover's sweep in 1928—21,392,190 votes to Smith's 15,016,443, carrying all but eight states, with 444 to eighty-seven electoral-college votes—was due to other factors equally decisive: Smith's urban, Northern, big-city liberalism; his stand on Prohibition; negrophobia; and Smith's image as a "city slickster." But the *bête noire* of his religious affiliation stuck and was to remain a truism of politics until John Fitzgerald Kennedy buried the myth once and for all.

If Smith was unusual as an Irish politician, Boston's James Michael Curley followed the pattern cut from whole cloth as if he had designed it himself. "Curley was less powerful than a party boss and more significant than a conventionally successful party leader. He was the idol of a cult, arbiter of a social clique and spokesman of a state of mind."* The state of mind was undoubtedly, "They've had theirs—let's get ours." No matter what he did, Curley's role as the defender of the "little man"—in this instance, the Irishman who was still denied a full role in the making of American society—rendered him near invincible in his political career, one of the most astonishing of all time. He was four times elected to Congress and four times mayor of Boston and he held other offices from alderman to governor. Yet he was also defeated once for the House of Representatives, once for the Senate, twice for the governorship and six times for mayor of Boston.

Curley was not only an important figure in the politics of Boston and Massachusetts, but an influential national figure because of his image as the successful Irish politician. He was not a "boss" in the classic sense of Jersey City's Frank Hague, Kansas City's Tom Pendergast, the Bronx's Ed Flynn, or Chicago's Richard Daley. He developed an Irish charisma the people loved, and his powerful personality, not the party machinery or the precinct workers, carried him to victory. And when he did need the party organization behind him, it alone could not deliver enough votes and he consequently suffered his defeats.

Curley remained on the political scene until he was seventy-one, when he was convicted of mail-fraud and served five months in prison. He was defeated for office when he ran for mayor for the last time in 1949. But Curley's booming voice, his eloquent rhetoric, made him a legend among the Irish, and, if he did wrong, they still loved him. He was theirs, and they had made him. To most of the Irish working class, Curley symbolized resistance to the white Protestant power structure, which had excluded the Irish for so long.

In Boston, the first city to have total Irish Catholic control, the transition from a city of Protestant Brahmins to one of Catholic laborers was made in the comparatively quick span of one generation. In 1851, Boston hired its first Irish Catholic policeman, and thirty-five years later, in 1886, it elected

* Shannon, p. 203.

its first Irish mayor. The Irish won a majority of the seats in the City Council in 1899 and elected their second mayor, Patrick Collins, in 1901. Their third mayor, John "Honey Fitz" Fitzgerald, the maternal grandfather of President Kennedy, succeeded Collins.

It is interesting to note that the move to gerrymander the city and change the city charter came from the Irish. Until 1909, the year of the changeover, the City Council had had ten negro council members from the Republican and predominantly negro Tenth Ward since 1895. But the Irish, stimulated by both their race prejudice and their political opposition to negroes, who were Republicans, chopped down negro political power in its ascendancy.

While Irish power was solidifying its control over Boston and New York City, it was following a similar pattern in other major cities—Jersey City, run ruthlessly and dictatorially by Frank Hague; Chicago, controlled in its incredibly open vice, corruption, and crime by Ed Kelly; and Kansas City, run by Tom Pendergast, who personally hand-made President Truman's career; the Bronx, by Ed Flynn; and Philadelphia, run by William Green.

If Pendergast can claim credit for Truman's accession to the Presidency on the basis that he made him U.S. Senator, James Farley is the one politician who can claim the major share of the credit for Franklin D. Roosevelt's election in 1932. Farley, a genius at organization, ran Roosevelt's first two campaigns with loving efficiency.

Successful organizers, Irish politicians have invariably been conservative in their political views, staunch anti-Communists, opponents to negro advancement, and rigid bureaucrats. This partially explains Al Smith's 1936 break with Roosevelt, whom he accused of preparing America for a Communist takeover. Jim Farley, who had seriously expected to succeed Roosevelt, bitterly left him in 1940 over the third-term issue and from his disappointment that Roosevelt had no intention of choosing him as a successor.

The Irish Catholic's unreasoning opposition to anything that remotely recalled Communism or "left-wing" ideas found its champion in Senator Joseph McCarthy's mid-1950 crusade against Communists. McCarthy's heavy-handed tactics and sweeping accusations at anybody who had ever had even a tangential association with Communism or a Communist or a Communist-front organization brought a new word into the English language—"McCarthyism," a twentieth-century synonym for witch-hunting. McCarthy's wild jousting with the Communists he believed to be under every bed in America achieved for the Irish what Moynihan described as a "strong temporary advantage . . . that may or may not prove of permanent value. In the era of security clearances, to be an Irish Catholic became prima facie evidence of loyalty. Harvard men were to be checked; Fordham men would do the checking."* This close-minded mentality of excessive patriotism has carried over into the late sixties, and Irish Catholics are still viewed

* Glazer and Moynihan, p. 271.

as the purest of anti-Communists in America. Protestants are suspect, and Jews are tainted.

Irish political power was at its fullest bloom, both locally and nationally, in the Roosevelt and Truman years. Both Presidents relied heavily on the big-city machines for their majorities, and these machines were under the domination of Irish Catholics. One of Roosevelt's closest advisers was Thomas "Tommy the Cork" Corcoran. It was Roosevelt who kept up the tradition of an Irish Catholic on the U.S. Supreme Court, and he chose a spectacular prototype of Irish Catholicism, Frank Murphy of Michigan.

Murphy was considered such a staunch Catholic that when his appointment was rumored, a former high official of the Department of Justice remarked to a friend: "If the President appoints Murphy to the Supreme Court he will have achieved his Supreme Court Plan, because when Murphy goes on the Court so do the Father and the Son and the Holy Ghost."*

Murphy was appointed to the U.S. Supreme Court in 1940. He was the Court's second Irish Catholic, the first having been Pierce Butler, who was appointed in 1922 by President Harding and whose death in 1939 paved the way for Murphy.

It is now a fundamental law of politics that the U.S. Supreme Court must include a Catholic as one of its nine justices. The current Catholic representative to the U.S. Supreme Court is William J. Brennan, Jr., of New Jersey, who was appointed by President Eisenhower in 1956 to a recess appointment and nominated and confirmed in 1957.

The seat of national Irish political power has been New York City. Of that city's last ten mayors, as of 1967, seven have been Irish Catholics, if Mayor Wagner, who is half Irish, is included. A third of the New York State delegation to the 1960 Democratic national convention was Irish. In 1961, both the chief justice of the City Court and the chief city magistrate of New York were Irish. In 1962, nine of the nineteen Congressmen from New York City were Irish, but, as of 1967, this figure has declined to six. A "balanced ticket" for New York State and City elections must still include an Irish Catholic.

In the Congress of the United States, Irish Catholics have political power far out of proportion to their percentage of membership in the House. Before the death of Robert F. Kennedy, the two most famous Irish Catholics in the Senate were the Kennedy brothers, Edward of Massachusetts and Robert of New York State. Furthermore, the Majority Leader of the Senate is Mike Mansfield of Montana. In the Eighty-ninth Congress, Catholics became the largest religious group in Congress with 108 members; the Methodists were second with 102. The majority of Catholics in the House, of course, are Irish. The Speaker of the House, John J. McCormack, is such

* Wesley McCune, *The Nine Young Men* (New York: Harper & Brothers, 1947), p. 142.

a staunch Irish Catholic that he is sometimes called "The Bishop." The Chairman of the Democratic Study Group, composed of the self-anointed liberals in the House, was Frank Thompson of Trenton, N.J., in the Eighty-ninth Congress, who was succeeded in the Ninetieth Congress by another Irish Catholic, James O'Hara of Detroit, Mich.

In the House there is an informal Irish Catholic clique that meets casually but regularly to discuss issues which affect their constituencies and their political relationship with the Church.

The influence of Irish Catholic politicians is declining slowly, not because of a lessened interest in politics, but because of their faster absorption into the American body politic as unhyphenated Americans and the concomitant rise to power of other ethnic groups which have challenged them for political supremacy in certain states and cities. Jews, Italians, and, to a far lesser extent, Poles and negroes are now coming into their own as political strategists and wielders of power.

The decline of Irish power is a perverse tribute to American religious tolerance. But if this tolerance has meant a reduction of Irish power at the local level, it has meant a rise of Irish power at the national level, signified by the election of Irish Catholic John Fitzgerald Kennedy as the thirty-fourth President.

Kennedy's election in 1960 was a sharp turn of events from 1884 when the slogan "Rum, Romanism, and Rebellion" was directed at the Democratic Party by the Republicans, who had begun to fear the influence of Irish Catholics in politics. The Irish and the Democrats reacted angrily to the open display of religious bigotry. It is believed that enough Catholic Republicans were alienated by the anti-Irish slogan to vote for the Democratic candidate, Grover Cleveland, who defeated the Republican candidate, James G. Blaine.

The Irish and the Negroes

The attitudes of the Irish toward negroes were shaped by the early years of contact between the two groups. The Irish not only feared the negroes as potential competitors for jobs, but responded with the same ingrained racial hostility as other whites. Shannon describes the early development of Irish attitudes toward Negroes:

> Irish opinion was almost unanimously opposed to abolition. Daniel O'Connell wrote his friends in America urging them to oppose slavery, and although the Pope issued a papal bull against the slave trade, these outside influences were not decisive. As the newest and least secure members of society, the American Irish were the most rigid and least generous in extending their sympathy to a submerged minority like the Negroes whose circumstances they scarcely comprehended. There was also an element of economic rivalry, since Irish working-men feared the upward thrust of the Negro would further depress their own

circumstances in the job market. This fear was not, however, the controlling motive. The number of free Negroes in northern cities was simply not great enough to pose that threat in clear terms. The basic cause of Irish opposition to abolition was an obsessive preoccupation with their own problems.*

But the groups also had opposite ideological positions. Whereas negroes tended to be liberal in their political philosophy, the Irish were conservatives. Undoubtedly the rigidity of Catholic religious attitudes was a significant factor in their stand-pat outlook. The Irish wanted respectability, and the only way to achieve it was to become part of the existing society. Negroes wanted equality, and the only way to achieve it was to change the whole pattern of society so that it might admit them to membership.

The Irish thus had a vested interest in keeping the black people down and preventing them from changing the society in which they passionately sought full membership. It was natural for such prominent Irish Catholics as George Meany, president of the AFL-CIO, to be a rabid and almost fanatic anti-Communist but a wishy-washy equivocator on the problem of racial exclusion of black workers from the labor unions. The Irish hierarchy of labor unions worked hard to bar negroes from membership, and Meany's decisive antinegro influence in the labor movement has given it an ideological cast that it will take years to lose. Labor unions today are as responsible for racial discrimination and segregation of negroes as industry, and the Irish Catholic labor leaders have been in the vanguard of this effort.

In the major cities where the Irish politician has controlled the political machine, integration of negroes into policy-making councils and the distribution of patronage have been agonizingly slow. Very few advances have been made under local Irish politicians, and the granite resistance of political bosses like Chicago's Daley to full integration in political jobs, education, and employment is characteristic of Irish hesitancy to accord full equality to negroes.

Under the efficient management of Irish bosses, the political machines of Tammany's Tweed, Murphy, and Sullivan; Chicago's Kelly and Daley; Kansas City's Pendergast; Jersey City's Frank Hague; and the Bronx's Ed Flynn dutifully got out the black vote on election day. Negroes were not rewarded with jobs, however, but were given chicken dinners and paid for their votes. Negroes could be had cheaply. The Irish knew it, and they treated negro demands with contempt. No Southern politician has been so obstinate about righting negro injustices as has Chicago's Richard Daley.

Irish Impact

The impact of Irish politicians on American politics is permanent and historically absolute. If they operated venally corrupt machines—and they

* Shannon, *The American Irish*, pp. 54-55.

did—it is because the system lent itself so ably to such dishonesty and exploitation. The Irish professionalized American politics and gave it style. The seriousness of purpose and the intensive organizational background work that Kennedy brought to his quest for the Presidency was typical of the Irish capacity for minute detail so prevalent in earlier political machines. When Kennedy entered the White House, he brought with him the "Irish Mafia," a not ungracious term which described those closest to him—not only those who were responsible for his election, but those responsible for the day-to-day decisions of his administration.

If Boss Tweed had built a New York City political empire on corruption and bribery of public officials, Boss Daley has built a Chicago dynasty on syndicated crime and subsurface corruption. Daley represents the "new look" of the Irish political boss. He believes in and practices what he calls "good government," and builds expressways, housing projects, and new downtown civic centers. He appoints outstanding citizens to public office and personally intervenes in crippling strikes. He is a model mayor. But Daley has done nothing to curb organized crime, which not only continues to run Chicago, but is a heavy contributor to the Democratic Party, both in Chicago and at the national level. "Whenever we needed some quick cash —and I mean large cash, like $10,000—during the campaign, we just called Chicago," a high official of the Democratic National Committee told the author in 1964 after the Presidential election.

There are now more than a thousand unsolved gangland murders in Chicago. Restaurants are still fire-bombed and blown up at will. Witnesses for "juice-racket" trials are intimidated and their cars destroyed by bombs in front of court-houses. The 1963 political murder of negro Alderman Benjamin Lewis of the Twenty-fourth Ward has never been solved and nobody seriously expects that it will. The illegal "jitney" racket continues to flourish on the South Side, and organized crime and vice is very much a part of Chicago politics. But nobody protests, and even the State Street businessmen support Daley because he devotes so much time to urban renewal. The Irish political boss has become a sophisticated and urbane statesman. He is what Jim Farley described as his "own figurative secretary of state."

Irish political power has diminished as a controlling force in American politics because of the increasing absorption of American Irish into the anonymity of American society. Immigration from Ireland is down to a trickle, and within a couple of generations, the percentage of foreign-born Irish will be smaller than one-hundredths of one per cent of the total population of America. The election of President Kennedy was the fulfillment of Irish power, bringing it from the parochial wards and precincts all the way up to the Presidency. Now that it has become a fact of political life, Irish power has already begun to give way to Italian power, Jewish power, Polish power, and, in the not too distant future, Black Power.

Italian Political Power

Probably the main reason the Italians were late coming into political power is that they were late coming to America. Although more than five million Italians migrated to this country between 1820 and 1963, large-scale immigration did not begin until 1880. By that time, the Irish had already taken over Tammany Hall in New York City, and within six years were to elect Boston's first Irish Catholic mayor.

Like the Irish, the Italians tended to concentrate in a few areas. The Italians chose New York City, Massachusetts, Connecticut, and New Jersey. As of 1960, 2,550,245, or 50 per cent of all the foreign born Italians living in America, were concentrated there.

Like the Irish, the Italians immediately staked out a field. For many Irish, it was politics. For many Italians, it was organized crime. Not that the Irish were not involved in the underworld; they were. The Irish were able to transfer the legitimacy of political power to themselves only with the help of corruption and Irish gangsters. In New York City, the Irish gangsters were succeeded by the Jewish crime syndicate and, as a scholar has noted, "Arnold Rothstein, 'Czar' of the New York underworld in the 1920's, was as closely linked to Democratic judges in Jimmy Walker's day as Frank Costello was fifteen years later. After the middle thirties, the most prominent gangsters in New York were of Italian origin, though their careers had begun in the 1920's."*

Italian political power in America goes back to 1736, when the first Italian to hold public office, Onorio Razzolini, settled in Annapolis, where he was appointed Armourer and Keeper of the Stores of Maryland. "In 1861, G. A. Pacetti became Mayor of St. Augustine, Florida. By 1880 two Italians were serving in the Texas Legislature and one (Antonio Ghio) was Mayor of Texarkana. In 1892 Constantine Lawrence Lavretta was elected to the Alabama Legislature and in 1894 he became Mayor of Mobile. Frank L. Monteverde was Mayor of Memphis, Tennessee from 1918 to 1921."**

These were all exceptions to the political rule. In none of the above-mentioned cities did Italians control the apparatus of government as the Irish did in Boston and New York City.

The first Italian to achieve national political prominence was Fiorello Henry LaGuardia, affectionately dubbed "The Little Flower." After being elected to Congress in 1916 from New York City—the only Italian-American

* Glazer and Moynihan, *Beyond the Melting Pot*, p. 210.
** Michael A. Musmanno, *The Story of the Italians in America* (Garden City, N.Y.: Doubleday, 1965), pp. 251-52.

in the Congressional delegation—LaGuardia served two more terms in Congress before becoming the first Italian-American to be elected mayor of New York City in 1933. Re-elected in 1937 and in 1941, he bucked the Tammany Hall machine as a Republican with the devoted support of the liberal American Labor Party.

As mayor of New York City LaGuardia became a national institution. Short, fat, and possessor of a voice that rasped its inflections, the ebullient Fiorello was a tornado of incessant energy. His unlovely face, which sometimes looked like a sculptor's unfinished clay model, became the symbol of good government as he cracked down on corruption and graft, read the funnies to the city's kids on Sunday morning, chased fires, and became New York City's first example of what Mayor Lindsay now calls "visible government." His success as mayor led President Roosevelt to appoint him Chief of the U.S. Office of Civilian Defense, and, in 1946, director of the U.S. Relief and Rehabilitation Administration. He died in 1947.

LaGuardia had broken down the barrier against Italians, and only three years later, in a special city election for mayor, all three major candidates were Italian—Acting Mayor Vincent Impelliteri, who ran as an independent after Tammany Hall refused to slate him; Ferdinand Pecora, the Democratic and Liberal candidate; and Edward Corsi, the Republican candidate.

One of the issues, raised by Corsi, was support of the underworld. On November 1, he accused both Impelliteri and Pecora of being backed by prominent criminals, claiming he had proof. Corsi cited a visit Pecora was supposed to have had with Frank Costello and denounced the other two candidates' association with "the Costellos, the Genoveses and the Adonises" (all Italian criminals and leaders of the Mafia).

This was comparable to three negro candidates running for office today and one accusing the other of association with "the Stokely Carmichaels and the Rap Browns." Such a charge would have almost no impact in the black community since all three men are heroes to a greater or lesser degree. Corsi's charge likewise made little impact, particularly in the Italian community, and Impelliteri won the election by a margin of 219,527 votes. Ironically, this election was held because of the resignation of Irish Catholic Mayor William O'Dwyer, under a cloud of bribery and corruption in his office.

A factor in the slating of three Italians for the office of mayor undoubtedly was Tammany Hall's election of Carmine DeSapio as its leader in 1949. The Italians were doing more than just "cleaning up" New York City, as that irreverent tag line suggests. They were running it. Their rise to political power, however, was aided by what Glazer labels their "involvement with crime." As Daniel Bell has noted, in The End of Ideology,* there has always existed an intricate relationship between crime, American life, and politics.

* The Free Press, Glencoe, Ill., 1960.

Some ethnic groups, however, become more proficient in forging the alliance between the underworld's needs and City Hall's aspirations in order to facilitate their political advancement. The Italians simply followed a pattern carved out for them by Irish gangsters and thugs who controlled the polls on election day by strong-arming voters or the Jewish gangsters who built financial empires with the cooperation of bribed public officials.

But the Italians improved upon the criminal modus operandi by taking over certain industries, such as construction and public trucking, by muscling contracts from frightened or bribed public officials. As Glazer describes the process, "Opportunities for wealth and prominence came slow and late to Italian Americans. Meanwhile, gambling, drugs and the waterfront succeeded industrial racketeering and bootlegging as the major sources of illegal wealth."*

In the public mind, the Italian Mafia became synonymous with organized crime. Names such as Frank Costello, "Lucky" Luciano, Tony Anastasia, Vito Genovese, Al Capone, Joseph Valachi, Joe Adonis, Albert Anastasia, and Momo Salvator Giancana were the kings of the underworld and the crime syndicate. The frequency with which their names were associated with organized crime, and several other factors, combined to create the impression that Italians were primarily responsible for the criminal pattern infecting American politics: the famous "Appalachian meeting" in upstate New York in 1959 where the so-called leaders of organized crime gathered for a "summit meeting"; the 1951 Kefauver investigation into organized crime (which paraded a long list of Italian names); and the use of the Italian word "mafia."

But organized crime exists only because public officials can be corrupted to permit it to flourish. Public officials are Irish, Polish, Jewish, German, Scandinavian WASP (White-Anglo-Saxon-Protestant), and negro. It cannot be denied, though, that there is a connection between politics and the leadership of organized crime. In Chicago, the alleged boss of the "Cosa Nostra" (crime syndicate) was Momo Salvator (Moe) Giancana of Italian extraction. It is no coincidence that Giancana's son-in-law, Anthony Tisci, was secretary to Representative Frank Annunzio of Illinois. Also of Italian extraction, he is Congressman from the Seventh Congressional District, which includes the First Ward of Chicago, home of organized vice and prostitution, represented by John D'Arco, Democratic Committeeman and the underworld "boss" of the ward. Ever since Al Capone's reign, that city has been the major source of criminal activity throughout America—to a large extent, guided by brilliant men of Italian extraction.

But if the Italians were the geniuses of the underworld, the Irish Catholics made the relationship between crime and politics work. Chicago's powerful Democratic boss, the late Mayor Edward J. Kelly, and the present Democratic

* Glazer and Moynihan, p. 211.

mayor, Richard J. Daley, have closed their eyes to the syndicate's operations and permitted them to control the city. Where the Italians have become a significant proportion of the population, they have concentrated on winning political office. This they have done successfully in four areas: Connecticut, where they number 237,146; Massachusetts, 311,053; New Jersey, 525,100; and New York, 1,476,946. The total for these states is 2,550,245—56 per cent of all those in the United States born in Italy or born of such parents.

Of the 1,476,946 Italians living in New York State, over half—858,602, or 58 per cent—live in New York City. New York City's Italians represent 11 per cent of that city's population, but in all three branches of the city and state government, they have held more than their proportional share of political offices and appointments. Of the city's nineteen Congressmen, three, or 16 per cent, are Italian. Of the three top elected officials in city government in 1967—the mayor, the president of the city council, and the comptroller—the third is an Italian, Mario A. Procaccino. Of the five borough presidents, one, Mario J. Cariello, is an Italian, although the former Richmond Borough President Albert V. Maniscalo had held unlimited political power in Staten Island for a number of years. Of the city's twenty-eight state senators, three are Italians. In the state assembly there are 150 seats, sixty-eight of which represent New York City. Of those sixty-eight, seventeen, or twenty-five per cent, are held by Italians. This explains why the most powerful position in the Assembly, the speakership, is held by an Italian, Anthony J. Travia of Brooklyn. Travia is so powerful that he has been promised a Federal judgeship even though he was not unanimously endorsed by the various bar associations. By the time this book is in print, his Federal judgeship will probably have been ratified.

In the executive branch, only one department of the state's seventeen major departments is headed by an Italian, John P. Lomenzo of the Department of Motor Vehicles. An Italian, Frank A. Sedita, was the Democratic nominee for attorney general in 1966, but was defeated by the Jewish Republican incumbent, Louis J. Lefkowitz.

Italians have never yet developed enough political power to elect a governor of New York State, even though they have had nominees for all of the other top state posts in both parties. The closest Italians came to the governorship was the succession of lieutenant governor Charles Poletti as acting governor on December 2, 1942, when Herbert H. Lehman declined to run for re-election. (Lehman, incidentally, was the first Jew to become governor of New York State.) When Lehman announced he would not be a candidate for re-election, the Democratic State Committee, which was under the control of the Irish Catholics, slated one of their own, Attorney General John J. Bennett, instead of Poletti, who would have been the logical nominee to step up.

There have been Italian governors in states where Italians do not comparably wield as much power: Foster Furcolo and John Volpe in Massachusetts; Albert D. Rosselini in Washington; Michael Vincent DiSalle in Ohio; John Pastore, Christopher Del Sesto, and John A. Notte in Rhode Island.

In New York City, the unusually high proportion of Italians in the Department of Sanitation has tended to reserve the post of commissioner of sanitation for Italians, just as the police commissioner has usually been an Irish Catholic because of the predominance of Irish on the police force. Paul R. Screvane, deputy mayor under Mayor Robert F. Wagner, started as an outstanding administrator when he was commissioner of the sanitation department.

The judiciary of New York City and State is where the Italians have been able to command a greater proportionate share of the political spoils than their numerical percentage of the population would warrant. Although they constitute 11 per cent of New York City's residents, Italians have the following percentages of judgeships in the various courts:

COURT	NUMBER OF JUDGES	ITALIAN JUDGES	PER CENT
Civil Court of New York City	95	27	28
Criminal Court of New York City	77	13	17
Surrogate Court (5 Counties)	6	2	33
Court of Appeals (New York State's highest court)	7	1	14
Supreme Court (Appellate Division— 2 Departments)	17	2	11
Supreme Court (5 Counties)	91	15	16

It is significant that in the Surrogate Court, probably the wealthiest of all the courts in the state and where millions of dollars pass through probate, there are two Italians out of six.

Italians are now a significant force in New York City and, to a somewhat lesser degree, New York State. Having already elected a number of officials, Italians are confident their political power is no longer dubious. In the future, it is only a question of whether such power can survive at its present level or will increase. The only unconquered goal for New York City and State Italians remains the governorship.

In Massachusetts, the U.S. Census Bureau in 1960 counted 311,053 Italians, a mere 5 per cent of that state's population. But the tenacity of ethnic pride among Italians and their strong cohesion as voters enabled them to elect their first governor, Foster Furcolo, in 1956. Furcolo, a two-term Congressman, resigned in 1952 to accept appointment as state treasurer to fill a vacancy and was the first Italian to hold an important state post. Two years later, he was the Democratic candidate for the U.S. Senate— another first for Italians—against Republican Leverett Saltonstall who defeated him.

Italian political power came of age in the Bay State, however, in 1964, when the Democratic and Republican candidates for governor were Italian —Francis X. Belotti and John Volpe, the Republican incumbent. The latter had had a popular administration, and despite the fact that President Johnson carried Massachusetts by a three-to-one margin, ticket-splitting enabled Volpe to defeat Belotti. The issue was obviously not an ethnic one, since both men were Italians. Volpe's popularity as a good administrator was decisive.

Of Massachusetts' twelve Congressmen, only one, Silvio Conte of the First Congressional District, who has held office for five terms, is Italian. In his district, Italians comprise only 4 per cent of the population.

In Connecticut, that state's 237,146 Italians represented, as of 1960, 10 per cent of the population. This is the one state where Italians are well on their way to establishing political hegemony over the state despite their comparatively small proportion in the population. According to Jack Zaiman, political editor of the Hartford *Courant* and one of the shrewdest political minds in the state, "the growth of Italian-American political power is one of the biggest political developments of the past few years and one of the least recognized." Italians occupy positions of great political influence at all levels of the executive and legislative branches of Connecticut's government.

In the executive branch, the offices of lieutenant governor and secretary of state are both held by Italians. In the legislative branch, Italians hold the key positions of president pro tempore and minority leader of the state senate, speaker of the house of representatives, and minority leader of the house.

Of Connecticut's six Congressmen, two, or 33 per cent, are Italian.

An Italian is mayor of Hartford (and, incidentally, is that city's first woman mayor, Ann Ucello), Waterbury (the state's fourth largest city), New Britain (the sixth largest city), Norwalk, Danbury, Derby, and Winsted.

In the state judiciary, of the thirty-six judges in the Superior Court, second highest in the state, eight, or 22 per cent, are Italian. In the Court of Common Pleas, which ranks just below the Superior Court, there are eighteen judges, of which four, or 22 per cent, are Italian.

Although an Italian has never been nominated for governor, it is generally believed that Emilio Q. Daddario, a Congressman, will be nominated after the present governor either retires or moves up to a higher political post.

Zaiman believes that the Italians have done so well in Connecticut because several factors opened up the political doors—the end of the "rotten borough" system, declared unconstitutional in 1964; reapportionment under the new state constitution, which allotted more political power to the urban centers where larger numbers of Italians are concentrated; the abolition of the small-town police courts; and so on.

The overriding impetus, however, to the sudden escalation of Italian political power has been both the cohesion of the Italians and their recognition of the value of uniting behind the most powerful Italian politician to achieve more power. As has been true nationally, there has been an imperceptibly low decline in Irish political power in Connecticut throughout the various committees, town and state, although an Irish Catholic, John M. Bailey, is still the Democratic state chairman (and also chairman of the Democratic National Committee, a post he has held since he was first appointed by President Kennedy).

The essential control of Connecticut is nonetheless still held by Irish Catholics. Not only is an Irish Catholic governor, but Irish Catholics hold seven of the fourteen positions in the governor's cabinet. Only one, the commissioner of the Department of Labor, is held by an Italian, Renato E. Ricciuti.

With their grip tightening on the councils of power throughout Connecticut, the Italians can be expected to increase their pressure for the governorship or a U.S Senatorship.

In New Jersey, which has a population of 525,100 Italians, 82,238 Italians, or 15 per cent of the state's total, live in metropolitan Newark and contiguous communities. This area has two Congressmen, Peter W. Rodino of the Tenth Congressional District and Joseph G. Minish of the Eleventh Congressional District. Both are Italian. Newark has an Italian mayor, Hugh Addonizio, a former Congressman. Italians do more than dominate the city government. They have a stranglehold on it. The mayor's administrative assistant (who is slated to become the first director of the Community Resources Administration, overseeing all antipoverty, welfare, and job programs), the police director, the chief magistrate of the municipal court, the president of the city council, the director of public works, the business administrator of the city, and the assistant director of the city's Housing Authority are all Italians. Of the nine members of the city council, four are Italians, the only solid ethnic bloc in the council, which explains the election of an Italian as city council president. (There are two negroes in the city council, despite the fact that Newark is now estimated to be 51 per cent negro, compared to 20 per cent Italian, as of 1967.)

Of the four, Connecticut, Massachusetts, New York, and Newark, only Newark exemplifies total political control by Italians. It is a tribute to the strong organizational and family ties that characterize the Mafia that Italian politicians are able to control the politics of a state or city even when they are an ethnic minority.

At the national level, Italian political power came of age on July 14, 1962, when President Kennedy nominated Cleveland Mayor Anthony J. Celebrezze as Secretary of the Department of Health, Education and Welfare, the first Italian-American to hold a Cabinet position. Celebrezze had been elected mayor of Cleveland five times beginning in 1953, and, as Kennedy noted in announcing the appointment, won his fifth term "with a 73.8 per cent plurality carrying every ward in Cleveland." The *New York Times* noted that "political considerations played a large part in his selection."

Referring to Abraham A. Ribicoff, who had resigned as Secretary of Health, Education, and Welfare two days before to run for the U.S. Senate seat from Connecticut, the *Times* said: "The appointment could well help both Mr. Ribicoff and Gov. Michael V. DiSalle of Ohio in their bids for re-election. Connecticut and Ohio both have large numbers of voters of Italian extraction. By the same token, the appointment could also be expected to help Edward M. Kennedy, the President's brother, in his race for the Senate in Massachusetts."

Celebrezze's appointment was an indication of the power and importance of the Italian vote and the extent to which it overshadowed the negro vote's vaunted power.

In the weeks preceding Ribicoff's resignation, there had been considerable talk of appointing the first negro Cabinet officer to succeed him. Most of the speculation centered on Home and Housing Finance Administrator Robert C. Weaver as the likely choice, in view of the fact that Kennedy had announced in January of that year that Weaver would have been his choice to head the proposed Department of Housing and Urban Development. Because Kennedy had slyly implied that perhaps Mr. Weaver's race was a factor in the Congressional rejection of the proposed Department, angered Republicans, led by their hoary-voiced spokesman Senator Everett Dirksen, all indicated they would quickly approve Weaver as the successor to Ribicoff.

By this time, the Italian voters were getting restless and disenchanted with the Kennedy administration for ignoring them in political appointments. The powerful New York State Italian-American Federation warned that Italians could not safely be considered loyal to any one political party. There were similarly repeated expressions from other Italian groups around the country.

Kennedy's response was the appointment of Celebrezze, which electrified the Italian community. Whereas Celebrezze's appointment was not able to stave off defeat for DiSalle of Ohio, it did help Ribicoff and Ted Kennedy win their races. The political gamble had paid off. Negroes would just have to wait for the next turn at bat.

In the U.S. Congress, there are sixteen Italians—two from California, two from Connecticut, one from Florida, two from Illinois, one from Massachusetts, three from New Jersey, three from New York, and two from Pennsylvania.

In the Senate, one of the most influential Senators, John O. Pastore, former governor of Rhode Island and now chairman of the Senate-House Atomic Energy Committee, is Italian. A dynamic speaker, Pastore is considered one of the serious contenders for Senate leadership. His political base, Rhode Island, is another one of the states where a heavy concentration of Italians has enabled them to wield political clout. They constitute 9 per cent of the total population in Rhode Island and are that state's largest identifiable ethnic group.

During the early days of the Johnson administration, one of the advisers closest to the President and one of the most influential was Jack Valenti, Special Assistant to the President. A current Special Assistant to President Johnson is Joseph A. Califano, Jr. Because of his responsibility for overseeing most of the President's critical legislative proposals, Califano is probably one of the most powerful Italians in the country.

Italians currently hold a series of subcabinet positions in the Federal government. An Italian has never been appointed to the U.S. Supreme Court, and there are currently no Italians serving on the nation's second highest court, the U.S. Circuit Court of Appeals, which has three negroes among its eighty-eight justices.

An Italian, Michael A. Musmanno, is a judge in the Pennsylvania Supreme Court, and Adrian Bonnelly is Presiding Judge of the County Court of Philadelphia.

In other parts of the country, the ethnic hold on Italians continues to dominate their lives. In Cleveland, Ohio, where a black man was elected mayor in 1967, an effort was begun in the spring of 1968 to unite Greater Cleveland's Italian-American population (first and second generations) into an all-inclusive organization. According to an article in the *Cleveland Press* on May 30, 1968, "Initial step is the designation of 'Italian Day' in Euclid Beach Park on Aug. 4. General chairman for the day is Frank Capriato, the builder, who has enlisted the help of a general committee of more than 12 prominent members of the Community. There are close to 40 clubs and organizations in the county. Among the initial groups helping Capriato in promoting 'Italian Day' are Italian Sons and Daughters of America; Sons of Italy; Society for Liberty and Progress, and the Italian Co-operative Club of America."

Italians and Negroes

The Italians, like the Irish, have resisted the political advancement of black people. In some instances, Italians have been more sympathetic only because they have realized that society has tended to regard them as unsavory and disreputable in some instances as it has black people. But the political tensions, racial conflicts, and (in East Harlem) violence between

Italians and negroes have flared periodically. Still, Italians do not seem to be afflicted with the same depth of ethnocentrism—and its outward manifestations of hostility toward black people—as are the Irish. Italians and negroes have been able to sit down to discuss the distribution of the spoils. The Irish have always simply informed the negroes what they were going to be given.

No Irish Catholic politician has been so devoted and loyal to the cause of equality for black people as was one of the most controversial Italian politicians who ever lived, Vito Marcantonio. A dynamic, colorful, and indefatigable politician, Marcantonio came out of the bowels of New York City's East Harlem. A lawyer and passionate believer in civil liberties, he was elected to Congress seven out of eight times between 1934 and 1948.

Considered by many a Communist, Communist sympathizer, or follower of the Communist line during the 1940's, Marcantonio was first a Republican and a protégé of LaGuardia's. His left-wing politics and statements soon immersed him in troubles, and the Democrats and Republicans not only joined hands to defeat him, but they gerrymandered the Eighteenth Congressional District to put him out to pasture.

The black people and Puerto Ricans of East Harlem loved him and continued to send him back to Congress until his final defeat. Marcantonio died on August 9, 1954, at the age of fifty-one. Although he had spent his entire career fighting for the deprived and the poor, Marcantonio is not remembered kindly by many Italians. It is a sorrowful commentary on the bias of some historians that Marcantonio's name is not mentioned once, for instance, in *The Story of the Italians in America* by Michael A. Musmanno, a distinguished Italian lawyer, jurist, and writer.

It is conceivable that when New York State is able to elect an Italian as governor and he becomes recognized nationally as an outstanding administrator and politician, the country may be ready for an Italian candidate for President. John F. Kennedy destroyed the myth that a Catholic could not be President. But the Irish are considered the royalty of Catholicism. It will take a few years before the country accepts an Italian, but it is not an impossibility, particularly if he can combine the political ingredients of a LaGuardia's lovability, DeSapio's back-room machinations, Poletti's statesmanship, and Pastore's fiery oratory.

Jewish Political Power

The only ethnic group in America that has sought, acquired, and controlled political power as an ethnic group and simultaneously managed to convince the country that it was not acting as an ethnic group has been the Jews. A remarkably sturdy people who have survived centuries and civilizations of persecution and, in the last quarter of a century, one of the most savage occurrences of genocide, the Jews have been faced with the same dilemma confronting black people in America: How much of your ethnic self should you perpetuate as an exercise in racial unity, and how much of the larger majority culture will you absorb, thus losing your identity?

Ever since nations and peoples were able to single out Jews, it has been this continual differentiation that has perpetrated witch hunts. To survive, the Jews have had to cling desperately together, build a sense of community, and further their sense of religious nationhood, at the same time trying to foster an impression that they really were not a separate group selfishly taking care of its own and concerned first about its existence and growth. This has been necessary, for the Jews have always been accused of "Jewish conspiracies." Hysterically racist documents such as the "The Protocols of the Elders of Zion," distributed nationally by a no less authentic American than Henry Ford, have tended to nourish in the susceptible racist minds of Americans the fantasy that some sort of conspiracy did indeed exist.

The myths about Jewish togetherness or Jewish unity are many. "The Jews own Wall Street" is one, when in fact Jews have long been barred from many WASP-ish firms. "The Jews control Hollywood" is another popular American belief, and, while ownership of the studios has resided largely in Jewish hands, Irish Catholics, Greeks, and Italians have played decisive roles in the motion-picture industry.

Jewish political power has been able to grow far out of proportion to numerical strength in the population because of the tradition of charity and the spirit of giving that characterizes the Jewish community. Perhaps more than any other ethnic group—and here again the principal reason is one of survival—Jews take care of their own first. Jewish schools, Jewish hospitals, and Jewish old people's homes are significant parts of many large communities.

The state of Israel could never have been started or sustained without American Jewish financial support. Along with the power of the dollar, the Jewish community has been able to muster allies who were either civil libertarians committed to freedom for all people or politicians who knew that large Jewish financial donations to their opponents could defeat them. Successful manipulation of the quid pro quo of politics has always been an accomplishment of the American Jew.

So eager have Jews been to dilute the impression that they are a unified, passionately endogamous ethnic group that they have rarely missed the opportunity to say otherwise. This has produced within the Jewish community a certain ethnic schizophrenia, comparable to that of the negro.

(The whole Black Power thrust, with its separatist overtones, has collided openly with the long-standing, acceptable movement toward racial integration, and there are increasing emotional pressures on the negro to reject integration and develop a black culture which would be at least equal in status and power with the existing white culture. It is this decision that black people are now being asked to make—choosing to be black people first, just as Irish, Italians, Jews, and Poles have made the similar choice.)

In May 1960, Dr. Jacob Prinz, president of the American Jewish Congress, delivered the keynote address before the AJC national biennial convention. He said:

No dictator, no anti-Jewish laws, not even surface anti-Semitism forces us to accept our Jewish identity.

But in choosing to be Jews, we must reject the idea of isolation, self-containment and ghettoization.

. . . Obviously, we owe no political allegiance to the State of Israel. But we must emphasize the bond of kinship we feel with the people of Israel.

The basic theme of Dr. Prinz's speech is the element of choice—the same sense of ethnic allegiance that motivates the Irish, Italians, Poles, and, to a lesser degree currently in America, the negroes. But, once that decision has been made, the foundation for ethnic solidarity and eventual political ascendancy and economic control has been laid.

Still, the Jewish community, covertly united, has projected a public image of diffusive integration and little ethnic cohesion. This image was merchandised to the heights of absurdity on September 2, 1960, when, for some strange and unknown reason, the American Jewish Congress issued a public statement denying that there was such a political animal as a "Jewish bloc vote in national elections." So powerful is the Jewish community in an election that both Presidential candidates, Richard M. Nixon and John F. Kennedy, issued statements endorsing the AJC's position paper and both took pains to deny dutifully that such a thing as a "Jewish bloc vote" or any kind of ethnic bloc vote existed—and both candidates knew they were lying. The AJC statement denounced what it called the "divisive myth of bloc voting" as jeopardizing the "American process of democratic elections." It took exception to the "current tendency to imply that a Jewish vote, as such, exists in national elections." While there might have been some substance to the statement, the AJC then became carried away with its own ethnic rhetoric and stretched credulity to a breaking point by concluding that in New York City, where Jews constitute more than one-quarter of the population, there never has been a Jewish vote!

To the contrary, there have been repeated published instances of the public recognition, the political acceptance, and the electoral necessity of a Jewish bloc vote comparable in scope and intensity to the Irish Catholic bloc vote, the Italian-American bloc vote, the Polish-American bloc vote, and the negro bloc vote.

But few politicians will publicly admit these exist. It is far more American to perpetuate the myth of the melting pot, the one-big-happy-family syndrome of American nationalism.

The Jewish-owned *New York Times* has particularly tried to avoid giving the impression that a Jewish bloc vote existed. But its news columns have contradicted its hypocritical editorial policy. In the *Times* of July 4, 1965, an article describing the Liberal Party of New York State said: "Ethnically the party is largely Jewish, and its voting strength comes mainly out of middle-class Jewish neighborhoods." In the *Times* of July 21, 1965, a column by the chief of its Washington bureau, Tom Wicker, wrote, in discussing the appointment of Supreme Court Justice Arthur J. Goldberg as U.S. Ambassador to the United Nations:

> But there is another interesting effect that may follow Mr. Goldberg's appointment, and the new prominence he will receive. Whether or not it was in the President's mind, Mr. Goldberg at the U.N. probably will pay handsome dividends among the nation's 5,500,000 Jewish voters. [Wicker is obviously far off in his statistics. As of 1967, the Jewish Statistical Bureau estimated a total of 5,721,000 Jews in America. It would have been more accurate for Wicker to refer to that number as the Jewish community rather than as voters.]
>
> Of these, 2,517,000 are in New York State, mostly in New York City, where Mr. Goldberg's new activities will be most visible.

Mr. Wicker then goes on to confirm the charade that American politicians play in denying the existence of the ethnic vote:

> It is fashionable, of course, to deplore ethnic and religious appeals as un-American, un-democratic and demagogic. But the fact is that ethnic and religious groups are there, like Mount Everest, and as long as they respond to appointments and appeals, politicians will make them.
>
> It is plainly better to attempt to pull, say, Irish, Jews and Italians together behind one ticket in New York City than for any one or two of these groups to divide against another.

Again, in the *New York Times*, on March 12, 1967, an article by Richard Witkin analyzed the political possibilities of Goldberg opposing New York Senator Jacob K. Javits in 1968: "Mr. Goldberg has never run for office but is generally considered to have wide public admiration. He would also challenge Mr. Javits' hold on the large and independent Jewish vote in the state."

A July 19, 1967, column by Washington's leading journalistic muckrakers, Drew Pearson and Jack Anderson, discussed the possibility of New York Representative Joseph Resnick as a candidate against Javits:

> . . . Democrats have long been looking for a Jewish candidate who could take on Jake Javits. Javits has been a good senator and aspires to be president.
>
> Part of his political strength lies in his religion which nets him a preponderance of Jewish-Democratic voters in New York City who cross over to the Republican ticket where Javits is concerned. They even voted for him and against Franklin D. Roosevelt, Jr. for attorney general.

That last sentence carried an element of awe and admiration since "Roosevelt" has always been believed to be one of the most magic names in the Jewish community.

In any event, comparison of these articles decisively buries the myth that there is no Jewish bloc vote. In fact, both the American Labor Party and the Liberal Party in New York State were founded by Jews as an outlet for their political preferences. Also, the early exclusion of Jews from political offices by the Irish Catholic-controlled machines necessitated the formation of a third party as a balance of power lever.

Jewish writer Nathan Glazer, in discussing the Jewish vote, writes:

> What attracts Jews is liberalism, using the term to refer to the entire range of leftist positions, from the mildest to the most extreme. The Jewish vote is primarily "ideological" rather than a party or even an ethnic one. There is little question that Jews are moved, as other groups are, by issues that affect them alone, such as policy toward Israel. But it is impossible to test the effect of pro-Israel feeling on voting, for political candidates in New York City all profess an enthusiasm for Israel.*

What Glazer does not say in that last sentence, however, is that the principal reason all New York City candidates profess this enthusiasm for Israel is the enormous political and economic power of Jews in New York City. An anti-Israel candidate risks his political career if for no other reason than the Jewish domination of New York City's media. Of the three newspapers in New York City, as of 1967—the *New York Times,* the *New York Post* and the *New York Daily News*—two, the *Times* and the *Post,* are Jewish-owned and exhibit an extraordinary pro-Jewish bias in their news columns and editorials. This bias is reflected in the exceedingly favorable placement of news articles and the number of pictures of Jewish newsmakers that appear in both papers. The election of the president of a prominent synagogue always rates a picture in the *New York Times,* while the election of a prominent negro to an important post rarely does.

"The Jewish liberal voting pattern has been of great persistence," writes Glazer. It is this overriding affection for liberalism that has sometimes dislodged the Jewish voter from his Jewish loyalty. As Glazer points out, the 1960 Democratic primary between Ludwig Teller, the regular organization candidate, and his challenger, Irish Catholic William Fitts Ryan, in the heavily Jewish-populated Twentieth Congressional District was really a contest between the entrenched Tammany Hall machine and the Reform Democrats, of which Ryan was a symbol. Ryan soundly defeated Teller.

This fact also accounts for Democratic candidate Abe Beame's failure in the 1965 race for mayor of New York City to win the Jewish vote against tall, attractive, and liberal Republican John Lindsay. Beame, an unattractive candidate, simply did not appeal to the broad cross-section of voters, including the Jewish voters. In a culture that cultivates sex appeal, television imagery, and charisma, the Jewish voter is as susceptible to these factors as all other voters.

* Glazer and Moynihan, p. 167.

Nevertheless, in a choice between an attractive, intelligent, and liberal Jewish candidate and an attractive, intelligent, and liberal non-Jewish candidate, the Jewish candidate will win the Jewish vote hands down.

This has happened repeatedly in the career of New York Senator Jacob K. Javits, who has successfully bucked a Democratic tide to climb to his present office.

In 1948, when Javits won re-election as a Congressman from the heavily Jewish Twenty-first Congressional District of Washington Heights, he defeated Democratic Paul O'Dwyer, brother of Mayor O'Dwyer, by a scant 66,455 to 64,297. Only two other Republicans won Congressional seats in New York City that year—Coudert of the traditionally Republican Seventeenth "Silk Stocking" District and Latham in Queens' conservative Third District. But Javits' area, normally Democratic and represented for years by Jewish Joseph Zaretzki in the state senate, switched their votes for him.

This happened again in 1954, the year of a Democratic sweep in the state when Averell Harriman was elected governor. Javits defeated the popular Franklin D. Roosevelt, Jr., for attorney general. In 1956, Javits ran for the U.S. Senate and defeated New York City Mayor Wagner. Again, a reading of the heavily Jewish neighborhoods in Manhattan, the Bronx, and Brooklyn showed that normally Democratic voters switched to Javits.

The growth of Jewish political power, both nationally and in New York State and City, is described by Glazer:

> The Jewish commitment to the Democratic party is virtually complete today because the Democrats, since 1928, have nominated liberal candidates for the Presidency.
>
> . . . German Jews, coming to political maturity and consciousness in the period of the Civil War, were perhaps predominantly Republican. . . . In the 1860's and 1880's Greenpoint had Jewish Republican leaders and there were Jewish Republican county leaders in Brooklyn before the end of the century. In the 1920's Meier Steinbrink and Samuel Koenig were Republican county leaders in Brooklyn and Manhattan.
>
> . . . Woodrow Wilson aroused some enthusiasm among Jews in 1912 and 1916. Henry Morgenthau, Sr., was chairman of the Democratic Financial Committee in 1912. Bernard Baruch was one of the President's advisers, Louis D. Brandeis became the first Jew to serve on the Supreme Court. But it was Al Smith who challenged the power of the Socialists on the East Side and taught Jews to vote for Democratic and national candidates. In 1922, with Smith heading the Democratic ticket for Governor, four Jews—three Democrats and a Republican—went to Congress from New York City. . . . It was in 1922 that Sol Bloom, Nathaniel Dickstein and Emanuel Celler began their long service in Congress, in seats that became as safe an any in the South.*

It is interesting to note President Wilson's liberal attitude toward the Jews, undoubtedly influenced by banker Henry Morgenthau's fund-raising efforts. Wilson was a racial bigot toward negroes; under his administration,

* Glazer and Moynihan, pp. 168-69.

negroes had fewer Federal appointments than at any time since Ulysses S. Grant's administration.

Franklin D. Roosevelt rewarded Morgenthau's heavy financial contributions to the Democratic Party by appointing his son, Henry Morgenthau, Jr., as Secretary of the Treasury in 1934, a post he held for eleven years. Morgenthau was the first Jew to be appointed to a Cabinet position.

The fact that Jews were able to win appointments to the Supreme Court and the Cabinet before Irish Catholics, even though the latter controlled the election machinery in most major cities, conclusively demonstrates the importance of money and the ability to raise money for political campaigns in shaping political attitudes. Political campaigns required money, and Jews performed this role for the Democratic Party, just as they later were to accomplish the Herculean task of raising millions of dollars to sustain Israel. It paid off in political appointments and a large share of patronage in the better-paying and more powerful positions in government.

Glazer confirms these observations:

> They have received a high proportion of the judicial posts and nominations for the past thirty years. One-third of the Congressmen from the city, and rather more of the judges, State Senators, and Assemblymen are Jewish. Jews have in fact held more judicial and elective offices than their numerical strength in the organization would seem to warrant. Their prominence in this respect reflects their financial contributions to electoral campaigns, the large number of lawyers among them and their high rate of voting participation, rather than strength on the clubhouse floor.*

That last factor is equally important—the Jewish "high rate of voting participation." No other ethnic group in America, or no other group, for that matter, has a more intense and constructive civic consciousness than Jews. While others usually bemoan the state of affairs, the Jewish community invariably takes the lead and does something about the shoddy state of politics. The Reform Democratic movement in New York City was Jewish-sponsored, -led, and -financed. It resulted in better government and more participation by all groups in the electoral process and the machinery of government.

To move from generalities to specifics, the measurement of Jewish political power in the three branches of New York City's government substantiates the role numbers and ethnic cohesion have played in the political success of the Jewish community.

Of America's 5,721,000 Jews, 1,836,000, or 32 per cent, live in New York City. In addition, 545,000 Jews live in the surrounding counties of Nassau, Suffolk, and Westchester. When the 68,000 Jews who are estimated by the Jewish Statistical Bureau to live in Albany, Buffalo, Rochester, and Syracuse are added to those two totals, 2,449,000, or 42 per cent, of America's Jews live in New York State. This explains the considerable political power Jews

---

* Glazer and Moynihan, op. cit.

have been able to acquire in the Empire State. One of the first Jewish governors in America was Herbert H. Lehman, who succeeded Roosevelt as governor, was elected in 1932 and re-elected for successive terms, declining renomination in 1942. (In the same year, 1933, that Lehman was elected, three other states also elected Jewish governors: Henry Horner of Illinois, Julius Meyer of Oregon and Arthur Seligman of New Mexico.)

Other metropolitan areas with comparatively large Jewish populations are: Los Angeles, 490,000 Jews; Philadelphia, 330,000; Chicago, 270,000; Boston, 169,000; Miami, 92,000; and Baltimore, Cleveland, and Detroit, with 85,000 each.

In all three branches of government in New York City, Jews have been able to fill positions in a greater proportion than their numerical percentage in the population—as have the Irish and the Italians.

Of the thirty-seven city councilmen, fifteen, or 40 per cent, are Jewish. Of the thirty-three major departments in the New York City government, as of 1967, fourteen, or 42 per cent, were headed by Jews. Of the thirty school districts of New York City, eighteen, or 60 per cent, are headed by Jewish assistant superintendents. (This is not surprising, since the Jewish community has been especially devoted to the advancement of education not only for itself as a means of survival, but as a fuller commitment to public service. Nevertheless, this monopoly on the top jobs in the educational system has produced tensions between Jews and negroes, the latter demanding a larger share of such positions in proportion to their numbers.)

The judiciary is where Jews have excelled in acquiring a persistently greater number of appointments than their proportion in the population. While other ethnic groups have tended to fluctuate in their proportion of the total of judgeships, that of the Jews has been consistently higher. As Glazer indicated, however, one of the factors responsible is the larger number of lawyers among them.

COURT	NUMBER OF JUDGES	JEWISH JUDGES	PER CENT
Civil Court of New York City	95	45	47
Criminal Court of New York City	77	77	45
Surrogate Court (5 Counties)	6	2	33
Court of Appeals (New York State's highest court)	7	2	28 (includes the Chief Justice)
Supreme Court (Appellate Division— 2 Departments)	17	8	47
Supreme Court (5 Counties)	91	44	48

In the nineteen-member New York City Congressional delegation, there were seven Jews, or 36 per cent, as of 1967. This percentage closely approximates the percentage of Jews in New York City's population—32 per cent.

Of New York City's twenty-six state senators, twelve, or 45 per cent, are Jewish. Of the city's sixty-eight state assemblymen, twenty-five, or 38 per cent, are Jewish, including the majority leader, Moses M. Weinstein.

In the executive branch, two of the state's top four elective offices are held by Jews, the comptroller, Arthur Levitt, a Democrat, and the attorney general, Louis J. Lefkowitz, a Republican. (If there is no such thing as a "Jewish bloc vote," somebody's bloc vote has been doing some very sophisticated vote-splitting for these two offices.)

Chicago and Baltimore are examples where the Jews as a small minority have nonetheless been able to play a decisive role in the political councils. For a few years in the late forties, one of the most powerful political bosses in the country was a Jew. In 1947, Colonel Jacob M. Arvey, a prominent Jewish politician, succeeded former Mayor Edward J. Kelly, an Irish Catholic, as chairman of the Cook County Democratic Central Committee and, by virtue of this position, the political boss of Chicago. Several political scandals in the Kelly administration had opened the door for so-called reform. It was on the wave of this emotional cry for change that Arvey was able to take command of the Democratic Party. Arvey was not a typical political boss. He believed in good government—at least for the people. Faithful to the Jewish tradition of political liberalism, Arvey engineered the election of Martin H. Kennelly, a respectable, clean, and very bland Irish businessman, as the "reform" mayor in 1947. In 1948, Arvey was instrumental in getting a distinguished University of Chicago economics professor, Paul H. Douglas, elected to the Senate and a well-known liberal, Adlai Stevenson, elected as governor. These two men were responsible for Truman's sweep of Illinois. Both ran ahead of Truman in that state.

But Arvey made two political mistakes, and the second was to cause his undoing. In 1949, a local newspaper revealed that he and four associates had purchased valuable property near Chicago's West Side in 1946 after the land had been condemned for a superhighway. Arvey admitted they had paid $900,000 for the property and later received a condemnation award of more than $1,200,000—making a profit of $300,000.

Then, in 1950, Arvey selected Captain Daniel A. Gilbert, a chief investigator for the state attorney general's office with eighteen years' experience, as the Democratic nominee for Cook County sheriff. Known as the world's richest cop, Gilbert was not regarded as an apostle of trustworthiness and honesty in government, and he was soundly defeated by a virtually unknown Republican who ran up a 300,000-vote margin over Gilbert. Gilbert dragged down to defeat with him U.S. Senator Scott W. Lucas, the Senate's Majority Leader, who was defeated by Everett M. Dirksen.

Arvey blamed the defeat on the Korean War and the attendant public uncertainty. But he did take full responsibility for the nomination of Gilbert. A week after the election, Arvey resigned. He was succeeded by Irish

Catholic Joseph L. Gill. The vice-chairman elected was a fast-rising little fat man named Richard J. Daley, who was to step up a year later as the real boss of Cook County because of his murky ties to the underworld. (The crime syndicate still controls Chicago. Daley rules by sufferance.)

Arvey's success as the first Jewish political boss of Chicago—and one of the few in the country—was an unusual accomplishment in view of the small proportion of Jews in that city—5 per cent. But a shrewd political mind and the financial power of the Jewish community enabled him to move into the political vacuum left by the scars of the Kelly administration.

In Baltimore, Jews comprise approximately 9 per cent of the population and have played a decisive role in the politics of that city. This also has enabled them to become an important political force in the state because of Baltimore's size as the largest city in the state.

One of the city's most powerful political bosses has been James H. (Jack) Pollack, who has controlled the Fourth District and who built what became known as the Pollack machine. It was natural for Pollack, a Jew, to control the district since it was predominantly Jewish. Pollack, however, worked hard to maintain Jewish political suzerainty.

G. James Fleming, a distinguished professor of political science at Morgan State College, describes Pollack's continuing assignment of the political plums to Jews, even though the district was becoming predominantly negro:

> Until 1954, all candidates for the legislature and city council from the 4th District were Jewish. The *Baltimore Sun* observed on June 4, 1958, that "a Pollack-backed candidate was invariably white and Jewish." In a later editorial (September 30, 1958) the *Sun* added: "As long as the Pollack machine held undisputed control in the 4th District . . . [the] machine backed no candidate who was not Jewish. Negroes had no place in the organization planning when it came to elective office."*

In 1967, the picture has changed radically. Pollack is still the political boss, but the three city council seats in the Fourth District are held by negroes. Jews control the three seats in the Fifth District. (There are eighteen seats in the council.)

Pollack's power, however, has guaranteed a Jew in key political positions at the Federal, state, and city levels. Of Baltimore's three Congressmen, one, Samuel N. Friedel, is a Jew who has held that office for eight terms.

Of the three top elective offices in Baltimore—the mayor, president of the city council, and comptroller—the third position is held by a Jew, Hyman A. Pressman. Of the three top state elective offices—governor, attorney general, and comptroller—the third is also held by a Jew, Louis L. Goldstein. (It should be noted here that in New York State, Maryland, and Baltimore, the comptrollers are all Jews. In addition, the present U.S. Com-

---

* G. James Fleming, "An All-Negro Ticket in Baltimore," *Case Studies in Practical Politics* (New York: Holt, Rinehart & Winston, 1960), p. 2.

missioner of Internal Revenue, Sheldon S. Cohen, is Jewish, as was his predecessor, Mortimer Caplin. The importance of controlling the financial or budgetary facets of government has long been one of the primary aims of Jewish political power as insurance for their political survival.)

Nationally, Jews have long been significant forces in both the executive and legislative branches of government. The Kennedy administration was the first to have two Jews in the Cabinet at the same time, Abraham A. Ribicoff as the Secretary of Health, Education, and Welfare and Arthur J. Goldberg as the Secretary of Labor. In addition to Caplin as the Commissioner of Internal Revenue, Myer Feldman was Deputy Special Counsel to the President, second to Theodore Sorenson, Special Counsel to the President and most powerful of all the Kennedy advisers.

While Jews were either heads or deputies in several of the independent agencies, none matched the power of the Cabinet positions or the proximity to the President.

One of the most outstanding appointees of the Truman administration was a petite and brilliant Jewish lady, Mrs. Anna Rosenberg, who was Assistant Secretary of Defense for Manpower and holder of one of the most powerful posts in the Federal government, second only in influence to Secretary of Labor Frances Perkins under Roosevelt.

Ever since President Wilson established the "Jewish seat" on the U.S. Supreme Court with his appointment of Louis D. Brandeis in 1916, that tradition has been maintained by President Roosevelt, who appointed Felix Frankfurter to succeed Brandeis in 1939, and by President Kennedy, who appointed Arthur J. Goldberg after Frankfurter left the bench.

In the U.S. House of Representatives of the Ninetieth Congress (1966), there were fifteen Jews, or 3 per cent of the total of 435 Congressmen. This percentage is greater than that of the national population, 2 per cent. The Jewish Congressmen, as of 1967, were: Sidney Yates of Chicago, Ill.; Samuel N. Friedel of Baltimore, Md.; Charles Joelson of Paterson, N.J.; Richard Ottinger, Joseph Y. Resnick, Herbert Tenzer, and Lester L. Wolff of New York State; and Emanuel Celler, Jacob H. Gilbert, Leonard Farbstein, Benjamin S. Rosenthal, James H. Scheuer, and Seymour Halpern of New York City; and Joshua Eilberg of Philadelphia, Pa. Not surprisingly, all are Democrats, with the exception of Halpern, a Republican.

There are two Jews in the U.S. Senate, Ribicoff, a Democrat, of Connecticut and Javits, a Republican, of New York.

There is another aspect of political power that no other ethnic group has been able to develop so successfully as the Jews. This is the occupation of some of the most important middle-line and policy-making positions in government. In certain departments and agencies, the critical jobs in statistics, budget, planning, and personnel are held by Jews. There are several departments in certain agencies that have become known as Jewish departments. In the Department of Labor, for example, several of the key jobs in the divisions of manpower administration, solicitor, administration, international labor affairs, and labor statistics are held by Jews. In the Bureau of the Budget, one of the most important officials in that agency, which is virtually a fourth arm of government, is the assistant director for budget review, Samuel M. Cohn. The chiefs of several of the other divisions within the Bureau are also Jews. This is especially true of the Small Business Administration. (The present chairman of the Securities and Exchange Commission is also Jewish.)

The ability to accept the superficially drab middle-line position and expand its power has been one of the factors responsible for a high percentage of Jews in policy-making posts. There has likewise been the tendency for Jews to hire other Jews, a characteristic true of all other ethnic groups except black people, who have not yet been able to develop the security or racial pride to hire other black people. While most ethnic groups seek to surround themselves with members from their own group, black people seek just as diligently to insulate themselves from other black people. There is the understandable fear of some negroes that a preponderance of black employees in the department will either lower that department's performance (an implicit acceptance of white propaganda) or will resegregate the department and, concomitantly, reduce its prestige.

Jews and Black People

In his brilliant study, "The Police and Minority Groups," sociology professor and criminologist Joseph D. Lohman maintains that "racism, or race prejudice, in the United States is of four major types: prejudice against the Negro, the Oriental, the Mexican and the Jew. . . . [It ranges] from unofficial and covert discrimination against Jews to the official and overt practices of segregation and discrimination practiced against Negroes. They are not confined to the South, but are found in variable degree throughout the United States."*

There is a tendency for people to believe that if two minority groups are mistreated and abused or have a legacy of persecution, an emotional identification and sympathetic relationship will exist between the two.

This fact, to some extent, explains why the Jewish community has been so deeply involved with the black civil-rights struggle and has contributed so heavily to its various organizations (the NAACP whose Jewish president has been in office for a quarter of a century, the Urban League, etc.). Jews have played major—and at various times, the principal—roles in most of the civil-rights groups. Had it not been for their financial efforts and labors of dedication, there is no question that the American negro's freedom

* "The Police and Minority Groups" prepared by Joseph D. Lohman and directed by Roger F. Shanahan, chief of police, Chicago Park District, Chicago, Illinois, 1947; p. 9.

struggle would not have reached its present stage, or even attained its current dimensions. Jews have identified with the miserable plight of black people because of its similarity to their history of oppression.

It has been suggested by some critics of Jewish involvement in the civil-rights struggle that they were motivated first by a desire to "save their own skins," that they believed it a fundamental necessity for ethnic survival to create a political atmosphere of racial equality. The poisonous plant of race hatred feeds on itself and ferments a venom that engulfs other racial groups. If one race is attacked and tormented, the permissive climate to attack another exists. An ethnic group such as the Jews, which has endured a 2000-year legacy of ethnic crucifixion, is far more sensitive to the social nuances and implications of race hatred against other groups as it tangentially affects Jews.

On the other hand, there is a deeply ingrained tradition of service in the Jewish community—service to its own members first and service to humanity. Such brotherly concern for other Jews has spilled over into the relationships Jews have with other peoples. Black people have been prime beneficiaries of this heedfulness.

Yet, strains have been placed on the relationship. Because of their superior financial resources and organizing ability, Jews have tended to assume a paternalistic control of black organizations. Jews have tended to decide for black people how hard they should push or how fast they should run. The parent has been reluctant to let the child stand on his own two feet and direct his destiny.

Anti-Semitism among black people and racial hatred for black people among Jews are two facts of American life. Of the many attempted explanations and rationalizations for these two conditions, none has been more brilliantly delineated than that of Oliver Cromwell Cox in a book which is perhaps the most definitive in the field of American race relations. Cox writes:

The question has been frequently raised as to the possibility of Negroes and Jews, as "minority groups," collaborating for the purpose of advancing their social position. Recently Dr. Werner Cahnman put it this way: "Both Jews and Negroes are threatened by the same hatred and the same hostility. Upon the strength of this they could unite in action. But their reaction to the situation is different: the Jews are cautiously defending where the Negroes are militantly attacking." Yet it is doubtful whether Jews and Negroes have a common basis for continuing action against the dominant group. In reality they are not "threatened by the same hostility," and there is some probability that there is as much reason for antagonism between them.

In so far as Jews are bourgeois-minded businessmen and manufacturers, they are likely to be, at least implicitly, race-prejudiced. . . . As Negroes become increasingly assimilated in the larger society, the likelihood is that they, too, will become intolerant.*

* Oliver Cromwell Cox, Caste, Class and Race (Garden City, N.Y.: Doubleday & Co., 1948), p. 396.

Analyzing the difference between anti-Semitism and race prejudice, Cox continues:

Anti-Semitism is an attitude directed against the Jews because they are Jews, while race prejudice is an attitude directed against Negroes because they want to be something other than Negroes. The Jew, to the intolerant, is an enemy within the society; but the Negro, to the race-prejudiced, is a friend in his place.*

The clarity and logic of Cox's thinking help to explain the growth of tensions between black people and Jews during the last few years, particularly as the black community has grown more militant. Moderately liberal Jewish businessmen have become disenchanted with the new radicalism of Black Power and the new emphasis on black control of all predominantly black civil-rights groups. Furthermore, Jews have fled integrated neighborhoods as rapidly and compulsively as their Gentile cousins. The Jewish employer and businessman has been quicker to hire blacks than other white employers, but it is difficult to trace this enlightened attitude as one steeped in morality or in economics. The motivation has determined the subsequent relationship between blacks and the Jews.

But where the two ethnic groups have really locked horns has been in the political arena. Jewish politicians have vigorously resisted all efforts to accord increased political representation to black people. Whether a Pollack in Baltimore, an Arvey in Chicago, a Ribicoff in Connecticut, or a Celler in Brooklyn, the Jewish politician has fought attempts of black people to gain political power. The classic example of this attitude rooted in racial hostility has been Brooklyn Congressman Celler's fight to prevent his Tenth Congressional District—31 per cent black in 1960 and an estimated 45 per cent black in 1967—from being gerrymandered to facilitate the election of a Negro Congressman from Brooklyn. As Chairman of the House Judiciary Committee, which oversees legislation dealing with reapportionment, Celler has been as stubbornly opposed to any legislation increasing negro representation as the most bigoted racist from the South.

In the future, as black people press harder against some of the tender political spots now filled by Jews, tensions between the two groups will in all probability increase. The Jewish merchant, the Jewish landlord, heretofore not the most popular citizen in the black community, will encounter a harsher and more violent form of anger. Concomitantly, the Jewish community can be expected to move closer to the majority group in its attitudes and practices toward black people. In a curiously perverse way, these twin developments will lead to a normalization of relations between the two groups. The polarization will hasten the ultimate political confrontation as blacks attempt to eliminate the remaining residue of Jewish power remaining in the black community and in the various civil-rights organiza-

* Cox, p. 393.

tions. If nothing else, the Jewish-black political relationship will finally become one based on honesty and a realistic acceptance of the hard ethnic facts of American political life.

Polish Political Power

Few ethnic groups have a more passionate involvement in their heritage and nationalistic ties than Polish-Americans. In defiance of the mythical melting pot, Poles have clung stubbornly to their traditions, proudly created "Little Polands" wherever they have settled, vigorously supported their Catholic parishes, and maintained newspapers published in their mother tongue.

This ethnic unity has fostered an emotional togetherness that has subsidized their political advancement. As a result, whenever Poles have comprised at least 10 per cent of the population in a city, Congressional district or state, they have been an influential factor in its politics.

Also exerting a powerful impact on the various "Polonias" (Polish ghettoes) in America have been the thousands of Polish-American organizations, both national and local. Some of the largest and most potent organizations are the Polish-American Congress, the Polish National Alliance, and the Polish Women's Alliance of America. All have been dedicated to preserving the Polish culture and simultaneously looking out for the Polish community by aggrandizing it leaders.

By remaining in their self-made ghettos, they were able to maintain their political power. They felt no shame from living in "Polonia."

It became the goal of almost every Polish family to live within walking distance of its own church around which not only religious but all sorts of social activities centered. Thus, in many cities, densely populated Polish neighborhoods developed. But these were seldom areas of tenement slums. Unable to express their peasant love for the land in any other way, Polish industrial workers scrimped and saved to buy homes of their own with at least a backyard in which to raise vegetables. In Bayonne, New Jersey, Americans of Polish descent stock own sixty per cent of all real property. More than four out of five of Chicago's Polish-American families own the houses they live in. Hamtramck, Michigan, the most solidly Polish city in America, is also the one with the highest ratio of home owners in the nation.*

Poles were among the latecomers to America. While there was a constant dribble of Polish immigrants to this country, the first big wave did not begin until 1890. Between that year and 1895, over 99,000 Poles came to America. Then, there was a tapering off, and not until 1921 did another upsurge of

* Albert Q. Maisel, *They All Chose America*, Thomas Nelson & Sons, New York, N.Y., 1957, p. 214.

Polish immigration take place. Between 1921 and 1925, over 200,000 Poles came to America.

By then, the Poles had already developed some political expertise, and in 1914, the first Polish-American, a lawyer named John C. Kleczka, a Republican, was sent to Congress from Milwaukee.

According to the U.S. Census Bureau, there are an estimated 2,780,026 Polish-Americans—or 1 per cent of the country's population—as of 1960. This figure is based upon the Bureau's "two-generation" test (foreign-born and the children of foreign-born or mixed parentage).

As have other ethnic groups, the Poles have tended to concentrate their settlements in certain states and cities. Over half of America's Poles, 54 per cent, or 1,512,319, reside in five states: Connecticut, with 117,663; Illinois, 358,916; Michigan, 255,467; New York, 683,610; and Wisconsin, 93,663.

In *They All Chose America*, Albert Q. Maisel discusses the early introduction of the Polish-Americans to politics:

Coming from lands where the opinions of Poles—and particularly of peasants —were never consulted, the immigrants had no experience to guide them in American politics. But as they bought homes and became municipal taxpayers, they developed an acute interest in city affairs. Thus, the first Poles elected to office were Chicago aldermen who promised to get the streets cleaned in the Polish wards. Later, as the immigrants discovered the power their geographically concentrated votes could wield, they sent their first young lawyers to the state assemblies.*

This group awareness of political power and the value of ethnic cohesion accounts for the fact that the Poles have been able to acquire representation in the various legislatures even when they were one of the smallest minorities in the population.

Michigan's first Polish-American Congressman, John Sosnowski, elected in 1924 from Detroit, was also a Republican. With the Roosevelt landslide in 1932 and 1936, many Poles began their political careers as Democrats. One was Detroit's John Lesinski, who was Chairman of the Education and Labor Committee when he died in 1950.

Despite their comparatively large number in New York State—683,610— Poles have not been able to exert much influence in state politics. On October 1, 1962, the New York State Council of Polish Democratic Clubs passed a resolution expressing dismay that a Pole had not been included in the make-up of the state ticket, but nevertheless voted to support the slate. In Buffalo, where the 71,633 Poles comprise 13 per cent of the population, they have been able to elect a Congressman, Thaddeus J. Dulski. Over half of Buffalo's Poles—41,585—live in Dulski's district. The comparative political power of the Poles and the negroes can be measured in this instance because of the near similarity in numbers. The 73,388 negroes in Buffalo

* Maisel, p. 219.

also comprise 13 per cent of the population. Yet, the election of a negro Congressman from that city is almost an impossibility. Because they are white, Poles are able to make political alliances with other white ethnic groups to elect one of their own to office. Dulski, incidentally, is now Chairman of the Committee on Post Office and Civil Service in the U.S. House of Representatives, the second Polish-American to hold a Committee chairmanship.

Wisconsin's two Polish Congressmen are Clement J. Zablocki, a Democrat of Milwaukee, and Alvin E. O'Konski, a Republican of Mercer. Although that city's 39,296 Poles comprise only 9 per cent of the population, Milwaukee has developed the reputation of being a Polish town. Poles hold a high proportion of the political jobs in City Hall.

In Connecticut, until Congressional reapportionment, the seat of Congressman-at-large was usually reserved for a Pole to accommodate the industrial New Britain area, which has the largest concentration of Poles in the state—29,823. But when that area became the Sixth Congressional District, its Polish Congressman, Bernard F. Grabowski, who had served at large in the Eighty-eighth Congress and had been re-elected to the Eighty-ninth Congress as the Sixth District's first Congressman, was defeated by an Irishman in the 1966 race for the Ninetieth Congress.

While Connecticut's 117,663 Poles are almost exactly half of the state's 237,146 Italians, the Poles do not have one-tenth of the political power of the Italians, who almost have a monopoly on the most important jobs in both the legislative and executive branches of government.

Chicago is where the Poles have really been able to exert a strong political influence.

Chicago's 258,267 Poles constitute a mere 7 per cent of the population, but they control a hefty 33 per cent of that city's nine man Congressional delegation. The three Polish Congressmen are: John C. Kluczynski of the Fifth District; Dan Rostenkowski of the Eighth District; and Roman Pucinski of the Eleventh District. Rostenkowski is also one of the fifty ward committeemen who comprise the Democratic Central Committee that runs Chicago. A member of the all-powerful House Ways and Means Committee, he sometimes has been mentioned as a possible successor to Mayor Daley. Kluczynski is a chairman of one of the subcommittees of the Public Works Committee and in such a position has considerable power over the allocation of funds to various Congressional districts for public-works projects. In addition to those three Congressmen, a fourth Polish Congressman from the neighboring community of South Holland, which, like Chicago, is part of Cook County, is Edward J. Derwinski

Again, by way of comparison with the political impotence of negroes, the Poles have almost five times the number of Congressional seats represented by their proportion of the population.

While Chicago's 812,637 negroes* comprised 23 per cent of the population in 1960, they have only one Congressman, or 11 per cent of the city's Congressional delegation.

Although Chicago's Polish population is one-third of that city's black population, the former have almost as many aldermen in the fifty-man City Council. As of 1967, there were seven Polish aldermen and ten negro aldermen.

Poles control 20 per cent of the judgeships on the municipal court and have membership in almost all the policy-making bodies of both the city and county. But they have set their hearts on capturing one of the U.S. District Court judgeships in Chicago. A *Chicago Daily News* story of November 16, 1967, mentioning the possibility of a District Court judge moving up to the U.S. Circuit Court of Appeals then said:

A promotion of this type would create a vacancy on the U.S. District Court bench. Francis S. Lorenz, state director of public works, has been mentioned as a possibility to satisfy the Polish-American community.
The appointment of Judge Alexander J. Napoli, an Italian-American, to the U.S. District Court bench last year made a number of Polish-American leaders unhappy.

Nationally, Poles struck political oil on September 9, 1963, when President Kennedy announced his intention to appoint the first Polish-American to a Cabinet post, John A. Gronouski, a former Wisconsin tax commissioner, as Postmaster General. The political power of the Poles is mirrored in the manner the appointment was made known. The night before Kennedy's announcement, Milwaukee's Polish Congressman Zablocki announced at a dinner of the Polish Legion of American Veterans that Gronouski would be named. Gronouski had earlier been one of the two finalists under consideration by Kennedy for Commissioner of Internal Revenue. The other finalist was Mortimer Caplin, a Jew. Because the Jews have more national political influence than Poles and also make a point of controlling, wherever possible, the financial budgetary posts in government, Caplin was appointed. But the political debt was still owed to Gronouski. That was one of the two factors in his appointment. The other factor was described in a *New York Times* story on September 10th:

The appointment was expected to be received with favor by the large group of Polish-Americans in such major cities as Chicago, Detroit and Buffalo.
. . . The second factor was Mr. Gronouski's Polish descent. Polish-Americans vote heavily in many major urban cities—including Milwaukee—and political experience has shown they often vote in blocs and for one of their own.

Thus, the Poles, with a national population of only 2,780,026, compared

* The 1960 Census figures are used because that year's figures were also used for the number of Poles. Later figures on the number of Poles in Chicago were unavailable. As of 1967, it is estimated that there are over 1,000,000 negroes in Chicago.

with 18,849,000 negroes, were nonetheless able to get a Cabinet post first, even though President Kennedy had previously indicated on two occasions he had intended to appoint a negro. The national importance of Polish political power has been recognized by both Democrats and Republicans. On October 1, 1960, President Eisenhower addressed the Polish-American Congress in Chicago and on May 5, 1963, Vice President Lyndon B. Johnson addressed the same group.

The Congress indicates once again the comparative superior political power of the Poles vis-à-vis the negroes. As of 1967, there were nine Polish Congressmen (four from Illinois, two from Wisconsin, one from New York, and one from New Jersey) and only six black Congressmen (including Adam Clayton Powell). There is presently one Polish Senator, Edmund S. Muskie of Maine.

Poles and Black People

Of the four ethnic groups considered in this chapter—the Irish, the Italians, the Jews, and the Poles—none are as antagonistic to black people as the Poles. Some of the worst racial tensions and flare-ups in northern urban areas have been caused by Polish residents when a black family moved into their neighborhood. In Chicago and Milwaukee during the last two years, racial violence has been spawned when black people encountered Poles. There has never existed much cordiality between black people and Poles, nor has there been any sympathetic appreciation or assistance by Poles for black civil rights. Politically, Polish Democrats have gone along with their party in voting for civil-rights measures when such measures did not threaten their political sanctuaries. But when the question of open housing has come up, the Poles have retreated from their mansion of liberalism into the outhouse of racial prejudice. This shift in political attitude can partially be explained by the intense endogamy of Poles and their deep affection for the ethnic exclusivity of their neighborhoods.

Perhaps the Poles might well recall the example of one of their heroes, Tadeusz Kosciuszko, who, along with Casimir Pulaski, played a critical role in the success of America's Revolutionary War.

After the war, Kosciuszko went back to Poland to help his country's continuing fight for freedom. He returned to America.

Maisel describes what happened:

Cheering crowds unhitched his horses from his carriage so that they might draw it themselves through Philadelphia's streets. Jefferson hailed him as the "purest son of liberty I have ever known." Congress voted him a grant of five hundred acres and a cash award of over twelve thousand dollars. But Kosciuszko never used these funds. As he boarded his ship to return to Europe, he handed

Jefferson his will, directing that his estate be used to purchase Negro slaves and give them their liberty.*

A Summary of Ethnic Political Power

The dominant fact of ethnic political power, more specifically the political power of the Irish, Italians, Jews and Poles, is the ability of these groups to control a higher proportion of the high elective and appointive offices than their percentage in the population warrants. They all have perfected the mechanics that control the theory of proportional equality. For them, proportional equality is an accomplished fact of political life.

In every single instance in various city, state, and Federal situations where these ethnic groups are a measurable statistic, they have been able to grab their proportionate share of the political spoils and, in most instances, more. This has been facilitated by the disorganization of other ethnic or economic groups. More particularly, it has revealed the extent to which the WASPS are unorganized.

In several cities and states and certainly at the Federal level, WASPS are in the majority. But the WASPS are not only not organized, they do not conceive of themselves as an endogamous group. Instead, the WASPS are Episcopalians, Baptists, Methodists, wealthy businessmen, poor laborers, teachers, social workers, doctors, etc. The controlling ethic of their economic status or their religion is not ethnically based. Because they are a secure majority—and believe America is really *their* country—they do not feel the need to cleave together. In contrast, the nationalistic and religious ethic of the Irish, Italians, Jews, and Poles in America *is* ethnically based. These four groups are oriented inwardly toward their group first, their country second.

To be an Irish Catholic or an Italian-American or a Jew or a Polish-American is to have a specific identity, an awareness of past glories and future power. It is an emotional in-gathering of peoples who may have a vague geographical sense of community, but are gripped by a fervent preoccupation with the solidarity of their ethnic background. For them, this is the most salient fact of life. In a collision between divergent or conflicting claims for their loyalty, the claim of nationality or religion tends to prevail. It is to this communal unity they can always return for survival and advancement. Many politicians know this and become "professional Irish" or "professional Jews" or "professional Italians" or "professional Poles" when running for office. (After Gronouski had served as Postmaster General, he was appointed ambassador to Poland. Although his identification with the Polish community was not so rabid and devoted as that of some Polish

* Maisel, pp. 210-11.

Congressmen or public officials elected because they are Poles, Gronouski still got considerable mileage out of his Polish background, returning to the motherland and taking lessons to become fluent in Polish.)

Until black people are able to acquire the same loyalty to the fact of their race—and the new ethic of Black Power appears to be a big step in hastening such identification—they will not receive their share of the political spoils that their percentage in the population demands. American politics has been a history of ethnic politics. The melting pot myth has been used by ethnic groups as a cover for the attainment of group power while paying lip service to the American creed. What really has existed has been an "emulsion bowl" of ethnic particles each seeking its own level, its own unity, its own loyalty.

The black achievement of real political power, the ability of black people as a group of people according to Max Weber to "realize their own will in a communal action against the resistance of others who are participating in the action," will only occur when their racial identity overrides all other facets of their lives.

CHAPTER EIGHT

New York and Chicago: No. 2 Tries Harder

The American system of ours, call it Americanism, call it Capitalism, call it what you like, gives each and every one of us a great opportunity if we only seize it with both hands and make the most of it. . . . My rackets are run on strictly American lines and they're going to stay that way.

—AL CAPONE
1929 interview quoted by Claude Cockburn, *In Time of Trouble*, 1956

As long as I count the votes what are you going to do about it?
—WILLIAM MARCY ("Boss") TWEED,
The Ballot, 1871

The two largest cities in America—New York City and Chicago—are also the two most efficient practitioners of the Four C's of big city government: crime, cronyism, clannishness, and corruption. Without those four elements, neither New York City nor Chicago—nor any major city in America for that matter—would be able to govern. In every city over 100,000, government is influenced, dominated, controlled, and even perfected in varying degrees by the Four C's. The political bosses or the most powerful cliques in government choose candidates and appoint public officials because of ethnic requirements (clannishness). In New York City and State, the balanced ticket is mandatory for victory.

Public officials, in turn, tend to hire persons who are friends and associates. If two men are eligible for a position in government, the one who knows the appointing officer will always be given the job (cronyism). The concept of civil service is one of the most successful frauds ever conceived in government under the guise of "good government." The extent and depth of racial discrimination and segregation in government proves this.

Public officials, in turn, are wined and dined and quite often given secret financial considerations for advance information on urban-renewal projects, construction contracts for highways, roads, public housing, schools, and government buildings, and contracts with cities for such services as sanitation, the purchasing of supplies and real-estate development. No matter how scrupulous a procedure is developed to ensure impartiality of selection, some public official or even public servant of lesser stature is able to communicate the desired information to certain businessmen who, in turn, perfect the rare ability to always be the lowest bidder. Kickbacks and financial rewards for such information are commonplace in municipal government (corruption).

Every political campaign needs money. The more important the office, the more money needed to successfully conduct a campaign. Political liaisons are made by many candidates with the underworld on condition the latter will be permitted to continue to operate in peace without police interference. Thus, "the numbers," book-making, narcotics, and prostitution exist only because of pay-offs to the police. The police, however, do not permit crime to dominate a city. They "manage" it. Management is doing business with the crime syndicate, which in turn is responsible for a certain amount of internal policing of its areas of operation. If, for example, there is a murder wave, the police are forced to crack down. Because of this hand-in-glove operation between members of the crime syndicate who manipulate many legitimate businesses and public officials, the latter are inclined to wink at illegalities and corrupt activities within government. Housing inspections of slums are rarely made because housing inspectors are paid off by slumlords with contacts in City Hall through their contributions to political campaigns. Police pay-offs are so flagrant, particularly in the ghetto, that they are sometimes observed by residents. But the "system" internalizes these procedures, and either politicians accept it or they are removed by the political machine.

Since the days of "Boss" Tweed of New York City and Al Capone of Chicago, those two cities are not so openly corrupt or so outlandishly contemptuous of public opinion. Corruption is far more sophisticated today. Yet, occasionally a newspaper reveals, as it did in Chicago, how a real-estate broker was able to purchase city property at something like one-tenth of its market price or a New York City department head resigns because of uncovered associations with criminals and is subsequently indicted for receiving alleged kickbacks.

In Chicago, less than five years ago, on February 28, 1963, Twenty-fourth Ward Alderman Benjamin F. Lewis, a swaggering and shrewd fifty-two-year-old black politician from that city's crime-dominated West Side, was found murdered in his office with his hands handcuffed in front of him. Police observed that he was shot at close range. Lewis had been overwhelmingly elected only two days before his political assassination. The murderer has not been found to this day, and nobody in Chicago seriously believes that he ever will be. But Mayor Daley turned up at the funeral and made many solemn vows, as he always does in such situations, to see that justice would be done. It was the kind of statement that a mayor who runs a corrupt city is supposed to make.

Today, in Chicago, restaurants are fire-bombed with impunity and the number of unsolved gangland murders in that city is over a thousand. Every few months, a body is found stuffed in a car trunk or some hoodlum, gangster, or businessman is discovered murdered in a fashion to insure recognition of the crime's syndicate's authorship. Mayor Daley has been able to build highways and housing projects, but has been totally unable to reduce crime.

Chicago's compulsion for violence is historic.

In Chicago, violence is accepted as a way of life. . . . It was in Chicago that labor unrest burst out into such landmarks of violence as the Haymarket Riots, the Pullman Strike of 1893 (when the Federal troops were sent to the city to quell the rioters), and the Republic Steel strike of Memorial Day, 1937, when ten persons were killed and more than 100 injured.

It was in Chicago that organized crime blasted its way to national infamy and international notoriety with a crime that has been virtually canonized in the annals of violence: the St. Valentine's Day Massacre.

It is in Chicago that racial unrest was ever punctuated with violence. In 1919, 38 people were killed, about 500 injured and 1000 left homeless in a race riot that lasted for six days. In 1951, when Negroes moved into a large apartment building in Cicero—on the western fringe of Chicago—a mob gutted the building.*

Chicago's legacy still operates freely and has enormous acceptance among both the white and black populations. Chicago is the bellwether of American violence.

The second largest city in America, Chicago has worked hard to build a civic pride that would make it "No. 1" in accomplishments, if not in population. As "No. 2," it has always tried harder.

For black people, Chicago has, in many ways, been a leader in political advancement, not political power, but political progress.

Perhaps this political progress goes back to the 1790's, when the first man to settle in what is now known as Chicago was a black man named Jean Baptiste Pointe duSable, generally recognized as Chicago's first settler.

In 1871, the first black man to hold any elective office in Cook County was John Jones, who became a county commissioner. (It should be noted

* Article in October 3, 1963, issue of the *Washington Post* by William B. Furlong, "Chicago's Trouble Is That It's Still Just a Young Tough," p. E3.

that Cook County embraces Chicago as the main municipal component. For example, according to the 1960 U.S. Census, of 5,129,725 persons residing in Cook County, 3,550,404, or 69 per cent, lived in Chicago. The Chicago Democratic machine has usually controlled the majority of Cook County offices, but occasionally the Republicans are able to break through and elect a sheriff, a couple of members of the Metropolitan Sanitary District of Greater Chicago, the president of the board of commissioners which controls the County budget, and a few other administrative offices.)

Chicago also produced in the 1890's one of the shrewdest black politicians in American history, Edward H. Wright, whose ability to manipulate and control the black vote for black political gains compared in brilliance to Memphis' Robert Church and New York City's J. Raymond Jones. Wright held the offices of assistant corporation counsel in Chicago and commissioner of the Cook County board of commissioners. He understood what power was and used it. Once, during the 1890's, he refused to vote for an appropriation to run the office of State's Attorney Charles S. Deneen until Deneen had fulfilled a promise to appoint a black man to his legal staff. When Deneen made the appointment, Wright backed the appropriation. That was black power in action. But Wright was the first black politician in Chicago to play a determining role in the politics of that city.

He rose to power in the administration of Republican William Hale ("Big Bill") Thompson, who had probably one of the most corrupt and racially integrated administrations in American history. Thompson was mayor from 1915 to 1923 and 1927 to 1931. During his administration, he appointed so many black men to political offices (Bishop Archibald E. Carey to the Civil Service Commission, Wright to the Corporation Counsel's office, etc.) that City Hall became known as "Uncle Tom's Cabin," and Thompson's final defeat came because of a white backlash candidate whose supporters openly campaigned with calliopes filled with black-faced persons singing "Bye, Bye, Blackbird," indicating that if their candidate was elected he would throw the black people out of City Hall. (He, the Democratic candidate, was, and he did.)

It was also during Thompson's regime that Chicago elected its first black alderman, Oscar DePriest, in 1915. He subsequently became Chicago's first black Congressman in 1928, the first black Congressman since 1901. (New York City did not elect its first black City Councilman, Adam Clayton Powell, until 1941 and its first black Congressman, Powell, until 1944. It is interesting to note that these two black trail-blazers were similar in political style—flamboyant, handsome, and colorful orators.)

But, facilitating the early rise of black political power in Chicago was its recognition by the white power structure, in this instance, a sympathetic mayor, Big Bill Thompson. Given two conditions, the readiness of the political machine to treat black voters equitably in the distribution of the spoils and a simultaneous existence of a black political leader, such as Wright or DePriest, who can control his constituency, black political power can become a reality. But it must be stressed that black political power does not exist in a vacuum. Unless the two conditions are present—a sympathetic white power structure and strong black political leadership—black political power atrophies.

On the other hand, New York City, the country's ethnic melting pot and the most sophisticated of American cities, did not accelerate black political advancement as rapidly as Chicago. New York City was the home of Harlem, black capital of the world. But Harlem represented the black arts, black music, black poets, and the black literati. Harlem was a twenty-hour party.

Probably the first black political boss and first black man to acquire any significant power in New York City was the Harvard-educated Ferdinand Q. Morton, who presided over the Harlem electorate as if it were his private domain. He ran a political club, the United Colored Democracy, through which all black patronage was channeled. Because of UCD's success in delivering the black vote to the Democrats in the mayoralty race (73.6 per cent of Harlem's vote), Mayor John F. Hylan appointed Morton chairman of the Municipal Civil Service Commission, a lucrative post which enabled him to tighten his patronage control over his "Black Tammany."

But Morton was a member of the Robert Church-Edward H. Wright-J. Raymond Jones school of practical politics. When Mayor LaGuardia agreed to reappoint him to the Civil Service Commission on condition that he break with the Democratic Party, Morton switched to the American Labor Party, a political affiliate of LaGuardia's, and told one of his friends: "We should take this political situation as a cold-blooded business proposition. We should treat it as an honest-to-goodness shopping trip. Politics . . . is but a theoretical bargain counter, to buy wares and get the best we can in bargains." In this instance, however, "we, the black people" became "I, Ferdinand Q. Morton." When the chips were down, the political boss looked out for Number 1, not his people.

It was not until 1935 that Harlem was finally able to elect its first Assembly District leader, Herbert L. Bruce, one of the toughest and ·most independent-minded black political leaders ever to work in politics anywhere in the country. In fact, Bruce's stubborn refusal to compromise black people, as had Morton, cost him his position. Tammany Hall was opposed to any black man who spoke his mind or refused to wrap a handkerchief around his head and shuffle his feet. J. Raymond Jones subsequently emerged as the main political force in Harlem with the backing of his political mentor, Mayor O'Dwyer.

Harlem politics is governed by two facts of life: its West Indian population and Adam Clayton Powell.

Proud, hard-working and independent of thought, West Indians who migrated to Harlem in waves during the late 1890's and early 1900's had not been raised in a subculture of inferiority. Nobody had told them in their country—which *was* their country, despite British rule—that they were not as good as the white man. Consequently, when they plunged into politics, it was with the idea of controlling their political territory and sharing fully in the spoils, not simply acting as messenger boys.

Bruce, the first Assembly District Leader, J. Raymond Jones, the first black man to head Tammany Hall, and Hulan E. Jack, the first black man to be elected Borough President of Manhattan were all West Indians. Despite the friction between Harlem blacks and West Indians the latter were responsible for most of the political advancement and power of Harlem.

Black Political Power in the Two Cities

As of 1967, which city had more black political power? Which of the two cities appears more likely to be the future citadel of black political power?

Using Stone's Index of Proportional Equality as a standard of measurement, a comparative assessment can be made. The Index compares the percentage of black people in the population with the percentage of black representatives in six areas of political activity as U. S. Congressmen, city councilmen or aldermen, state representatives, members of the mayor's cabinet or heads of major departments, judges, and members of the board of education.

Both New York City and Chicago have black postmasters general, Henry McGee in Chicago and John R. Strachan in New York City. McGee, however, was not only appointed before Strachan, but had held one of the highest positions in the U. S. Post Office as regional personnel director.

On the political balance sheet, Chicago does come out ahead of New York City in the political power wielded by black people.

Yet, there are other considerations which must be taken into account. Of the five New York Borough Presidents, one, Percy E. Sutton, is black. The first black Borough President was Hulan E. Jack, who resigned in 1960 during a scandal affecting his office. Otherwise the office has been a stepping stone to higher political office. Jack was succeeded by Edward R. Dudley, who is now a New York State Supreme Court Justice. After Dudley, Mrs. Constance Baker Motley occupied the office, and she was subsequently succeeded by Sutton, one of the most articulate, attractive, and outstanding black politicians in America. Sutton is one of the few black politicians who made a political name for himself in a comparatively non-

OFFICE	NEW YORK CITY	CHICAGO
City's black population (1967 estimate)	*(In per cent)*	*(In per cent)*
	21%	31%
U.S. Congressmen	5% (1 out of 19)	11% (1 out of 9)
City Councilmen or Aldermen	5% (2 out of 37)	20% (10 out of 50)
State Representatives	7% (5 out of 68)	16% (10 out of 62)
Heads of Major Departments	5% (2 out of 34)	0% (0 out of 24)
Members of Board of Education	11% (1 out of 9)	15% (2 out of 13)

Judges (New York)
Civil Court	5% (5 out of 95)
Criminal Court	6% (5 out of 77)
Family Court of New York State	3% (1 out of 33)
Surrogate's Court	0% (0 out of 6)
Supreme Court (1st, 2nd and 11th Districts)	3% (3 out of 95)
Supreme Court (Appellate Division for New York City)	5% (1 out of 17)
Court of Appeals	0% (0 out of 7)
U.S. Customs Court	11% (1 out of 9;

Judge Watson appointed from New York City)

U.S. District Court	4% (1 out of 24

from Southern District)

U.S. Court of Appeals	0% (0 out of 9)

Judges (Chicago)
Associate Judges, City of Chicago	8% (3 out of 36)
Circuit Court	6% (5 out of 76)
Appellate Court	0% (0 out of 12)
Supreme Court (state's highest)	0% (0 out of 7)
U.S. District Court	8% (1 out of 12)
U.S. Court of Appeals	0% (0 out of 9)

racial area. As a state assemblyman, Sutton played a key role in the legislative success of the drive to reform the abortion laws. Sutton also is one of the few black politicians who would prefer to rise in the political hierarchy at the city or state level without necessarily transferring to the national scene as a U.S. Congressman, which so many have expected him to do (i.e., succeeding Adam Clayton Powell). Sutton's ambition was to become the first black lieutenant governor in New York State's history. He temporarily abandoned this pursuit for political power within the state when he announced his decision to run for the U.S. Senate in March 1968. Sutton had hoped to win Liberal Party support if he was successful in the Democratic primary. But, once again, the reality of ethnic politics reared its head. The Liberal Party broke a 24-year record of supporting Democratic candidates at the state level and voted to support Republican Senator Jacob K. Javits for re-election instead of Sutton. The extent of ethnic factors in this decision was reflected in Javits' uncertain, almost contemptuous response to the endorsement which he had not sought and for which Sutton, in his own words, "had begged." But Sutton was black and Javits was Jewish. The Liberal Party was only following the dictates of ethnic politics—take care of your own first.

Sutton subsequently withdrew from the race for the U.S. Senate Democratic nomination, privately fearful that a crushing defeat (highly likely without Liberal Party support) would severely damage his chance of becoming the first black lieutenant governor. At the time of this writing, unless unforeseen national political events intervene or there is a re-shuffling in the state hierarchy of the Democratic Party, Sutton is still an inside favorite for his party's nomination to the state post he covets.

New York City black people have also held more important administrative positions than Chicago black people. This discrepancy is explained by the nature of the cities themselves. While neither city is a tower of good will for black people, New York City is perhaps more sophisticated in its attitudes toward black people and more willing to accept them as heads of departments. During the Wagner administration of 1959, a black man, James R. Dumpson, headed the Department of Welfare. A black man in Chicago, William Robinson, was not appointed director of the Cook County Department of Welfare until 1966.

A black man, Robert Lowery, is now Fire Commissioner in New York City, an almost unthinkable appointment for Chicago to make.

But Chicago black people have been able to carve out a larger proportion of elective office. Yet, if the current New York State redistricting plan stands up, New York City will send its second black man (or woman, since Assemblywoman Shirley Chisolm is a leading candidate) to Congress from the borough of Brooklyn. The area to be represented by the black Congressman is Bedford-Stuyvesant, which now has a larger black population than Harlem and is one of the most solidly black communities in the country.

It is possible that Chicago's black electorate may become sufficiently restless to demand a second black Congressman from the predominantly black West Side Sixth Congressional District. (One of the most prevalent rumors concerning the political assassination of West Side Alderman Lewis in 1963 was that he had acquired so much personal power that he had decided to run for Congress—whether Mayor Daley and the Democratic machine backed him or not—and Lewis could have won without party support. The machine would have been seriously crippled in the black community if Lewis had been able to pull off his political coup.)

In both cities today, the Four C's are still the dominant fact of political life. In New York City, judgeships are still purchasable, and in Chicago, votes are still purchased and dead people are voted with monotonous efficiency. A headline in the October 12, 1964, issue of the *Chicago Tribune* declared: "Ghost Vote 'Homes' Found" and revealed the results of a Republican investigation which showed that there were:

1. Thirty voters registered under addresses at 752 to 754 Oakwood Blvd., although there were no buildings on the lots.

2. Nine registered as living in a vacant building at 3670-72 Indiana Ave.

3. Another nine registered as living in a vacant building at 3639 Michigan Ave.

4. Sixteen registered in a house at 3663 Michigan Ave. which is vacant except for the basement.

Many other buildings in the three Loop and west side wards which registrants recently gave as their addresses have been boarded up for years, the canvassers found.

On November 4, 1964, a headline in the *Tribune* pointed out that "Reporters Spot Vote Buying in Chicago Wards." The story stated that "Teams of *Tribune* reporters who toured traditional ballot stealing areas of the city witnessed money changing hands before and after voters visited polling places." Mayor Daley came to power on the back of a corrupt, crime-dominated, crony-saturated and ethnically clannish political machine. He has not changed it, but made it less blatant and more awesomely efficient.

Other Cities

Besides Chicago and New York City, the other cities which currently have black Congressmen are Philadelphia, Detroit, and Los Angeles. According to the special U. S. Census Report of 1967, the black proportion of the populations in those three cities and three other cities with similarly large black population was as follows (according to the size of the cities) in 1965: Los Angeles, 17 per cent black; Philadelphia, 31 per cent; Detroit, 34 per cent; Baltimore, 38 per cent; Cleveland, 34 per cent; and St. Louis, 36 per cent black.

Two questions are obvious. Why does Los Angeles, with a 17 per cent black population, have one black Congressman, when the three cities of Baltimore, Cleveland, and St. Louis which have black populations twice that percentage do not have one black Congressman? Why does Detroit, with a 34 per cent black population, have two black Congressmen and again, those same three cities not have even one?

The answer lies in several factors. In Detroit, industrial unionism recognized that black workers must be incorporated into the unions and taught that some of the techniques of organizing paid political dividends. There is a high political consciousness in Detroit's black community, and the liberal Democratic machine of both the city and the state has recognized the need for greater black representation. Also, Detroit's 1943 race riot, one of the worst in U.S. history, undoubtedly sensitized the Democratic Party of both the city and the state to move faster to meet legitimate black demands.

In Ohio, Maryland, and Missouri, the state legislatures have ignored black pressures for a black Congressman and, with racist contempt, gerry-mandered Congressional districts in those cities to avoid the possible election of a black Congressman. In Ohio, however, the state legislature has finally bowed to black restlessness and altered the Congressional District boundaries to ensure the election of a black Congressman from Cleveland in 1968.

It is grimly apparent that the only strategy which is going to influence the state legislatures of Maryland and Missouri to redistrict Congressional boundaries to guarantee the election of a black Congressman is the unleashing of a series of black rebellions so devastating in their angry destruction that the justifiability of black demands will be recognized. Until this happens or black communities in these cities can generate the organizational genius of an Edward H. Wright, a Robert Church, or a J. Raymond Jones or the charisma of an Adam Clayton Powell or Oscar DePriest, the black electorate will continue to wallow in the mire of political second-class citizenship.

CHAPTER NINE

Four Black Men in the White Power Structure

> We do not seek to be mere recipients
> from the decision-making process but par-
> ticipants in it.
> —"Black Power: The Politics of Libera-
> tion in America" by STOKELY CAR-
> MICHAEL and CHARLES V. HAMILTON,
> p. 183.

"NEGRO POLITICIANS"

"Negro politicians" have frequently been portrayed in some political-science texts as creatures sui generis—political animals that can be catalogued with the assumption that they spring from no previous forebears. While such artificial compartmentalizations have made "experts" out of white political scientists with ingrained racial biases and white axes to grind, they have not seriously increased our knowledge or our understanding of the negro politician.

A negro politician exists as a negro because of only one fact of American life—white political racism.

As a black man, he is denied full participation in the political process because of his black skin. No other ethnic group has had to contend with such a sociological liability in this country. To be a negro businessman or a negro politician or a negro educator or a negro historian or a negro political scientist is to be a negro first. Skin color qualifies the level of excellence, the depth of performance, the range of visibility. But to be a politician in the American political process is to conform faithfully to the expectations politicians must fulfill. There are only so many methods, approaches, and techniques American politicians can utilize. The political apparatus of

159

American democracy delimits them. The requirement of maneuverability within the body politic circumscribes them.

A politician can do a number of things in his climb to power. He can maneuver stealthily behind closed doors, playing off one faction against the other until he solidifies his own power base and then takes over a debilitated and divided group as its dearly awaited leader (as did Chicago's Mayor Richard Daley). He can steal votes to win elections by buying votes or by using names of dead people on the voting rolls to control the outcome. If he is a political boss he can blackmail his candidates to control their fidelity. He can be a demagogue, mesmerizing the masses with his oratory, his charisma, thus retaining power solely through his authority, fulfilling either minimum needs or maximum dreams of the electorate, but nonetheless remaining in power primarily through his attractive personality.

He can ally himself with the crime syndicate, permitting it to legitimately manage a certain amount of organized vice (prostitution, book-making, loan-sharking, etc.), and become a respectable but unknown surrogate for the syndicate which controls him and determines his vote or policy for him. He can be the statesman, rising above common machinations of ward-heelers and precinct leaders, and be elected as the prototype of the good leader, the incorruptible public official. He can be a political flunky, ingratiating himself with the majestic powers in the Valhalla of decision-makers, even rising to a position of prominence and power by trading favors and making questionable alliances within the group to ensure his future.

To be elected, to control a political machine, or just to survive, the American politician incorporates one of the above methods into his political modus operandi. He does this whether he's black or Irish or Italian or Jewish or Polish or Puerto Rican or Mexican-American. If he is black, he can be characterized as an Uncle Tom if he is subservient and rarely speaks out on issues. If he is white, he becomes known as a "brown-noser," or if he is a Mexican-American, a "Tio Tomas." If he has the advantage of being simply a white WASP politician, he is known as a moderate or a conservative. If he is black, he is a militant. If he is white, he is a radical. But the uncontrollable flamboyance and aggressiveness in action are the same for black or white.

Yet, some white political scientists have become authorities on the negro politician by analyzing him as a different species of homo sapiens, not endowed with the same drives, the same weaknesses, and the same strengths.

The only factor which differentiates the black politician from the white politician and precludes the former's exercise of unlimited power and his reverie in impossible dreams is his black skin.

Whites have had their Pendergasts and their Hagues.

Blacks have had their Bob Churches and Ray Joneses.

Whites have had their Jimmy Walkers and their Fiorella LaGuardias.

Blacks have had their Oscar DePriests and their Adam Clayton Powells. Whites have had their William O'Dwyers.

Blacks have had their Hulan Jacks.

The stage has been smaller in each instance, but the role and the styles have been identical.

In the last five years, 1962-1967, four black politicians have captured the national spotlight and remained the focus of continuing public attention: Illinois Representative William L. Dawson, New York Representative Adam Clayton Powell, Chairman of the New York County Committee (Tammany Hall) J. Raymond Jones and Massachusetts U.S. Senator Edward W. Brooke.

Each of them attained the heights of political power at a given time, if not in the exercise of actual power, certainly in a position to which power is attached.

All four acceded to their positions of power through different techniques, different styles, and different political circumstances. All four occasioned varying reactions in whites ranging from hysterical rage and race hatred for Powell and suspicion and respectful wariness for Jones to unthreatened acceptance of Dawson and paternalistic affection for Brooke.

Powell could never have been elected U. S. Senator in Massachusetts, and Brooke would have never survived in Harlem. Yet, both, by altering their styles to meet the different requirements of the constituencies, might have attained some other level of political success.

In terms of the American color line that ultimately decides the behavioral patterns of black politicians, these four political successes could be characterized as follows: Brooke, "Mr. Non-Negro Politics"; Dawson, "Mr. Establishment Negro Politics"; Jones, "Mr. Organizational Negro Politics"; and Powell, "Mr. National Black Politics."

Those designations are used only to capsulize political tendencies as they are affected and determined by the black community. Obviously, Brooke would be considered by most whites as a national politician. And Jones certainly has played ball with the establishment almost as frequently as Dawson, but Jones, a proud and brilliant man of independent thought, has occasionally fought the establishment. Dawson never has.

If a spectrum of popular conceptualizations is drawn, Brooke and Dawson could be considered conservatives or Uncle Toms, Jones a moderate or negro leader in the traditional sense of the term, and Powell a radical or militant.

One could hastily draw the conclusion that political black militants are doomed to ultimate destruction, as Powell was. But Hulan E. Jack, former Manhattan Borough President, a conservative and viewed by the black community as an "Uncle Tom" while in office, was chopped down by an investigation into alleged bribery of a public official and forced to resign.

The lesson is unforgettable. The black politician walks on eggs through-out his whole career and can never pause to relax in the comforting security of permanent success. Some white politicians are untouchable. No black politicians are.

If a black politician becomes too powerful—i.e., exercises whatever power flows from the perquisites of offices—he is regarded as a threat to the white political establishment, unless, of course, he can be contained and in turn, accepts containment. He must be willing to compromise far more fre-quently than white politicians because of the peculiarities of American racism, which demand that he not be too independent, too audacious, or too unpredictable. No white person likes an independent, audacious, or unpredictable darkie.

To pursue the acquisition of power is American in the most noble tradi-tion of American politics. For a black man to pursue political power and then exercise it has not been universally accepted yet.

Brooke, Dawson, Jones and Powell all had one thing in common: They all wanted to be participants in the decision-making process; they no longer wanted to be its recipients. In this shared desire, they rose beyond the ordinary confines for black politicians. Their careers have flourished in the tradition of South Carolina's Robert Brown Elliott, Louisiana's P. B. S. Pinchback, Tennessee's Robert Church, and Illinois's Oscar S. DePriest. All these black politicians were historical figures who were able to operate as successfully as white politicians. They understood and played the political spoils game with relentless cunning and imagination. At all times, they sought to be politicians, not negro leaders—a concept that is a figment of the white man's imagination.

"NEGRO LEADERS"

One of the most serious afflictions crippling the forward progress of America's black people has been the pathological fact of life known as the "negro leader."

No custodian of political or economic power, no Machiavellian manipu-lator of elections or corporations, he has been assigned this honorific status in life because the white power structure knows he is safe. What makes him safe are his predictability and his absolute control by white people.

The "negro leader" has no true power base. He is a "spokesman," actually a ceremonial personage. He remains a "negro leader" only as long as he can be controlled by the white establishment. He makes no unexpected demands upon the conscience of white Americans. Nor does he push American society beyond its conservative limits in the arena of black-white relations.

"Negro leaders" fall under two categories: "Uncle Toms" and "ceremonial negro leaders." The author evolved the concept ceremonial negro leader in 1963. It differs from the Uncle Tom in several ways. Within the total power structure of a community, the ceremonial negro leader only retains power. The ceremonial negro leader is not an Uncle Tom. Yet there are certain identifiable similarities:

1) Neither is feared by the white power structure. They are invited to sit on committees because they willingly "go along with the program."
2) Both are totally predictable.
3) Neither is prepared to disturb the basic infrastructure of our society, retaining their position as "Negro leader" at the white man's whim.
4) Both bargain and negotiate on the white man's terms, at his calling, on his home grounds and on his timetable.
5) Neither is capable of energizing an entire community into a frontal assault on racial segregation in the community, nor are they prepared to utilize any latent possible power they may possess to do so.
6) Both prefer talk to action.
7) Both are the prime beneficiaries of the more militant posture of other civil rights groups.

But the differences between the Uncle Tom leader and the "Ceremonial Negro Leader," while not more in number than the similarities, are more significant in their substance.

The Uncle Tom operates from a position of naked fear.

The "Ceremonial Negro Leader" maneuvers from a posture of hesitant caution.

The Uncle Tom openly and at all times accords white people superordinate status.

The "Ceremonial Negro Leader" is at least prepared to challenge the periphery of the white power structure—but on a limited basis and with the previous approbation of white liberals.

While the "Ceremonial Negro Leader" is constantly checking in with the white power structure, he never fails to keep his political tracks covered in the Negro community. Whenever he is rebuffed in the white community on a particular issue, he will invariably turn to the Negro community for help, totally involving himself in maneuvers with the Negro community to achieve that particular goal.

Once having gained his point, he returns to his previous position of rebuilding his image in the white community as the "moderate" and "responsible" leader. He then repeats his frequent checking in process.

On the other hand, the Uncle Tom never involves himself with the total Negro community, but instead limits his contacts to just a few close associates.*

One of America's first negro leaders was neither, and in this sense, he was an anomaly—Frederick Douglass. A militant, Douglass was a fiery orator, an uncompromising activist, and a disciplined militant. He was the beloved and respected representative of the black man's radical struggle against slavery, and the small groups of white people who listened to him were friends and helpers who were so deeply concerned about slavery that they never regarded him as a threat to the established order.

* Chuck Stone, *Tell It Like It Is* (New York: Trident Press, 1967), pp. 62-63.

Because of the unique circumstances of slavery, Douglass was the first black man to obtain some form of political power without the ballot box. He antedated the Black Reconstruction politicians of his era.

One of the most powerful negro leaders of all time was Booker T. Washington, the first in a long line of successful and respectable Uncle Toms. Washington was exactly what the white community had been yearning for. There had been no public delineation by any black man of the black man's goals after his emancipation. Washington, in his famous 1896 Atlanta Compromise address, settled those fears. He promised white people that black people really wanted a status of "separate and inferior." Black people would become skilled laborers, artisans, and mechanics.

This philosophy was tailor made for white supremacy, and white people overnight lionized Washington. He was an eagerly sought speaker and was even invited to the White House to dine with President Theodore Roosevelt. Washington made sense for white people in his time and they acclaimed him as a national negro leader. This designation enabled him to wield political influence in a period when there was a virtual black-out on negro politicians.

Today, the black community is still burdened with its negro leaders. America is ruled by politicians, bankers, corporate executives, and industrialists. The black community is ruled, according to the wishes of the white community, by negro leaders who are heads of civil-rights organizations totally beholden to white financial sustenance.

The National Urban League's Whitney Young, the NAACP's Roy Wilkins, and the A. Philip Randolph Institute's Bayard Rustin are 1968's version of Booker T. Washington. Against the backdrop of today's excruciating racial tensions, their national influence would be negligible if they were outright Uncle Toms. Even the white community might recoil from their ineffectual embrace. Besides, the mood of the black communities in 1968 is more militant. Therefore, they more closely approximate the posture of the ceremonial negro leader. In this respect, they are powerless, as power is understood and played in American society. Their power is derivative. It is handed down by whites with specific proscriptions attached.

It is possible for a negro politician to become a ceremonial negro leader. In fact, most of them are. This is because the negro politician has still not understood one basic fact: His power comes from the black masses. If they are organized by him, can be controlled by him, and will continue to follow his leadership, his power base will remain secure. He can negotiate from a situation of strength.

As outlined in the chapter on the Irish, Italians, Jews, and Poles, this organizational identification with the masses of people within their own ethnic group was the one fact that has perpetuated the political power of these ethnic groups. But the black politician has never understood this fact, or even believed it could have implications for his survival. Instead, the negro politician has tried to sail a middle course between the Scylla of integration, which acts to eventually destroy his political base, and the Charybdis of blackness, which amalgamates his power but tends to separate him from the white political mainstream.

Until the negro politician makes a clear-cut choice and begins to head in one direction or the other, his emotional oscillations will erode his capabilities for long-range political leadership. The negro politician will eventually be confronted with the same two questions which plague all black people today: How black do you want to be, and how black *can* you be?

Four black men, Brooke, Dawson, Jones and Powell, all answered those questions in their own way with their own style and, to a great extent, achieved their own brand of success.

EDWARD W. BROOKE

"Mr. Non-Negro Politics"

"I do not intend to be a national leader of the Negro people.
I intend to do my job as a Senator from Massachusetts."

Boston, in so many ways, has been the cradle of liberty for American democracy's growth to white manhood. Because it has, black people there have enjoyed its blessings, participated in its making and, at the same time, made their own history.

Crispus Attucks, a black man, was the first person to be killed in the Boston Massacre on March 5, 1770, by British troops.

Two black brothers in Boston were perhaps the first black men in America to challenge their obligation to pay taxes if they could not vote.

The first two black men to be elected to an American legislature assembly in 1866 were both from Boston, Edwin G. Walker and Charles L. Mitchell. In Boston's already established tradition of fair play, one was a Republican and the other a Democrat.

In the years of the "Great Black-out," 1877-1929, negroes were prevented from voting in the South and frozen out of the political machinery in the North. In Boston, however, negroes were elected to the Common Council regularly between 1895 and 1909 when the city charter was reorganized.

Boston has never been a center of negro activity. Negroes living in Boston have always considered themselves Bostonians first and black people second. Black consciousness has found little fertile earth in which to spawn the tree of black power, although Harvard University educated one of the intellectual forerunners of the black power movement, W. E. B. Du Bois. This brilliant writer and scholar was the first black man of distinction to challenge Booker T. Washington's proclaimed subordinate status for black people. In his book, *The Souls of Black Folk*, Du Bois in a chapter, "Of Mr. Booker T. Washington and Others," exposed the folly of Washington's position and called for black people to become integral and equal parts of American society.

In 1960, according to the U.S. Census, Boston's 68,493 black people represented 9.8 per cent of the municipal population. State-wide, Massachusetts' 111,842 black people were a mere 2.2 per cent of the total population. Obviously, there was no foundation for state-wide black political power.

And yet, in 1966, Massachusetts elected the first black United States Senator since 1881, Edward W. Brooke.

Brooke's success was a combination of luck and his own personal determination.

A native of Washington, D.C., Brooke graduated from Howard University, served in Italy as a captain with the all-black 366th Combat Infantry Regiment, returned home to speed through Boston University Law School and marry a pretty Italian girl, Remigia Ferrari-Scacco, whom he had met while in Italy.

Like Adam Clayton Powell, Brooke was an authentic member of the negro middle-class contemptuously labeled the "black bourgeoisie" by Howard sociologist E. Franklin Frazier. Brooke's life was typically middle-class Washington negro—a father who was a government employee, attendance at an Episcopal church chosen as much for its color lines against dark-skinned negroes as its weekly dosage of pasteurized religion, residence in a pleasant Northeast segregated community of comfortable homes and well-manicured lawns and an active social life amongst Washington's negro middle-class, most of them fair-skinned, proud and believers in "separate but equal" societies for light-skinned prosperous negroes and dark-skinned improverished blacks.

After his graduation from Boston University and inter-ethnic marriage, Brooke settled down in Boston. In 1950, he was persuaded by friends to run for the Massachusetts state legislature. He entered both the Democratic and Republican primaries, survived the latter and by that very fortuitous circumstance became a Republican. Defeated, he tried again in 1952, was narrowly defeated and decided to withdraw from politics after his confrontation with public innuendos about his interracial marriage.

In 1960, however, Brooke was persuaded to run for Secretary of State and lost another close race to Kevin H. White, who was to be elected in November 1967 as mayor of Boston over a "white backlash" candidate. Choosing his political options carefully, Brooke rejected an offer to join the staff of Gov. John Volpe, an Italian. He instead got himself appointed chairman of the Boston Finance Commission, a lethargic municipal agency.

Injecting new investigative energy into the BFC, Brooke uncovered enough corruption to force the resignation of several city officials.

He was now established in the eyes of the public as the "crusading, young 'District Attorney'" type. Handsome with his dark hair, Kelly green eyes and toothpaste-ad, infectious grin that spreads several miles across his pale face, Brooke also was an affable hand-shaker who managed to be acceptable by being firm enough to establish a public image but humble enough not to affront white people.

In 1962, he easily won his party's nomination for attorney general and won, becoming the highest elected black state official in the country. Brooke's victory was ascribed to two factors: First, a split within the Democratic party caused by the incumbent, Edward M. McCormack's, battle with Edward Kennedy for the nomination of U.S. Senator. Kennedy was the President's brother and McCormack was the favorite nephew of the Speaker of the U.S. House of Representatives, John W. McCormack, himself a very powerful man. Secondly, many Massachusetts Democrats crossed party lines to vote for this attractive negro whom they wanted to see make history as a symbol of the Bay State's traditional liberalism.

In 1964, the year of the Goldwater debacle, Brooke became a national figure when he ran up the highest plurality of any Republican running for a major office. While he was racking up a 797,510 plurality in a vote total of 1.5 million, Ted Kennedy was winning re-election with the Democratic landslide that also swept in Lyndon Johnson.

During his two terms in office, Brooke de-emphasized his race and emphasized good government. He was more against corruption than he was for civil rights for negroes. This credentialed him as a "moderate," and while the country was still recovering from two summers of black rebellions, Brooke calmly announced that he would seek the U.S. Senate seat of retiring Leverett Saltonstall.

Brooke had made known his intentions before Saltonstall's announced retirement and he was the first major Republican to declare his candidacy for the seat. This immediately put the Republicans in a quandary. To oppose Brooke was to oppose a proven vote-getter and a popular public figure. Furthermore, no matter how much the party would downgrade Brooke's race as a factor, it would appear to many that he was being denied the nomination because of his race. (Brooke himself admitted in an interview in *U.S. News & World Report* on February 1, 1965, that in his three state-wide races, "the racial issue has always been raised.")

Brooke won the nomination and went on to defeat former Governor Endicott "Chub" Peabody 1,213,473 to 744,761 votes. Brooke ran well even in heavily Irish Catholic wards where the white-press-created "white backlash" had been expected to materialize.

One of the ironic consequences of Brooke's victory over Peabody was that he defeated a man who was far more liberal on civil rights for black people than the black candidate himself.

Once again, Brooke's victory showed that many white liberal, guilt-ridden Democrats, all carrying the weight of centuries of their forefathers' racial persecution on their shoulders, crossed party lines to vote for Brooke. Massachusetts was determined to continue its liberal tradition.

From a strict interpretation of the phenomenon of negro politics, Brooke cannot be classified as a "negro politician." He does not owe his election to negroes. The black vote was not the balance of power in his election. Negroes comprise only 2.2 per cent of the state's population, hence Brooke does not represent a black constituency.

Brooke rose to his base of political power by obscuring the fact—as much as possible—of his race. This was rarely alluded to in his campaigns and his conduct in office. If anything, Brooke is more a symbolic achievement for institutions like *Time* magazine, which did editorial handsprings over Brooke's election, exulting in the fact that a negro other than Adam Clayton Powell had finally made national headlines. *Time*, which had made an editorial crusade out of hating Powell, had planned to do a cover story on Powell the week of his return in January 1967, but Powell refused to talk with *Time* reporters. *Time* persisted, then finally gave up.

Time then portrayed Brooke on its cover of February 17, 1968, timing the story to appear the same week after Powell had appeared before the Celler Committee investigating his conduct as Chairman of the Education and Labor Committee.

Clearly, Brooke, as a negro politician, was the answer to the white man's prayers. Despite the fact that he was a political anomaly, almost a political freak, as it were, white America has never missed an opportunity to point to Brooke whenever a discussion of Powell or other less popular black politicians has surfaced. It was a new twist of the old argument that if all negroes looked, acted and had the same kind of job as Ralph Bunche, white people would not object to their moving into their neighborhood. If all black politicians could only be like Edward Brooke.

The Junior Senator from Massáchusetts has maintained his tangential involvement with the black community by attending negro social affairs, occasionally making a tour of a negro poverty program and speaking before black fraternal and educational groups. He has carefully shied away from creating an identity as "the negro Senator" or the "civil rights voice of the Senate," and as has been true in many legislative instances around the country, there are several white Democrats who are more liberal and more committed to black equality than Brooke.

Still, many black people admire Brooke's achievement even though it does not materially change their economic or political status. It has opened a new door. It has polished the tranished gold of the "American dream" and encouraged young blacks to believe that the highest legislative office is now attainable.

Brooke is not a "negro politician" in the classic sense and is as far removed from the emotional ties of race relations as he can hope to be. According to a magazine report in early 1967, he had only hired two negroes out of a staff of 19. Brooke is "Mr. Non-Negro Politics" of his time, a colored American who successfully achieved one of the highest offices in the country for a colored man by working hard to convince white Americans to forget that very fact. He is a curious symbol in the era of Black Power and perhaps a daily reminder that there is some thrust left in the waning force called "integration."

WILLIAM L. DAWSON
"Mr. Establishment Negro Politics"

"Don't Get Mad, Get Smart."

A black Democratic Congressman from Chicago is probably the last person in the world a white Republican former president of General Motors would ever expect to help politically. But Charles E. Wilson, Secretary of Defense in the Eisenhower administration, did just that in 1954. Appearing in Detroit on October 11, 1954, for a fund-raising dinner for the Republican Party, Wilson held a press conference. Two of the topics discussed were the Korean War and the mounting unemployment in Detroit despite the increased war production in other industries. Wilson was asked if more defense contracts could not be assigned to Detroit to meet this problem and what could be done to combat unemployment which had increased the joblessness of 19- and 20-year-olds in some communities.

Wilson's reply, typical of his breezy self-made-man egotism, was a compound of sympathetic understanding and his old-fashioned let-them-eat-cake philosophy:

> "The idea that a 19-year-old boy could be drafted and sent to Korea to be shot at and he didn't have enough gumption to go 100 miles and get himself a job—I don't go for that.
> "And I've got a lot of sympathy for people where a sudden change catches them. But I've always liked bird dogs myself, you know, one who'll get out and hunt for food rather than sit on his fanny and yell."

To the Democrats, the statement was manna from heaven. Wilson was accused of everything from comparing unemployment people to dogs to implying that all unemployed people were lazy. Walter Reuther, president of the CIO, sent a letter to President Eisenhower demanding Wilson's resignation.

Because of the higher incidence of unemployment among black people, the black community was particularly incensed; the negro press wrote angry editorials.

At a political meeting in Chicago, Rep. William L. Dawson promised that "all of us dogs are going to get together and vote to get rid of those other dogs in Washington."

To those who were still chafing from Wilson's bootstrapmanship, Dawson paused dramatically and then roared:

"Don't get mad, get smart!"

Those five words became the slogan for a renewed vote drive in black precincts across the country. The slogan appeared on pamphlets and in Democratic literature.

"Getting smart" meant only one thing—voting.

Merely getting angry was an exercise in futility unless you were prepared to do something about it. A heavy Democratic vote was the answer to Wilson's Republican impudence.

"Don't get mad, get smart" has been used repeatedly in vote campaigns in the black communities. It is a tribute to a black politician who became in his time one of the most powerful politicians in Chicago and one of the most powerful black men in the country.

Dawson's political career began as a Republican when he was elected an alderman of the City Council from the predominantly black Second Ward on the South Side. He was known as a maverick, occasionally breaking ranks to vote for measures he believed would help black people. Born in Albany, Georgia, on April 26, 1886, Dawson finished Fisk University cum laude, graduated from the Kent School of Law and settled down to practice in Chicago.

A quiet man who listened as much as he talked, Dawson was an astute organizer. Democratic Mayor Edward Kelly recognized this trait in Dawson when he hand-picked him to organize the black vote for the Democratic Party. Dawson switched parties to become a Democratic Ward Committeeman.* With the help of the tightly organized and ruthless Democratic machine, Dawson built up an organization which dominated the South Side's politics. So powerful was he by 1942 that he decided to run for Congress to fill the seat left vacant by retiring Arthur W. Mitchell, who had served four terms.

Mayor Kelly had never contemplated Dawson running for Congress. He had only wanted a black plantation chief to control the black vote

* The 50 Ward Committeemen, not the aldermen, run the Democratic Party in Chicago. They comprise the Democratic Central Committee of Cook County. To be an alderman or Congressman and a Ward Committeeman is to control patronage for the ward as well as the office. Dawson is currently one of three Chicago Congressmen (out of nine) who is also a Ward Committeeman. Mayor Daley who rules the Committee with an iron fist is its chairman.

and assign patronage. But Dawson had nurtured the dream of Congressman since 1928 when he had run unsuccessfully for Congress, the year DePriest was elected from Chicago as the first black Congressman in America since 1901. This time, in full possession of the Second Ward Democratic political machine, Dawson was elected by a skimpy 1000 votes to Congress in 1942 at the age of 56 as the second black Democratic Congressman in American history. It was the beginning of the longest political career of any elected black official in American politics. In 1966, he was re-elected from the South Side Congressional First District for his thirteenth term.

Dawson, a loyal "organization man," learned quickly that the organization was the wellspring from which all progress, jobs and favors flowed. Dawson exercised his power carefully, prudently and patiently. He quietly built a black political machine that was as efficient and vicious as the city-wide Democratic machine.

As the various South Side wards became blacker, black aldermen were chosen to represent them. In each case, Dawson either decided who should be the candidate or he issued final approval. Six wards—the Second, Third, Fourth, Sixth, Seventeenth and Twentieth—were soon represented by negro aldermen. With the exception of the Fourth and the Seventeenth Wards, the others were all under the hegemony of Dawson's fiefdom. Dawson controlled those wards by deciding whether the aldermen should be both aldermen and Ward Committeemen. Because they were loyal Dawson lieutenants, the black aldermen in the Third, Sixth and Twentieth were also Committeemen. Dawson was the Second Ward Committeeman and has retained that post today.

As noted earlier, organized crime and violence control Chicago politics. These are the only two realities of that city's political structure. Anybody who challenges the system risks being murdered or declared persona politicus non grata and barred from employment by any of the official agencies and by those businessmen who rely on these agencies for necessary favors.

Dawson not only made an early peace with these conditions, he became an integral part of their operation. For their continued support of the Dawson machine, the numbers racket and other vices (organized prostitution, illegal book-making, etc.) were permitted to flourish on the South Side. Dawson's secretary, Fred Wall, was convicted of allegedly selling appointments in the Post Office. Nobody was shocked. This was the reality of the system, the way things really were.

One of the most iniquitously flagrant examples of politically protected activity is the South Side "jitney." A "jitney" is a taxi-cab which operates on South Parkway and Indiana Avenue as a sub rosa transit system. For fifteen cents, a person can ride from 26th Street and South Parkway to 66th

Street and South Parkway and approximately the same distance on Indiana Avenue. The jitneys stop faithfully at bus stops and pick up and discharge passengers anywhere along the Parkway. Over the years, the bus company has attempted to bring the jitneys into court as an illegal and hazardous operation. Various citizens groups have been formed to have the jitneys outlawed. The citizens groups have gone the way of *all* citizens groups in America and the jitneys are as solidly entrenched in Chicago's transportation as Lake Michigan and the dirty Chicago River.

The jitneys still operate and so does Congressman-Ward Committeeman Dawson. Without the jitneys, there would be no Dawson. Without Dawson, there would have been no Daley.

In 1955, Dawson, supported by a small group of party regulars, convinced the Democratic Central Committee of Cook County to dump the "reform" Democratic Mayor Kennelly for Richard J. Daley, an Irish Catholic Ward Committeeman who was a former majority leader of the state senate and the then Cook County Clerk. There was deep concern among many leaders that Daley's rumored ties to the crime syndicate would usher in a new era of crime control.

But Daley believed that "good government is good politics," and while his administration has continued to be dominated by the crime syndicate in its inability and almost pathological refusal to solve restaurant bombings, mob murders and political assassinations, Daley has given Chicago a refurbished urban renewal image.

When Daley was slated as the Democratic candidate for mayor in 1955, Chicago newspapers were furious. They knew who was behind the move and accused Dawson of hand-picking Daley as the candidate. Daley was elected over a strong Republican challenger, Robert Merriam, by approximately 125,000 votes. Daley's margin of victory, as was true of his re-election to a third term in 1963 and a fourth term in 1967, was provided by the slavishly loyal negro Democratic vote on the South and West Sides. For example, Daley squeaked through to victory over Polish Benjamin Adamowski with a 137,531-vote plurality or 55 per cent of the vote. The Dawson-controlled black vote provided the cushion of victory with 113,895 votes for Daley in the eight predominantly black wards, or 85 per cent of the black vote.

Dawson's decision to dump Kennelly and substitute his old machine friend, Daley, was probably his last passionate act for civil rights. Under Kennelly's regime, white police brutality had risen to scandalous proportions. Black people were beaten, harassed and arrested arbitrarily by white policemen. Kennelly, who had come to power as the "reform" mayor to clean up the city, interpreted this mandate to mean that city government should be run blandly and without scandal, not efficiently or for the black public good. Furthermore, Kennelly, who was not a civil libertarian, refused to take any official action to prevent the escalation of racial confrontations and tensions accompanying black people moving into previously all-white neighborhoods. There were several "move-ins" by black people and the police not only refused to protect the negroes, but actually permitted whites to destroy their property and assault them. Chicago became famous for its race riots in the Roseland area and at Peoria and 57th Streets.

Thus, Dawson was motivated in 1955 as much by his deep concern for the official mistreatment of his people as he was by his friendship for one of the members of the power elite of the Cook County Democratic Central Committee, Dick Daley. With his election as mayor, Daley became one of the most powerful machine bosses in the country.

Dawson's last aggressive act for black people in 1955 which was to ensure Daley's election was followed by the beginning of his new posture as the "establishment nigger" when he opposed the Powell Amendment (to bar Federal aid to segregated schools) in 1956. His refusal to speak out more forthrightly that same year on the Emmett Till lynching was the breaking point as far as the militant NAACP leadership was concerned. Its president, a brilliant and articulate labor leader, Willoughby Abner, whom many negroes viewed as the rightful and logical successor to Dawson in the new era of black awareness, sharply criticized Dawson in an open letter to the press.

As the civil-rights movement gathered momentum, Dawson retreated further into silence. He continued to do just three things: win re-election, control black patronage in Chicago and keep his mouth shut.

What was even more dangerous, the NAACP had begun to document the pattern of de facto racial segregation in Chicago's public schools, indicating disparities in allocations between black and white schools. The continued airing of these charges would only serve to embarrass Dawson's dear friend, Mayor Daley, and might even force Dawson to speak out more forthrightly for his people as he had worked for them in the past.

Dawson refused to take on the eloquent and popular Abner in public debate and declined to comment on the NAACP president's charges that he had gone "soft" on civil rights. Instead, the "old pro" did the only thing he knew how to do—he simply took over the NAACP.

Precinct captains were given the assignment of selling memberships in the NAACP, an obvious act of dedication to civil rights. When the next election was held for the presidency in 1957, the new "Dawson members" outvoted the regular members, defeated Abner's bid for re-election and installed as the new president a bland insurance executive named Theodore Jones who had ties to the organization and who could be expected to run the NAACP as an independent organization so long as it never embarrassed the Daley machine. Jones and his successors have done that. The NAACP has remained under the complete domination of Dawson's political machine.

"Don't get mad, get smart." The NAACP had gotten mad. Dawson had gotten smart. Dawson had won his battle—and the NAACP lost theirs.

Meanwhile, Dawson was becoming a powerful national figure. In 1944, he was appointed Assistant Chairman of the Democratic National Committee and subsequently became the first negro to be elected as its Vice-Chairman.

His long tenure in Congress finally paid off when he became the Chairman of the Committee on Government Operations in the Eighty-first Congress on January 3, 1949, and the first negro to head a Congressional Committee. At the time, there was some public discussion among Congressmen about a negro taking over the Committee. (If he had been prevented from taking charge, it would have meant a derogation of the seniority system, and few Southern Congressmen hated black people enough to destroy a system by which they had benefited more than anybody). Just how much Dawson had become accepted as a "safe nigger" and a member of the Establishment was revealed when several Southern Congressmen publicly stated that they could foresee no difficulty in serving under Dawson's chairmanship.

Dawson ran his quiet committee without any public fanfare or relationship to the black masses. Few black people in the country were aware of the fact that Dawson was a Committee chairman. By this time, he had developed an almost neurotic aversion to the press and to public statements. He claimed that his position was frequently misrepresented.

Like his partner-in-machinations, Lyndon Baines Johnson, Dawson could never understand why the press should poke, probe and unfrock.

An example of the extent to which Dawson was a faithful and true defender of the Establishment—even when it was wrong, which is 50 per cent of the time—occurred on October 12, 1964. In his capacity as chairman of the Government Operations Committee which issued its report of a two-and-one-half-year investigation of Texan Billie Sol Estes' multi-million-dollar scandal, he issued a public statement denying that President Johnson, who was Vice President during Estes' machinations, had had anything to do with the Texan millionaire's financial finagling. The report did not contain Dawson's public statement which said: "There is no evidence that the then Vice President participated in any way in the relationships between Billie Sol Estes and the Federal government or its agencies other than routinely referring to the department of agriculture correspondence, including complaints in which Estes was involved."

Several members of Congress found it a little "odd" that the report was released while Congress was out of session, but more particularly only a few weeks before the Presidential election.

In the last few years, a group of more militant and younger aspirants for Dawson's seat has begun to challenge him. The first serious challenge occurred in 1964 when a civil rights activist, an undertaker named A. A.

(Sammy) Rayner, ran against Dawson in the April primary. Rayner had run against Sixth Ward Alderman Miller in 1963 and lost by only a few votes. This was the first indication that the old Dawson ship of state was wobbling unsteadily in the storm of militancy. The Sixth Ward is composed of middle-class negroes who had come to resent Dawson's "old-line handker-chief-head" politics. As are many white middle-class voters, they are also anti-political machine.

Although he had the money and the organization, Dawson took no chances. He mounted a strong organizational campaign. Each of his Con-gressional District's 446 precincts has a captain and two assistants. They flooded the District with literature—and money. Dawson's Second Ward Secretary and 26th Precinct Captain Lawrence C. Woods sent out over his signature a mimeographed letter (which was published in the *Chicago Daily Defender* on April 21, 1964, much to the anger and embarrassment of the machine). The letter stressed why Dawson should be re-elected in the April 14th primary, and then two of its paragraphs read as follows:

I am very proud of you, and I always try to show my appreciation by thinking about you and your family at Christmas, Easter, and at the closing of school. After every election victory, a dinner basket is placed in your home. You under-stand how I feel about you and your families. Let no man come between us.

. . . When I bless my table on April 15, I shall bless the table of 582 REGU-LAR DEMOCRATIC VOTERS of the Twenty-sixth Precinct.

I sincerely thank you.

Yours very truly, etc.

The letter is just one of the techniques Dawson has utilized to stay in power. His hold on the electorate has become solidified by such favors, some outright vote-buying in certain South Side precincts (and very widespread vote-buying in the predominantly negro West Side precincts), patronage and intimidation of welfare recipients and public housing tenants.

No job is held in City Hall below a certain level without approval of the Ward Committeeman in whose ward the job-holder resides. The approval is usually written. A large number of welfare recipients have only been able to receive benefits after having gone to the Ward organization and having been instructed by the Committeeman or one of his assistants how to apply. Most of the recipients believe they can be removed from the welfare rolls, even though they are entitled to such relief.

But the Dawson machine knows no moral limits in its manipulations to ensure victory.*

---

* The author, while editor of the *Chicago Daily Defender*, stood outside one polling place near a public housing project on South State Street. As a shabbily dressed woman approached the polls, a precinct captain hailed her jovially and said: "Hi, there, Mrs. Johnson. How are you? And those wonderful kids of yours? I know you're going to do the right thing today, aren't you? Enjoying your apartment? We sure want you to be able to stay there. You're one of our favorite people. Good luck in there, now, okay?"

As would be expected, Dawson defeated Rayner by a better than two-to-one margin. Many thought Rayner would do better, although none expected him to defeat Dawson. But there was a strong civil rights fervor in the city. Two successful school boycotts on October 25, 1963, and again in February 1964 had kept over 250,000 students out of the public schools to protest de facto segregation. The Daley machine fought both boycotts with the full support of the white press, all of the negro politicians, petitions from parents who signed promising they would not let their kids participate and a constant blitzkrieg of statements from the mayor's office.

The success of the boycotts led many in the black community to believe this meant Dawson's grip had slipped. They were to be sadly mistaken. It was another example of the inability of the civil rights activists to translate the evangelical fervor of their cause to the sober pragmatism of the ballot box.

In 1966, Dawson was again challenged, by a young social worker named Fred Hubbard. Again, Dawson's machine began to grind out its propaganda. Leaflets saturated the black community, promising that "a dollar a minute will be given away" at a Dawson rally. $1000 in bonuses was promised to the precinct captains bringing in the most votes—$500 to the winner, $300 for second place and $200 for third place. $20 bills were raffled off at one of the black movie houses by a Dawson alderman.

Some of the Dawson faithfuls were still taking no chances. Only a few weeks before the election, Hubbard was shot at night in his political headquarters by "an unknown assailant" who, as was to be expected, was never caught. Hubbard was not wounded seriously. He refused to condemn either the Dawson or the Daley machine for the attempted political assassination and many disillusioned supporters quit his camp. Dawson went on to defeat Hubbard by 17,000 votes out of a total 65,000 cast.

In 1967, the aging Dawson is barely able to function physically. Hobbled by a wooden leg as the result of a World War I injury, he walks painfully over to the House floor each day, sits for a while during the debates, and then goes home. He is faithful in attendance and in answering roll calls, and his vote is as reliable as the first day he entered the House. But, at eighty-one years of age, how much can an ancient warrior who has lost contact with the black masses do?

Dawson, however, is still *the* black power in Chicago politics. He is still deeply respected by President Johnson and Mayor Daley, both of whom owe much of their political good fortune to Dawson's once-upon-a-time vigorous deployment of political resources.

Dawson has become such a faithful and dependable "Establishment Negro" in the declining power of his long career that he no longer even pretends to be the champion of black people he was fifteen years ago when he roared, "Don't get mad, get smart!" Forced to choose between supporting the plantation politics of the Daley machine and the politics of blackness, he predictably has supported the machine. This is why opposition to him is increasing on Chicago's South Side, particularly among the negro middle classes.

In 1968 Dawson was opposed in the Democratic primary by A. A. (Sammy) Rayner, an undertaker who had previously challenged Dawson in 1964 and lost by 20,000 votes. In 1967 Rayner, in preparation for his 1968 challenge of Dawson, knocked over a Daley machine stalwart, a black alderman named Robert H. Miller, coincidentally also an undertaker.

But Dawson's higher loyalty to the white machine over the color of his skin is proved by his tacit support of Third Congressional District Representative William T. Murphy, a mediocre politician of five terms in Congress. Murphy's district is now estimated to be 60 per cent black. For that reason he was challenged by a forty-two-year-old black publisher, Augustus A. Savage, in the June 11, 1968, Democratic primary. Murphy relied on the creaking, tyrannical, but still efficient Daley machine. Savage placed his hopes in an aroused and united black vote that would "vote black" before it voted party.

In the end, the Daley machine delivered for both Dawson and Murphy. The white Congressman overwhelmed his black challenger by more than 22,000 votes, and Dawson turned back Rayner by more than 10,000 votes. The difference in Dawson's plurality over Rayner in 1964 and in 1968 clearly revealed that it is just a matter of time before "the grand old black man" of politics is defeated.

If any one black man could expose some of the behind-the-scenes maneuvering and big political pay-offs at all levels, Dawson is probably that man. But he never will, and a grateful white political structure accords him the reward of remaining in office as long as he wishes. Dawson continues to faithfully attend the Second Ward organization meetings at his clubhouse at 3435 South Indiana Avenue. He is a creature of habit. He is a man who still appreciates the appreciation of his political flunkies and favor-seekers. Each Friday evening, they remind him of his greatness.

And in his way, Dawson has attained a certain measure of greatness. When he was in his prime, in the words of one South Side admirer, "he was a bitch." He was a strong politician who could hold his own in smoke-filled back-rooms where the real decisions are made by groups usually composed of white men. Dawson was one of the rare exceptions in America who early became part of the Establishment—and has stayed there, close to the top.

In an August 26, 1966, column in the *New York Post*, columnist Pete Hamill, an astute observer, wrote: "Dawson, of course, is a good example of how Chicago politics works. If Adam Clayton Powell has had black power for a quarter of a century and used it for himself, it can be said of

Dawson that he has had black power even longer and used it for the Establishment."

Dawson would consider that paragraph a tribute to his recognition of the realities of politics. And as he sat in his office in April 1964 asking the black editor of the *Chicago Daily Defender* why the editor did not want to support him for re-election in the primary, Dawson honestly did not understand that a black revolution was taking place in America. To get things done, one solicits the royal tenders of the Establishment. One does not negotiate with the rabble in the streets who stormed the Bastille, threw the tea in the Boston harbor, drove the British out of Ireland, and defeated the Arabs in Palestine.

Dawson has rarely gotten mad; he has always been smart. That is why he survives today, ruler of all he surveys, custodian of what opponents covet and member in good standing of the Establishment. He can stay as long as he wants because the Establishment told him years ago: "Well done, thou good and faithful servant: thou hast been faithful over a few things, I will make thee ruler over many things."

J. RAYMOND JONES

"Nobody ever does anything for nothing."

In the shabby household of American politics, there are a chosen few whose grace and elegant presence admit them to membership in its royal family. Just by their flair, they have given a tawdry and oligarchical system a new sense of purpose and a renewed belief in the universality of competence. Some have been world historical individuals. Others have enjoyed national fame. A few have only achieved local recognition. But they have all shared that indefinable quality called style—Andrew Jackson, Thaddeus Stevens, Franklin D. Roosevelt, Wendell Willkie, Fiorella LaGuardia and John F. Kennedy.

One of the few black politicians in America who could walk in their company is J. Raymond Jones.

The only man to have ever headed a sovereign political organization, Jones achieved this ultimate success through the nobility of his bearing as much as through his shrewdness of intellect. He made history for American Negroes on December 4, 1964, when he was elected leader of the New York County Democratic organization, otherwise known as Tammany Hall. For Jones, it was an office he was convinced early in life a black man could attain.

As has been true of Adam Clayton Powell, the physical appearance of J. Raymond Jones has been an important factor in his success. Six feet tall, solidly built of hard muscle that has finally begun to flab, silvery-white, closely cropped hair and a tonsorially perfect mustache, he is a man of enormous presence. When Ray Jones walks into a room and imperiously surveys its occupants, it is almost as if he were taking a last-minute check before presenting his credentials to the Court of St. James. Even his enemies respect his dignity and fear his sharp mind.

This mind, so thoroughly political, has earned him the cherished sobriquet of "The Fox." Like the fox, Jones has been wily, slippery, cunning, vicious, cautious, and always quick. His understanding of what motivates men and his ability to capitalize on their greed—even as he has gluttoned himself on the spoils of public office without sinking to their level (and occasional conviction)—have separated him from the others of his standing.

"Nobody ever does anything for nothing"; J. Raymond Jones has practiced what he has preached.

Niccolo Machiavelli paid tribute to the kingly attributes of such men as J. Raymond (The Fox) Jones when he wrote: "A prince being thus obliged to know well how to act as a beast must imitate the fox and the lion, for the lion cannot protect himself from traps, and the fox cannot defend himself from wolves. One must therefore be a fox to recognize traps and a lion to frighten wolves."*

In the end, when Jones finally resigned as County Leader in March of 1967, it was because he had not been enough lion. He was unable to frighten off the wolves—Senator Robert F. Kennedy and a reborn coalition of the Irish Mafia and the Jewish Mafia—and they devoured his leadership. Adam Clayton Powell, the lion, was also stripped of his leadership because he was not enough of "a fox to recognize traps. Those that wish to be only lions do not understand this."**

Born on St. Thomas in the Virgin Islands on November 19, 1899, John Raymond Jones, by the time he was 16, was a large young man of restless energy. His father was a schoolteacher, but he opted not to finish school and instead stowed away on an island schooner for Puerto Rico.

He arrived in New York City when he was 18 and worked at a succession of jobs, both physical and menial—longshoreman, porter, factory hand and ice helper. One of his jobs was to deliver ice to Harlem's Dunbar apartments, home of many prominent negroes, including W. E. B. Du Bois, who was one of Jones' customers.

An incident in 1921 triggered his interest and subsequent involvement in politics. He had become an inspector during a voter registration and was asked to deliver some registration books to the Cayuga Club, a "for whites only" clubhouse in Harlem. Insulted by the doorman, Jones recalls he decided on the spot to go into politics. A different story is recounted by Collis

* Niccolo Machiavelli, *The Prince* (New York: New American Library, 1952), p. 101.
** Machiavelli, p. 101.

Crocker, however, who helped Jones organize his political base in Harlem, the Carver Democratic Club: "When the doorman at the Cayuga Club said to Ray, 'you know you niggers aren't supposed to come in here,' Ray took those registration books and let him have it—a solid left hook."

Jones soon became the 13th Assembly District Leader and was immediately recognized as one of Harlem's finest political minds by Mayor William O'Dwyer, who appointed him as Deputy Commissioner of Housing and Buildings on January 2, 1947. O'Dwyer also let it be known publicly that Jones is "my man in Harlem" and his adviser on patronage for that area.

A year later, Jones was to get his first political scars in a skirmish involving the Surrogate Court, an institution that led to his undoing in 1966 and near political demise in 1948.

Mayor O'Dwyer was supporting the president of the City Council, Vinvent Impelliteri, for the lucrative post of Surrogate Court Judge. But the Tammany leaders, including Jones, voted against the mayor's choice and instead nominated General Sessions Court Judge Francis L. Valente. (Note that there was no ethnic conflict on this office. Both Democratic candidates were Italian.) On July 1st, O'Dwyer personally announced Jones' resignatior as Deputy Commissioner. A few weeks later, the peace pipe was smoked in the Tammany wigwam and Jones was reinstated.

Irish Catholic Mayor O'Dwyer, like some of his predecessors who ruled the Tammany roost, soon came under fire for a series of scandals involving bribery of public officials (with suspicion directed toward himself) and other corrupt practices. He resigned, Impelliteri assumed office and on December 13, 1950, Jones resigned at Impelliteri's request.

There were public denials that Jones' resignation was in any way connected with investigations by the District Attorney into corrupt activities of building inspectors under Jones' administration. The following year, Jones announced he would not be a candidate for re-election as District Leader, and the political career of J. Raymond Jones seemed permanently eclipsed.

Neither his career nor his reputation was aided by public disclosures on November 19, 1951, during a New York State Crime Commission investigation that Benjamin Bernstein claimed he could have had the municipal court judgeship in 1945 for $18,300, but refused it. Sidney Kansas says he also turned down the same offer and named Harlem District Leader Angelo Simonetti and Jones as having made the offer.

For seven years Jones led a quiet life, and then, in 1958, he came out of his political semi-retirement to master-mind Adam Clayton Powell's campaign to keep his Congressional seat.

Carmine DeSapio, the then leader of Tammany Hall, had decided that the obstreperous Powell should be taught a lesson for bolting the Democratic Party in 1956 to support Eisenhower. As a result, Powell was not slated by the Democrats as their regular candidate for Harlem's Congressional seat. The vote was taken on May 15th.

Harlem's leaders who viewed the move as a racist affront quickly agreed Powell's charisma and tremendous popularity could easily defeat Tammany in Harlem, but an organization would still be needed to get out the vote. Their virtually unanimous choice was a man many had already forgotten —"The Fox."

Jones took over with all of the punctilious authority of a Roman general. In a few short weeks, using Powell's Abyssinian Baptist Church basement as a headquarters to recruit volunteers (a large majority of whom came from Abyssinian's 13,000 membership), Jones whipped together an organization that was as briskly efficient as Tammany itself.

To take over Powell's campaign as its campaign manager, Jones had to resign his $12,000 job as a judicial secretary, a sinecure the Party had awarded him for faithful service in the hopes he would stay permanently retired. But Jones correctly reasoned that nobody could beat the charismatic Powell, and he gambled not only on Powell's future, but on his own.

On Primary Day, August 12th, 23,343 of Harlem's 50,000 registered voters had gone to the polls and endorsed Powell over Tammany's candidate, a lackluster newspaper columnist named Earl Brown, 14,935 to 4959 or a 3 to 1 margin.

As much as this was a victory for Powell and a defeat for Tammany Hall, it was the beginning of a comeback for Jones. He was clearly the guiding organizational genius behind Powell's victory, and the self-centered Powell never missed the opportunity to credit "my good friend, Ray" with responsibility.

In the years, the Powell-Jones alliance flowered. It was a perfect match— "The Lion and The Fox." When Powell wanted a political favor, he publicly demanded and threatened reprisals. Jones quietly worked behind the scenes securing the favor. Two such diverse personalities and methods of operation were bound to encounter strains and the two suffered a bitter split over a large amount of money Powell claimed was due from a business partnership the two had formed to bring more middle-income housing into Harlem. The Powell-Jones schism never reached the point of no return. Each had affection and extraordinary respect for the other. Even when they were on opposite sides of the political fence, they would invariably somehow manage to become reconciled.

In 1961, Jones, back as the 13th Assembly District leader and one of the accepted political powers of Harlem, risked his political career to support Mayor Wagner for re-election against Tammany's choice, New York State Comptroller Arthur Levitt. Powell backed Levitt. This was a curious turnabout. Powell, the maverick, was supporting the organization's man. And Jones, the organization man, was supporting the maverick.

Wagner was strongly supported by the reform wing of the Democratic Party which had already unseated DeSapio as Leader. Jones, a loyal organization man, nonetheless threw in with the Reform Democrats (whom he loathed as "idealists" and impractical neophytes who did not understand the hard realities of politics). Again, Jones' intellectual flexibility and his uncannily accurate assessment of what would happen paid off handsomely. Wagner overwhelmed Levitt and the Tammany bosses. Jones clearly emerged as one of the most powerful politicians in New York City, black or white.

After Wagner's victory over the organization, Jones was the logical choice for Tammany Hall Leader. But New York City Democrats were not quite ready for a black man to take charge. They instead elected a weak "consensus" candidate named Edward N. Costikyan whose tepid rule-by-factions nearly sundered the organization.

In 1962, Jones was elected to the City Council to fill out an unexpired term. The following year, Powell supported an opposing candidate, but Jones defeated him with a 5 to 1 ratio. Jones was still the organizational genius.

Two years later, Jones finally won the honor which should have been his in 1961 when he was elected head of Tammany Hall.

The first thing Jones did after his election was to take a telephone call of congratulations from one of Powell's aides who informed him that Powell would be delighted to meet with him. "The Fox" quickly recognized that he needed "the Lion" in the stratosphere of politics where everybody tries to undermine the leader. A rejuvenated alliance between Harlem's two most powerful leaders would forestall any such attempts.

Jones announced on the day of his election that he would go to Washington to confer with Powell. When questioned as to why he would go to Washington instead of Powell coming to New York City, the distinguished-looking political patriarch leaned back and said with a gentle and easy laugh that Powell was "the only district leader who is chairman of the Education and Labor Committee." (The real reason, of course, Powell could not come to New York City was his avoidance of an arrest order in connection with a libel suit. Jones was just enough of a politician and a friend to Powell to hide this fact.)

In 1965, some of Jones' power as the County Leader was diminished when the mayor personally selected a negro woman attorney for the NAACP Legal Defense Fund, Mrs. Constance Baker Motley, as his choice for Manhattan Borough President to succeed Edward R. Dudley who had been elected to the State Supreme Court.

Mrs. Motley's selection was made without the full concurrence of Jones who nevertheless graciously accepted the final choice. Powell, the Lion, did what Jones, the Fox, could not do. He publicly blasted Wagner for having made the choice without consulting the black leaders of Harlem.

Jones' final hurrah came in 1966 over a battle for the Surrogate Court judgeship.

As had been true in the past, the Republicans and the Democrats usually agreed on a candidate in exchange for other political favors. It was a tradition. Jones was a great believer in tradition.

But the Jewish-dominated Liberal Party which had backed Republican Mayor Lindsay's successful bid for mayor of New York City now felt big enough to take on Tammany Hall. Alex Rose, one of the chief tacticians of the Liberal Party, publicly charged that there had been a back-room Republican-Democrat "deal" in the selection of the bi-partisan supported State Supreme Court Justice Arthur G. Klein for the post. The Liberals enlisted the support of Senator Robert F. Kennedy, who agreed to intervene in this strictly County fight, a rare political move.

But the situation was itself rare. Whereas it had always been the tradition of the Democrats and Republicans to "make deals" on the Surrogate Court judgeship, this time there was widespread resentment at the thought of a black man deciding half of the deal. Nobody had ever challenged the system before when Italians or Irish governed Tammany Hall. But the Liberal Party, more committed to Jewish power than Black Power, decided it was time to knock off the most powerful black man in New York City.

Kennedy blissfully went along with this scuttling of Jones' leadership, labeling the Surrogate Court nomination as a "suspicion of corruption." With his open support, the Liberal Party and the Reform Democrats put up their own candidate, another State Supreme Court Justice named Samuel J. Silverman.

Jones recognized the threat to his position. He publicly accused Kennedy of a personal vendetta against him and of trying to take over the Democratic Party organization at the County level. "He who seeks to conquer aims at me, the office, the Court—all principle is shoved under the rug," declared Jones on June 2nd.

Most of Harlem's legislators and district leaders naturally united behind Jones and strongly hinted in a public statement that the attack on Jones' leadership (which even the devoutly liberal Franklin D. Roosevelt, Jr., admitted was behind the move) was racially motivated. They issued a public statement on June 9th, declaring their united support for Jones.

On June 13, a story on page 45 of the *New York Times* declared in a five-column headline: "Campaign for Surrogate Reflects Kennedy vs. Jones Struggle."

Kennedy had one thing Jones did not—money. An extraordinary amount of money was spent in an ordinarily drab race. Full-page ads were taken out by the Kennedy forces in the negro-owned *Amsterdam News,* and these ads were reprinted as posters and flooded Harlem like the Nile River on its yearly rampage.

In the end, "green power" was more potent than Black Power. Silverman defeated Klein by a plurality of 23,146. Had Harlem voters followed their political leadership, they might have been the balance of power. Only Powell and Sutton were able to carry their assembly districts for Klein; the other two Harlem districts went for Silverman as he picked up 21,085 Harlem votes.

While Jones has always been respected in Harlem and recognized as a "race man," there was just enough of his reserved, detached manner and his successful ability to get along with the white power structure to make some Harlem black people question how much Jones was dedicated to their best interests first vis-à-vis Jones' best interests. Thus, when he really needed the black voters to stand behind him, they did not. The issue was not clear enough for them. Maybe the white power structure did want to get rid of Ray Jones. Maybe there was a "Jewish conspiracy" to accomplish this. But Bobby Kennedy, brother of the late and beloved President Kennedy, was surely no racial bigot.

Jones was defeated not only by a monumental concentration of money and ethnic power, but a biased press which made no pretense of its sympathies. For example, when Alex Rose charged a "deal" had been made, the story was played at the top of the page of the *New York Times,* a two-column headline with a picture of Rose on June 1st. Two days later, when Jones accused Kennedy of unfair intervention, the story was placed on page 25 of the *New York Times.* When the Harlem leaders convened a press conference to announce their support for Jones, that story was played on page 42 of the second section of the *New York Times* with a one-column headline.

Jones got his political revenge a couple of months later at the New York State Democratic Convention when he rammed through the selection of upstate industrialist Howard Samuels as Lieutenant Governor over Orin Lehman, who was widely regarded as Kennedy's choice. Kennedy denied this, but many political observers privately declared that Kennedy had, indeed, "been had" by Jones.

Even if it were true, the gesture was a small and futile display of fading power. It was just a matter of time. With Kennedy able to control all Federal patronage as the highest elected official, with the re-election of Republican Governor Nelson A. Rockefeller and a Republican mayor in City Hall, Jones' patronage pickings were slim indeed.

He announced his resignation as Tammany Leader on March 10, 1967, with a public denunciation of Kennedy and of his efforts to prevent him from functioning as County Leader.

One rumor discussed in Harlem and Washington, D.C., was Kennedy's alleged secret purchase of the *Amsterdam News*, the large Harlem weekly newspaper. While there has been no subsequent evidence that this is true —the masthead has continued to list the same owners and there was no immediately discernible shift in editorial policy—there was speculation that a strong anti-Kennedy column written by the executive editor, James L. Hicks, during the Klein-Silverman battle had figured prominently in Hicks' sudden and unexpected resignation.

Political friends expect Jones to eventually retire to Virgin Islands, where his wife, Ruth, is a Customs Collector as the result of an appointment by President Kennedy. As to his financial ability to support himself, there are many rumors about his affluence. In an article in the *New York Times Magazine* on February 19, 1967 (the month before he resigned), the author wrote:

He [Jones] is commonly suspected of having engaged in all sorts of political intrigue. There are whispers that he has been involved in middle-income housing projects in Harlem and murmurs that he is senior partner in an elaborate brokerage of judgeships. These murmurs turned into shouts last spring during the primary battle between the forces of Samuel Silverman and Arthur Klein for the post of Surrogate.

. . . No one has ever pinned anything on Ray Jones, which is a tribute either to his integrity or to his cunning, both of which he possesses in large measure.

If, however, a politician truly believes in the axioms that guide his activities—and there is no reason to doubt that Jones fervently believes that "nobody does anything for nothing"—then, one must expect that integrity combined with cunning will ensure the implementation of the axiom at all times.

Jones, whom a woman editor of a negro newspaper once adoringly called "that gorgeous hunk of West Indian man," stayed with the organization when he believed it was right. When he believed it was wrong or that it sought to make a personal attack on him, his great pride in himself as his own secretary of state and as a negro, coupled with just enough dedication to his people, disturbed him into dissent.

This was what differentiated Jones from Dawson. The latter never challenged the righteousness of the organization even when it murdered people. Jones did. This ability to close one's eyes to unconscionable activity by whites against blacks is what made Dawson a loyal "Establishment House Nigger" and Jones only a loyal organizational man who appreciated the value of working through a system.

As a West Indian, Jones was one of many who helped to give Harlem what little political independence it has enjoyed. Independent of spirit and proud of their black skin as well as their heritage, West Indians have refused to accept a subordinate status. Many of the political breakthroughs in Harlem and in New York City (first negro Assembly District leader, first negro Manhattan Borough President) were West Indians. They taught Harlem negroes to be proud of their black skin and to fight white political oppression.

"Mr. Organizational Politics" is not known to as many black people in America as Adam Clayton Powell, although Democratic Presidents from Truman to Kennedy to Johnson have all had a profound respect for him. It would be no surprise if Jones came out of a second semi-retirement to play an active role in the 1968 Presidential campaign. He, along with Powell— "nobody ever does anything for nothing"—was one of the first to support Johnson for the Presidency back in March 1959.

Powell's impact on New York City's black people, of course, has been perhaps the most decisive factor in what little political sophistication Harlemites possess—and they possess very little.

But the real power—the power to decide who gets what jobs, who will be the candidate, who will be awarded a lucrative contract to do business with the city, who will get the opulent position of Surrogate—that power is only wielded by the Establishment through the organization. Jones never quite made it to the Establishment because they chose to destroy him. The Establishment in New York City—controlled by Jews and dominated by Irish and Italians—has not yet decided to permit a black man to be one of them. Ray Jones came as close as anybody.

He did briefly control "The Organization" as the perfect organizational man. When New York City elects its first black mayor, he will owe that achievement in part to a regal personality who will by then be a noble legend and a distinguished member of the archives of black politicians— J. Raymond (The Fox) Jones.

ADAM CLAYTON POWELL
"Mr. National Black Politics"

"Keep the faith, Baby."

A popular story in the Negro community concerns a black waiter who was hired for a dinner given by one of the most prominent white leaders in the city. The affair received much publicity and the waiter's friends vicariously reveled in his privileged access to the inner secrets of the white world.

The next day, several of his friends crowded around him in the barber shop to hear what had taken place at the dinner. The waiter was nonplussed. "Ain't no big deal," he said, with a contemptuous dismissing motion of his hand. "All they do is sit around and talk. They talked *all* evening. I'm told by the other servants that that's all they ever do is talk. They talk all the time."

"Lord, man!" exclaimed a friend. "What do they talk about?"

"Us!" the waiter replied.

In the last few years, Adam Clayton Powell is *all* the white community has talked about.

If any one black man has worried 180,000,000 white people, it has been Adam Clayton Powell. Symbol of black aspirations and black achievement to black people, Powell has been the national incarnation of debauchery and the profligate life to whites. Most white people regard black people as fun-loving, dancing, singing children. But they are unable to internalize the image of a brilliant and powerful black politician, not only throwing his political power around, but luxuriating in the sybaritic pursuits of life at the same time.

Adam Powell not only defied the great American conception of black people as submissive and speak-only-when-spoken-to "house niggers," fawning and shuffling when the white plantation master has given permission, he ungraciously destroyed it. He took away the white man's blanket of racial myths and left him little consolation.

A nation does not destroy its legacy overnight, no matter how repellent its antecedents. The legacy of white master-black slave has persisted in the subconsciousness of the vast majority of American whites. From the first grade, we are taught that Columbus "discovered America." He only discovered it for white people. It had been here all the time for the Indians.

The slaves were freed, but American history decreed that an apartheid mentality would be handed down from father to son. Black people were the workers, the hewers of wood, the Gunga Dins of American society. White people were the soldiers, the statesmen, the "baaskaps" (Afrikaaner for "bossman"). A hundred years is too short an interval to erase the cultural architecture built on this relationship. Adam Clayton Powell was molded in its image, a fact which he never accepted, and it led to his eventual destruction. Like Malcolm X, Powell met the white man on his own terms, his own level and his white logic. This was unforgivable and both men were destroyed (as white people gleefully love to point out, Malcolm by guns fired by his own people, and Powell by a libel suit by a black woman).

There are probably no adjectives left which have not been incorporated into the millions of words written about Powell in newspapers, magazines, books and pamphlets. Arrogant, audacious, flamboyant, irresponsible, self-centered, elegant, witty, charming, exciting, paranoid, perpetually happy, uncommonly brilliant and disturbingly handsome, Powell possessed so many natural gifts, he ignited deep resentment in the ordinary little white men who were his peers and were forced to tread in his shadow.

The tall, suave Harlemite whose wavy black hair, off-white skin, precisely trimmed mustache and provocative smile were as much a part of the national scene as the Federal budget was one of the few black men whose name became a household word in both the white and black communities.

So universal in appearance was he that Powell could have passed for a Greek cook, a Spanish nobleman, a Puerto Rican fisherman, a Sicilian gangster, an Egyptian businessman, a Brazilian politician or a Mexican actor—but never a "negro politician."

Always sensitive about a white skin that housed a black militancy, Powell was an early follower of Marcus Garvey's firebrand black nationalism. "Black is not a skin color, but a way of thinking," he often said. One of his favorite sermons during his many years as pastor of Abyssinian Baptist Church was, "Think Big, Think Black and Think Like a Child of God."

It is important to understand the impact of Powell's physical attractiveness in the black community. Powell grew up in a black culture which accepted its white-designated symbols of inferiority. That which was black was bad, that which approximated white, beautiful and good. This system of value judgments based upon the polarities of color was never more precisely summarized than in a racist poem black people jocularly recited in an almost sick rejection of their color:

> "If you're white, you're all right.
> If you're yellow, you're mellow.
> If you're brown, you can stick around.
> But if you're black, step way back."

Powell, in physical appearance, looked like a white man. Not only "tall, dark and handsome," he was for millions of black women their Gary Grant, their Gable, their Gregory Peck.

His good looks coupled with a magnificently resonant speaking voice and a theatrical flair when he preached that would have done justice to a Cecil B. DeMille spectacular made him one of the most beloved and worshipped matinee idols in the black community.

These were the ingredients of Powell's charisma which brought him to the political heights and also what helped to dethrone him. Powell during his entire life had never suffered a defeat or a reversal of fortune. When the conspiratorial forces in Congress, acting with the tacit approval of President Johnson, finally decided to unseat him, Powell could not believe that the cataclysms which ruin most men could dissemble the charmed circle of his protected life. At 57, the cat who had lived nine lives believed there was still one more left. This is what made his fall from grace such a bitter one. It came so near the end of a successful career that had overcome all previous adversity. He seemed immune.

Powell was born on November 29, 1908, in New Haven, Conn., where his father, the Reverend Adam Clayton Powell, Sr., was the pastor of a church. The family moved to New York in 1909, where his father assumed the pastorship of the Abyssinian Baptist Church and built it into one of New York City's largest Protestant memberships.

Powell attended Colgate University, then later acquired 'an M.A. at Columbia University. He was not a spectacular student, not because he was not bright, but because he did not study as hard as his courses required. He was, in fact, a playboy.

In 1937, Powell succeeded his father as pastor of Abyssinian and, with his incredibly exciting preaching, multiplied the church membership rapidly. During this period, he began his activist ministry, leading picket lines against white merchants in Harlem who refused to hire black employees. Powell's picket lines succeeded and the largest department store in Harlem agreed to hire black salesladies. Powell next turned his attention to the exclusion of black people from jobs as bus drivers and skilled workers for Consolidated Edison. The Greater New York Co-ordinating Committee for the Unemployment which Powell had formed in association with several black radicals, a few upper-class negroes and even a sprinkling of whites now turned its attention to the bus company and Con Ed. The latter was the first to capitulate and agreed to hire more negroes. Then, in 1940, Powell took on Mike Quill, the domineering Irish Catholic leader of the Transport Workers Union, which religiously barred negroes. Only Irish were hired.

A boycott of the bus company was set in motion which was to antedate by 17 years another more famous boycott in Montgomery, Alabama, also led by a young black Baptist minister, Martin Luther King, Jr. The boycott was successful. Powell called on black people not to ride buses in Harlem. "Beginning tomorrow," he declared in a rousing speech, "every negro that rides a bus is lynching the negro race."

Empty buses rode up and down Seventh Avenue. The bus company stood firm. Then, Powell's committee promised to march downtown and picket the company's offices. The resulting bad publicity plus the loss in revenues quickly brought the bus company to the bargaining table to sign an agreement with Powell's committee. The three-part agreement signed between Powell's committee, the company and the bus union stipulated the immediate hiring of 210 negroes as drivers and Grade I mechanics. A formula was also worked out for future hiring of negroes. It was one of the first significant employment victories for negroes anywhere in America.

Powell was now riding high. Harlem lavished its affection at his feet and his church membership swelled. In 1941, he became the first negro to be elected to the City Council. In 1942, he started his own newspaper, *The People's Voice*, which, for tough, uncompromising militancy, brilliant editorial writing and exciting layout, has rarely been matched. Powell's weekly columns when re-read in light of today's "Black Power" militancy clearly anticipated these developments. Any one of those columns can stand alone today as a "call to rally under the banner of blackness."

By 1943, Congressional reapportionment gave Harlem a Congressional district predominantly black. Powell announced his intention to run for

Congress, and in 1944 was easily elected. It was the beginning of a sensational career which was to irritate whites and titillate blacks. Powell was a consistent headline-grabber. His denunciations of President Truman's wife as "the last lady of the land," his loud calls during World War II for black soldiers to be permitted to fight instead of just serving as water-boys behind the lines and his relentless fights on the floor of Congress against all forms of bigotry endeared him to black people all over the country.

Within two years, Powell quickly became a national symbol of politics to all black people. Every black person considered him "our Congressman," our black champion.

He became known as "Mr. Civil Rights." More importantly, he was now "Mr. National Black Politics."

One aspect of Powell's life—his fast changes with women and wives—was never accepted by whites, but among blacks was shrugged off as part of a black ethos which could not get excited about a black man's sexual activities while America was starving its black people, lynching them, bombing their churches and decimating their self-respect.

Powell went through a quick succession of wives—each marriage more controversial than the previous. His first wife, a prominent Cotton Club showgirl named Isabelle Washington, nearly cost him his ministry, but when he threatened to resign, the congregation backed him. He subsequently divorced the fair-skinned Isabelle and married chocolate-colored Hazel Scott, then one of the most exciting jazz pianists in America. Later, he divorced Hazel, married a comely Puerto Rican girl named Yvette Diago. By 1961, that marriage was on the rocks and Powell began keeping company with an olive-skinned beauty named Corrine Huff, "Miss Ohio" in the 1960 Miss Universe contest, and Powell's secretary. During a campaign in Harlem, an opponent started to recite Powell's peccadillos and in the middle of his litany was interrupted by a loud bass voice: "Aw, quit it, man. The cat's livin'!"

In 1956, Powell pulled the first of his many unexplainable political switches when he supported Eisenhower for President. Powell claimed that the then Democratic candidate, Adlai Stevenson, was soft on civil rights. And while few would admit it, Stevenson clearly was. No man could talk more about civil rights and say and do less than Stevenson. He was the perfect representative of the fuzzy-minded white liberals who just as eagerly barred negroes from their inner circles as Southern white bigots.

Powell claimed his support of Eisenhower was for the record of the Eisenhower administration. More knowledgeable and politically cynical observers suggested a deal had been made between Powell and the Republicans to drop prosecution of an income tax case for Powell's support. Yet, even Powell's enormous popularity was still unable to deliver the negro vote to the fumbling general, although the 39 per cent of the black vote

Eisenhower won that year, the highest of any Republican Presidential candidate since 1936, can partially be ascribed to Powell's defection.

Despite the Republicans' alleged deal, public pressure soon forced an income tax trial, and the first of Powell's "nine lives" was expended. A hung jury failed to find him guilty in 1960 and the Federal government declined to prosecute further.

In 1961, Powell became the second black man to head a Congressional Committee when his seniority catapulted him into the chairmanship of the Education and Labor Committee. His selection was opposed in a nasty, angry statement by AFL-CIO George Meany, who criticized Powell's "irresponsibility." What Meany really was saying was that Powell's unpredictability meant that it would be difficult to control him. The labor movement has long tyrannized a number of Congressmen by underwriting their campaigns and, in many instances, under-the-table financial bribes for unswerving support of labor legislation. It is a common practice for certain key Congressmen and Subcommittee chairmen to receive from $5000 to $40,000 for their support of a piece of legislation dear to labor's heart or their sponsorship of labor-written legislation. Meany knew that Powell could not be "purchased," hence his condemnation of Powell's prospective chairmanship.

Powell had already arranged the chairmanship as the result of an early unspoken agreement between him and his close friend Speaker of the House Sam Rayburn of Texas. Rayburn was an early supporter of his Texas protégé, Lyndon Baines Johnson, for President in 1960. Perhaps if Powell would support Johnson, there would be no difficulty in that succession to the chairmanship. . . .

In March 1959, Powell astounded the black community by announcing his support for Johnson, who until that time had not acquired any image as a liberal or even a remote friend of negroes. But Powell was heeding the philosophical advice of two other astute black politicians—"Don't get mad, get smart," and "Nobody ever does anything for nothing."

After he became chairman of the Education and Labor Committee, Powell was a changed man. "Jesus answered and said unto him, Verily, verily, I say unto thee, Except a man be born again, he cannot see the kingdom of God."*

Becoming a Congressional Chairman was a rebirth for Powell. Widely criticized for his high absenteeism in Congress, Powell began running the Committee with an efficiency and dedication that astonished his most passionate detractors. He put together one of the sharpest staffs on Capitol Hill (and incidentally, the most integrated in the entire Congress), assigned bills with an appreciative eye for the political benefits a particular Congressman might receive back home, cracked the legislative whip on getting out important legislation, and became known among Capitol Hill reporters and

* John 3:3.

most of his associates as one of the most effective—if not *the* most effective
—chairmen in the Congress.

In his five years as Chairman, Powell's Committee passed 60 major pieces
of legislation which included increasing the minimum wage, fair employment practices, aid to elementary and secondary schools, manpower development training act, anti-juvenile delinquency, vocational rehabilitation,
school lunch program, barring discrimination in salaries paid to women for
the same work performed by men, Federal aid for library services and the
war on poverty.

Few could dispute his skilled admiralship in steering a bill through the
hidden reefs of Congressional whims and neuroses. Many times Powell
compromised on a section of a bill in order to get it through the House. At
this kind of maneuvering, nobody could surpass Powell, and his readiness
to compromise always surprised his enemies, who expected the arrogantly
stubborn and egotistical Powell to resist any watering-down of his Committee's bills.

But Powell fervently believed that legislation from his committee would
benefit black people—not a succession of meaningless civil rights bills, but
higher wages and the strong enforcement of antidiscrimination in employment and labor unions.

He took great pride when this fact was recognized, and a high point of his
career was a letter from President Johnson six months before the President
was to become an integral part of the political conspiracy to ruin Powell.
On March 18, 1966, Johnson wrote to Powell:

Dear Adam:
The fifth anniversary of your Chairmanship of the House Education and
Labor Committee reflects a brilliant record of accomplishment.

It represents the successful reporting to the Congress of 49 pieces of bedrock
legislation. And the passage of every one of these bills attests to your ability to
get things done.

Even now, these laws which you so effectively guided through the House are
finding abundant reward in the lives of our people.

The poverty program is rapidly paving new pathways to progress for those
whom the economic vitality of this land had previously bypassed.

The education measures are being translated into fuller opportunities for all
our citizens to develop their God-given talents to their fullest potential.

Minimum wage, long a guarantee of a fair return for an honest day's work,
has been increased and greatly extended.

And the problems of juvenile delinquency are being met and curtailed by
positive and determined action.

Only with progressive leadership could so much have been accomplished by
one Committee in so short a time. I speak for the millions of Americans who
benefit from these laws when I say that I am truly grateful.

Sincerely yours,
Lyndon B. Johnson
(signed)

While Powell was developing his proficiency as Chairman, he was simultaneously perfecting his acquisition of what he has always called his "creature comforts." As dedicated as Powell has always been to black people, to equal rights and justice, to black militancy, to Harlem, to better jobs for black people, to more legislation to improve America, and to the cause of universal liberty and world peace, he has never permitted any of these concerns to interfere with his fondness for the pursuit of pleasure. Most men seek pleasure. Powell was carried away by it.

In 1962, newspapers revealed his sojourn in Paris with two young ladies, both staff members, one white and one colored. A great cry of anguish rose from white America and Powell was denounced in editorials and even criticized publicly by some colleagues. Powell quickly flew home, but that trip was to be resurrected repeatedly and he was christened the "Harlem Globetrotter." Although Powell's travels were neither so extensive nor so frequent as those of certain other Committee Chairmen, Congressmen and Senators, the racist tag, "Harlem Globetrotter," pinned on him by anti-negro columnists stuck and became a part of his reputation.

On a March 6, 1960, evening television show, Powell made a remark that was to lead to a series of costly court battles, a $211,500 judgment eventually reduced to $46,500 which he paid, a criminal contempt order ordering his arrest if he set foot in New York City, a Congressional move to bar him from his seat and a factor in the eventual loss of his Chairmanship and exclusion from Congress in 1967.

Powell called a Harlem woman, Mrs. Esther James, a "bag woman" for the New York City Police Department. (A "bag woman" or "bag man" is a slang term for a person who acts as a go-between between gamblers and the police in collecting pay-offs for police protection for illegal gambling activities.)

Mrs. James sought an apology from Powell, who refused. She then started a million-dollar defamation suit. In February 1961 the television station and the sponsor settled out of court with Mrs. James for $1500 and were both dropped as defendants.

Powell, of course, intended no personal malice. He had never met Mrs. James and knew little about her, except from information which had been passed on to him from what he believed to be reliable sources.

His characterization of Mrs. James on the television show was a public extension of detailed remarks he had made on the House floor concerning the gambling syndicate's activities in Harlem. On January 7, 1960, he made his first public statement on the House floor in which he outlined "New York's Billion Dollar Racket." He included newspaper articles on numbers racket pay-offs to police. He listed names, places and meetings. The articles were from the *New York Times*, the *New York Post* and the *New York Journal-American*. All of them alluded to the existence of the numbers racket with some degree of police protection and, in some instances, connivance.

Then, on February 25th, Powell inserted the name of Mrs. Esther James as "extorting money from gamblers and those operating numbers in the uptown area for the purpose of transmitting this money to police officers." He also listed Mrs. James' address.

Powell's crusade of listing the addresses of "numbers drops," the controlling figures in the Harlem gambling syndicate, and the police refusal to take action against known illegal activities were a source of deep embarrassment to the New York City Police Department. None of them were unhappy when Mrs. James filed suit against Powell.

In fact, her suit was mandatory not only to clear her name, but to clear the reputation of the city police. Unless Powell were found guilty, it would have meant that there might have been some substance to his charges, not necessarily against Mrs. James, but against the police.

During the trial, Powell refused to make an appearance or testify on his own behalf. That was viewed as a serious mistake by many lawyers and friends. It was also believed by other lawyers, rightly or wrongly, that the occasion could be used by the plaintiff to go on a "fishing expedition" on Powell's personal and financial activities and his alleged connections with questionable figures in Harlem.

Naturally, the press and the public sympathized with Mrs. James against Powell. One of his chief journalistic antagonists, who took delight in "exposing" Powell's personal activities, Drew Pearson, supported Mrs. James. On February 14, 1967, after Powell had been asked to step aside and not take his seat, Pearson began to develop pangs of remorse and printed a column in the *Washington Post*, "Powell Accuser Had Long Police Record," in which he detailed Mrs. James' arrest record. Pearson pointed out:

Most courts permit all evidence regarding a plaintiff's career to be placed before the jury. This is because when a plaintiff sues for libel, it's important to see whether he or she has a good reputation and whether it has really been damaged.

However, Mrs. James' police record was ruled out.

Then, in an amazing underhanded tribute to Powell, Pearson wrote:

Charles T. McKinney, who defended the case for Rep. Powell, was handicapped by the fact that his client was as usual busy in Washington and elsewhere. He did not appear in his own defense. Juries are usually charged by the judge that the absence of the defendant cannot be held against him. Attorneys handling the Powell case could not remember whether Judge Aurielo so charged the jury.

McKinney at one point moved for a mistrial because a New York newspaper had published the fact that one juror had heard on television that Rep. Powell was going to attend the trial and the juror had announced this to the other jurors. When Powell did not appear, according to the newspaper account, the jurors showed visible signs of disappointment. Judge Aurielo overruled the motion for a mistrial.

Pearson's about-face was noteworthy. Had the facts of Mrs. James' arrests and these legal technicalities been published at the time of Powell's trial, he might have not been found guilty. But Pearson was one of the many who wanted to ruin Powell.

On April 4, 1963, Powell was finally found guilty and ordered to pay a $211,500 judgment. During the course of the various appeals and other legal strategies, over eighty judges heard the *James* v. *Powell* case as Powell fought vainly to overcome paying the judgment. He was never fully successful, although he did manage to get the sum reduced to the $46,500 which he paid in 1967.

But the most important factor in the jury's finding of guilt was his failure to appear during the trial. Both his non-appearance and Mrs. James' faithful appearance each day apparently touched off deep resentment against Powell and sympathy for Mrs. James. Repeatedly, as the attorney for Mrs. James sought to examine Powell's financial records to determine his ability to pay, he refused to appear in court, and the civil and criminal contempt charges mounted until by 1966, Powell was unable to appear in New York City on any day of the week without being subject to arrest as ordered by State Supreme Court justices.

The public was given the impression, through a barrage of racially hostile and morally sanctimonious editorials and stories, that Powell was "defying the court," a "scofflaw," "placing himself above the law," etc.

One of Powell's most virulent and ancient enemies, the *New York Times*, then launched a crusade to have Powell unseated.

Powell had been a special target of the *Times*' editorial page ever since his accession to the Chairmanship of the Education and Labor Committee.

A confluence of acrimonious denunciations over a period of five years had helped to create a climate of widespread hostility toward Powell which resulted finally in his being unseated by fellow members of the House. The lavish reporting by the press of his statements and the excessive concern for his personal life had been equally vital factors in the white public's contempt and almost visceral animosity for Powell.

But the black community enthusiastically continued to back him throughout the country. In the 1966 election, the Harlem electorate which had suffered exposure to the vitriol of the *New York Times*' editorials thumbed their collective noses at the paper when they re-elected Powell to his twelfth term with 44,991 votes or 74.1 per cent of the vote over his Republican opponent Lassen R. Walsh's 10,637 votes and the *New York Times*-endorsed Richard Prideaux's 3814 votes.

Despite his continued popularity in the black community, Powell's independence, his lack of concern for public opinion about his personal life, his defiance of the New York State courts, his retaining his wife as a staff member, and his continuing association with his secretary, slowly piled up a mountain of public opposition that finally buried him in an avalanche of retribution.

To whites, Powell was an irresponsible demagogue, a racist, pleasure-seeking playboy who was, to Theodore H. White, an "egregious and frightening" exception to the rule that elected Negro officials are, "by and large . . . among the finest men elected anywhere in the country."*

That this was a form of racism was substantiated by a Northern Democratic Congressman who declared in an interview: "Nobody blames me for Howard Smith or H. R. Gross. But whites all over America blame their congressmen for Adam."**

To black people, Adam was their Messiah, a savior, an uncompromising fighter who kept his finger and his fist in the white man's eye, who always heeded their pleas for help in getting a job or a promotion, who could be counted on to scream embarrassingly loud and clear if racial discrimination were involved, who did the unorthodox in ferreting out racial segregation, whose personal courage and defiant style were a symbol of resistance to American segregation and who, above all, gave them a profound pride in the beauty of their black skins.

Whereas most Congressmen would refer the complaint of a serviceman to the Congressman who represented the serviceman's home, Powell made a long-standing practice of investigating any black serviceman's complaint of racial discrimination in the armed services. Frequently, letters to him averaged 100 a week from black servicemen.

He wrote a personal letter every few months to the presidents of the country's 116 predominantly negro colleges to advise them of super-grade openings (GS 16-18) in the Office of Education and to ask for nominations; inform them of the availability of grants to universities from the National Aeronautics and Space Administration for research (in an analysis of universities receiving such grants, he had found only two negro colleges), and apprise them of the procedures in getting summer jobs for their students.

He sent a personal letter to every one of the black students who won a scholarship from the National Achievement Scholarship Fund (the only Congressman to do this).

He put together not only one of the most skilled staffs on Capitol Hill, but the most integrated, and on his Committee staff he employed more black professionals than existed in the entire Congress. Of the five top positions on his Committee—the Special Assistant, the Chief Clerk, the Education

---

* *The Making of the President 1964* by Theodore H. White: Atheneum Publishers, 1965; p. 253.
** *The New Republic*, January 21, 1967; p. 13.

Chief, the Labor Chief and the Staff Director—only the last two were white. The Chief Clerk and the Education Chief were black women. Of the Committee's 24 staff members, 12 or 50 per cent were black. No other Committee in the 16 Committees in the Senate and the 20 Committees in the House were as integrated.

Harlem was a direct beneficiary of his power as Chairman of the Committee. Not only did Harlem's HARYOU-ACT administer a two-million dollar antipoverty program that employed over 400 Harlemites, but members of Abyssinian Baptist Church which he pastored as well as the church itself directly benefited. Ten members of the church were employed by another Harlem anti-poverty program known as ACT and their total salaries came to $90,000. In addition, ACT rented space from Abyssinian, paying the church $45,927 a year in rent and $18,000 in maintenance.

If any black government employee had a complaint—legitimate or not—Powell ordered it investigated. His frequent public denunciations of racial discrimination in the Federal government attracted a constant flow of letters to his desk, each one of which he demanded be investigated and followed through until the situation was resolved.

One classic case of racial discrimination in the Federal government that only Powell was able to end involved a black woman who was a Phi Beta Kappa, had a master's degree in English, yet had remained a GS-5 for 18 years in the Department of Interior, one of the most rigidly segregated departments in the government.

When Powell received her well-written letter, carefully and logically pleading her case, he made the case a source of continuing personal concern. The woman stated she had been to the Urban League, the NAACP, its Washington representative, Clarence Mitchell, Jr. (whom Powell despised and called "Uncle Tom," to his face), and the Federal government's Equal Employment Opportunity officers.

Powell wrote a personal letter to Secretary of the Interior Stewart Udall with whom he had always had a friendly relationship. After an investigation of the woman's case, several meetings, phone calls and exchanges of letters, Udall handwrote a personal note to Powell on January 21, 1966, which said:

Dear Adam:
  It has taken much too long, but my people finally found a good promotion for [the woman's name]. She will serve as a research assistant in my Resource Program Staff at a GS-9 level.

Most sincerely,
Stew

This was the Adam Clayton Powell to whom black people looked. And if white people, such as Theodore H. White, were horrified by his headline-seeking antics, black people were awesomely appreciative of his militant efforts on their behalf.

Although President Johnson was to become an active part of the political conspiracy to strip Powell of his chairmanship, the relationship between the two men was still affable as late as July 21, 1966. On that day, Powell met with the President to discuss legislation. The President told him in their meeting that he was unhappy with the way most of his top black appointees were performing in their jobs. He wanted more vigorous action and he wanted Powell to show them how he (Powell) got things done. Would Powell get the ten top black appointees together for a luncheon ("You know, Adam, what we in Texas call a little barbecue"). Powell agreed, called Louis Martin, Deputy of the Democratic National Committee (whom Powell frequently referred to as a "B.S. artist with no power"), and asked his suggestions for the ten top black appointees. It was agreed, after Powell examined the list Martin had sent him, that those to be invited were: Secretary of HUD, Weaver; Federal Reserve Board member, Andrew Brimmer; Atomic Energy Commission member, Samuel Nabrit; Export-Import Bank member, Hobart Taylor; Director of the Community Relations Service Roger Wilkins; Assistant Secretary of Labor George L. P. Weaver; Assistant Secretary of HEW Lisle Carter; Associate Special Counsel to the President Clifford Alexander; Solicitor General Thurgood Marshall and Director Contract Compliance in the Department of Labor Edward Sylvester.

The meeting was never held. By then, the controversy around Powell was so hot, he thought it best to postpone it and not embarrass the black appointees who might be spotted by the press coming to Powell's office.

The controversy was one of the most dangerous of Powell's stormy career. It was a political struggle which was to lay the foundation for Powell's loss of his chairmanship and subsequent exclusion from Congress.

The principal antagonists were: AFL-CIO president George Meany (who acted only after a long consultation with President Johnson); Representative Frank Thompson (Meany's hatchet-man for the job); Representative Edith Green (a wizened little woman full of so much frustration and hatred for Powell, it almost seemed as if she would burst); Representative Sam Gibbons (the front-man for Thompson's assignment to strip Powell of his chairmanship powers); and Sargent Shriver.

It is difficult to assign priorities to which one was most responsible for "doing in" Powell or which action of the fiery black Congressman sparked the organization of the revolt against him. But five events were to provide the basis for the bitter determination to take away most of Powell's powers as chairman and eventually his chairmanship:

1. His pocket-vetoing of a prized bill of labor's—the situs picketing bill.
2. His postponement of floor action on the War on Poverty bill from June until September.
3. His opposition to Representative Green's sponsorship of an amendment to

an education bill that would have given the District of Columbia the right to elect a school board with independent taxing powers.

4. His assumption of leadership of the "Black Power" movement and decision to call a National Black Power Planning Conference at the request of Stokely Carmichael.

5. His call for the resignation of Sargent Shriver.

Which of the five was most significant cannot easily be determined. But all five situations came together in August and September 1966 in a gargantuan political explosion the repercussions of which will be felt for many years to come in the combat zone of black-white relations.

What really happened behind the scenes in the conspiracy between certain newspaper reporters, Congressmen, labor leaders, political leaders and the White House is a book in itself.*

Since the public has already been immersed in a Roman orgy-style account of the events during Powell's demise in the newspapers and magazines a brief summary will serve here.

Beginning with the public disclosure in August 1966 that Powell's wife had not been receiving her checks although she had been on his Congressional payroll, and a series of trips taken to Miami with a female companion (ostensibly on his way to Bimini, the Bahamas, where he spent considerable time), the House of Representatives launched an investigation in December 1966 under Ohio Representative Wayne Hays (D.-Ohio). Its conclusions stripped Powell of his chairmanship. When the Ninetieth Congress convened on January 10, 1967, he was denied his seat on a temporary basis. (He was asked to "stand aside" and was not administered the oath of office.)

The Speaker of the House was then directed to appoint a Congressional Committee under the chairmanship of Representative Emanuel Celler (D.-N.Y.) whose exhaustive investigations concluded that Powell should be fined and censured for his conduct. But a racist-oriented House of Representatives overrode the Celler Committee recommendations and voted to exclude Powell. He subsequently won re-election in April 1967 by an overwhelming majority in Harlem, but the House refused to recognize the election and Powell remained excluded, as H.Res 278 requires, for the duration of the Ninetieth Congress or until January 1969.

What happened to Powell was prefigured in Georgia in 1966 when the state legislature refused to seat newly elected State Representative Julian Bond of Atlanta, a former public relations officer for the Student Non-

* Because of the author's close association with Powell as a staff member during the fight to strip Powell of his chairmanship, the author has elected not to describe in detail many of the secret meetings between nationally prominent white leaders and the bribes offered to certain politicians for support in the chairmanship battle. Both Powell and the author, however, possess documents and memoranda from other political leaders which substantiate the existence of racism and political conspiracy. The full story will not be told until Powell retires from politics.

Violent Coordinating Committee, because of his public remarks advising young men not to serve in the Vietnam War.

The young and dynamic Bond took his case all the way to the U.S. Supreme Court, which quickly ruled that the denial of his seat was a violation of the First Amendment and a denial of Bond's right to freedom of expression. Bond was re-elected overwhelmingly by his constituency and subsequently seated.

What of Powell's future?

Nobody can prophesy the outcome of one of the most unpredictable political figures in American history. A mercurial personality who has wavered erratically between tub-thumping militancy and cowardly silence, Powell's greatest faults have been his massive egotism, his insensitive arrogance, his inability to discern between friend and foe, his failure to recognize the enormity of the conspiracy against him and his naive conviction that he would always be a member in good standing of the political *Übermensch*. To the end, he honestly believed that somehow he would be bailed out of his troubles as he was in his 1958 defeat of Tammany Hall, his 1960 income tax trial victory and his relative survival during the paring away of his chairmanship in 1966. When one has lived all his life never suffering a serious reverse, it is impossible to believe that finally, at the age of 57, his entire life will cave in.

Powell's good life and his paradise of "creature comforts" which he mercilessly pursued sometimes to the exclusion of political activities were finally dampered. There was nothing wrong with his hedonistic compulsions. What was wrong was that Powell failed to, in the language of the ghetto, "T.C.B."—take care of business. Had he stayed away from Bimini and fought as he had in the 1930's and the 1940's, he could have mobilized the black people of America into a new militancy and new revolutionary concern for true Black Power.

Powell could quickly forget the enemies he had made, because his greatest fault was his inability to harbor a grudge. Powell has never been a "hater." People double-crossed him regularly and a few months later or a few years later, when they returned to him to either ask forgiveness or simply continue to share his friendship, he gave it magnanimously. "The trouble with Adam," it has been remarked, "is that he really believes this Christian stuff. He really believes in forgiving people and they do him in every time." The Clarence Mitchells, the George Meanys, the Frank Thompsons, the Edith Greens, the Sam Gibbons, the *New York Times*, the Irish Catholic and Jewish liberals, the Roy Wilkins, the Whitney Youngs, the John Conyers and finally, the Lyndon B. Johnsons all forgot the great political contributions of Adam Clayton Powell. All forgot his symbolic importance to black people in America. Each of them, for his own special selfish reasons, wanted him expelled from his paradise. Had Powell been more of a Machiavellian, he might have survived. His Christian convictions compelled him to admonish one and all to "Keep the faith, baby." But Machiavelli added a caveat to this injunction. In the chapter from *The Prince* titled "In What Way Princes Must Keep Faith," Machiavelli advised:

. . . A prudent ruler ought not to keep faith when by so doing it would be against his interest, and when the reasons which made him bind himself no longer exist. If men were all good, this precept would not be a good one; but as they are bad, and would not observe their faith with you, so you are not bound to keep faith with them.

Powell could never accept this political truth. Powell cheerily kept the faith with black people and with white politicians, but in the end the whites betrayed him. At the time of this writing a Federal grand jury is inquiring into his Committee activities and may well indict him with the explicit intention of sending him to jail. Even so it would be folly to attempt to predict what will eventually happen to Powell. He may stage a political comeback. He may decide to come out fighting and attempt to regain his old power or he may simply resist the effort to indict him and remain in permanent exile in his Bimini hideaway.

Whatever finally happens, Powell's inner serenity continues to be reflected by his favorite quotation: "I have fought a good fight, I have finished my course, I have kept the faith." (II Timothy 4:7)

Black Politicians of the Future

Within the limitations for maneuverability in the American political system, black politicians can be expected to acquire more power as the ethnic consciousness of the black electorate intensifies. More black public officials will be demanded, and a higher proportion of black representatives in the executive, legislative, and judicial power structure will be sought.

This increased political sophistication of the black electorate will enable black politicians to be more militant and less compromising about their racial background. It is more likely that black politicians, particularly those who can only be elected with a significant black vote, will move toward an Adam Clayton Powell and J. Raymond Jones posture rather than an Edward W. Brooke and William L. Dawson public attitude. Black people will insist that black politicians be strongly identified in the public mind as black politicians, just as the Irish Catholic mayor did in 1906 when he referred to Boston as a "Catholic city."

Symbolic of the "new breed" of black politicians who are considered "soul brothers" by the black electorate yet remain attractive to both the white voter and the white political boss are Cleveland's mayor, Carl Stokes, and Los Angeles State Senator Mervyn Dymally. These two successful black politicians in the new era of "Black Power" and an unknown future for black-white relations have not run away from the fact of their race, yet their militancy has not been of the rancorous variety which alienates their white associates and electorate.

But black politicians will be as diversified as white politicians. There will continue to be black demagogues, black "brown-nosers," black connivers, black strategists, black bosses, black "foxes" and black "lions." There will also be black politicians who will represent predominantly white constituencies. In 1966, the Republicans slated five black men to run against five white Democratic incumbents in predominantly white districts. They were:

NEGRO REPUBLICAN	OPPONENT	CONGRES- SIONAL DISTRICT	PER CENT OF VOTE WON BY NEGRO	PER CENT OF NE- GROES IN DISTRICT
Henri O'Bryant, Jr.	Edward R. Roybal	California, 30th	33.1	15.6
Stephen Maxwell	Joseph E. Karth	Minnesota, 4th	40	1.8
Earl Harris	Peter W. Rodina	New Jersey, 10th	33	8.3
Clarence E. McCleod	Michael A. Feighan	Ohio, 20th	28.4	40
Frederick M. Coleman	Charles A. Vanik	Ohio, 21st	18.4	36

It is interesting to note that the highest percentage of the total vote won by any of the negro Republicans was in the district which had the smallest percentage of black voters. And the two districts with the largest percentage of black voters also had the lowest vote cast for the negro candidate. This pattern reaffirms the domination of party loyalty over race as a factor in deciding the voter's allegiance.

As has already been indicated, the Republican Party has usually taken the leadership in breakthroughs for black candidates in elective offices, and as the above table indicates, it continues this tradition.

The future pattern of black political activity may well result in black Democrats running from predominantly black districts and a few black Republicans running and—as did Edward Brooke in Massachusetts—winning in predominantly white constituencies.

It will be a long time in American politics before black people have another Adam Clayton Powell, with his style, delightful impudence, and power, and J. Raymond Jones, with his imperial manner, back-room machinations in the political machine and his organizational power. They belong already to a great legacy and a tradition of black political power, limited and circumscribed by white political power but nonetheless able to operate effectively in the combat zone of racial politics.

Because these two men lived, maneuvered and schemed—and to some extent, were sacrificed on the altar of white racism—future black politicians will owe them their success.

CHAPTER TEN

1967: Year of the Black Mayor

*For the day of vengeance is in my heart
and the year of mine redeemer is come.*
ISAIAH 63:4

For black people, their "day of vengeance" had begun with the black rebellions of Harlem, Bedford-Stuyvesant, Watts, Newark, Detroit and over
eighty major cities throughout America. But if the rebellions communicated
black discontent and alienation to apathetic whites, they also destroyed black
communities and, in many instances, black businessmen.

While America's black ghettoes were exploding in orgies of violence,
many black leaders were quietly pursuing power through another medium—
politics. They too were angry, and perhaps felt vengeance in their hearts.
But they sought a more constructive redemption through political achievement, especially in 1967.

For black Americans, 1967 was the year of the black mayor. It was a year
that witnessed the election of two black mayors in the eighth and seventieth
largest cities in America—Cleveland, Ohio, and Gary, Indiana.

It was a year that pressured a Texas-reared President to appoint a black
man as the "mayor" of the nation's capital.

It was a year which encouraged black men in six major cities to run
for mayor, and two got elected, for a political batting average of 33 per
cent.

Prior to the election of forty-year-old Carl Burton Stokes as mayor of
Cleveland and thirty-four-year-old Richard Gordon Hatcher as mayor of
Gary, there had already been seven black mayors of predominantly white
cities.

The following table lists them and the populations of their cities as of
1960, according to the U.S. Bureau of Census.

CITY	MAYOR	TOTAL POPULATION	NUMBER OF NEGROES	PER CENT OF NEGROES
Flint, Michigan	Floyd J. McCree	196,940	34,812	17.7
Saginaw, Michigan	Henry G. Marsh	98,265	16,550	16
Springfield, Ohio	Robert E. Henry	82,723	11,838	14
Ypsilanti, Michigan	John H. Burton	20,957	4,671	22
El Centro, California	DuBois McGee	16,811	1,684	10
Milpitas, California	Ben Gross	6,572	277	2
Disinore, California	Thomas Yarborough	2,432	345	14

Several all-black cities even in the North also had black mayors—for instance, Clarence Lee of Kinloch, Missouri (pop. 6501), a suburb of St. Louis.*

But none of the seven black mayors of the predominantly white cities had been elected in a city-wide popular vote, but were either elected mayor or head of the government by the City Council or City Commission.

In addition to the black victories in Cleveland and Gary, a black man, Walter E. Washington, was appointed Commissioner or "mayor" of the nation's capital, 66 per cent black Washington, D.C., by President Johnson under his Executive Reorganization plan accepted by the Congress in 1967. (Prior to Washington's appointment, a three-man Board of Commissioners had governed the city. One of these was the first black man to be appointed a District Commissioner, John B. Duncan, who was appointed by President Kennedy in 1961.) Washington, D.C., the ninth largest city in America, was 55 per cent black when Duncan was appointed.

What made 1967 "The Year of the Black Mayor" was not only the elections of Stokes and Hatcher and the Presidential appointment of Washington, but the candidacies of black men for mayor in the second largest city, Chicago, the fourth largest city, Philadelphia, the twenty-second largest city, Memphis, Tennessee, and the seventy-fifth largest city, Youngstown, Ohio.

In Memphis and Philadelphia, black men ran in the Democratic primary and were defeated; two black men running as independents in Philadelphia

* On May 21, 1968, a fifty-four-year-old black man, Matthew G. Carter, was sworn in as mayor of Montclair, N.J., a predominantly white suburban community of 43,000 residents. While not elected by a popular vote, Carter received the highest number of votes for the town's five commissioners (all white), and in turn, they elected him mayor. The town is approximately 25 per cent black. Carter is an executive of the Y.M.C.A.

were also defeated. In Youngstown, the Republican candidate for mayor, a black man, was defeated by the incumbent Democrat.

A black man also ran for mayor in the Westchester community of Mount Vernon. The Reverend Samuel Austin ran third in a three-way race with 3794 votes, or 14 per cent of the total vote of 26,751. A candidate of the "New Voice Party," he was opposed by the Democratic-Liberal incumbent mayor, Joseph P. Vaccarella, and the Republican-Conservative candidate, August P. Petrillo, who defeated the incumbent, 14,173 to 8784.

In this sleepy New York City bedroom town of 72,918, with an approximately 20 per cent Italian population and a 30 per cent black population, the candidates of both major parties were Italian. This was not unusual in view of the organizational expertise of Italians in unifying their small proportion of the population to virtually take over a city (as they have done in Newark) and the publicized invasion in Mount Vernon of the Italian-controlled gambling syndicate. On the other hand, the city's black people were able to give the Reverend Austin only 14 per cent of the total vote. He did, however, carry all twelve predominantly black districts in the city's twenty-one. It was the first time a black man had ever run for mayor in any of the communities of Westchester County, one of the country's wealthiest areas. A black man running for mayor in an upper-middle-class suburban community was one more political development establishing 1967 as "The Year of the Black Mayor."

The following chart summarizes the results in the candidacies of black men for mayor of their cities. (Population statistics, 1960 Census.)

CITY	RANK ORDER	TOTAL POPU-LATION	NUMBER OF NEGROES	PER CENT OF NEGROES	BLACK CANDIDATE	RESULTS	PER CENT OF TOTAL VOTE
Chicago	2	3,550,404	837,656	23.6	Dick Gregory	defeated in primary	2
Philadelphia	4	2,002,512	535,033	26.7	Lenerte Roberts	defeated in primary	2
Philadelphia	4	2,002,512	535,033	26.7	Cecil Moore Rev. L. L. Smalls	defeated in election	1 0.8
Cleveland	8	876,050	253,108	28.9	Carl B. Stokes	elected	50.8
Washington, D.C.	9	763,956	418,693	54.8	Walter E. Washington	appt. by President	
Memphis	22	497,524	184,725	37.1	A. W. Willis, Jr.	defeated in primary	12
Gary	70	178,320	69,340	38.9	Richard G. Hatcher	elected	50.6
Youngstown	75	166,689	31,905	19.1	Hugh Frost	defeated in election	21

An October 1967 report, "Social and Economic Conditions of Negroes in the United States," prepared jointly by the U.S. Bureau of Census and the Bureau of Labor Statistics (BLS Report No. 332), revealed that the percentage of black people in major cities had significantly increased. The

BLS estimate for the percentage of black people in the thirty largest cities in 1965 included five of the seven cities where black men had run for mayor (or were appointed, as in Washington) in 1967:

	1960	1965
Chicago	23%	28%
Philadelphia	26	31
Cleveland	29	34
Washington, D.C.	54	66
Memphis	37	40

The noticeable change to black people of their demographic status was watched more intently by aspiring black politicians. Most of the incumbent negro politicians had already made their peace with the white political machines that have stifled black progress. They could not be expected to challenge a system in which they had a vested interest for personal survival. Black insurgents, impatient, hungry for power, exhilarated by a new pride in the political leadership of black people and contemptuous of the black Rip Van Winkles in power, had begun to champ at the restraining bit of second-classmanship.

If nobody could agree on a precise definition of Black Power, a self-evident component was political power. Black Power meant, among other things, that black people should have more power and that this power should be in the decision-making councils of government.

At the same time, the black rebellions were firing up the discontent of the black masses for something more than a change in their cultural impoverishment. They wanted a hand in helping to effect the change. This was the real meaning of the year of the black mayor, 1967. For the first time, black people would do more than participate in the process of government: they would help control it.

In Youngstown, O., the Republican Party, as it has done in several history-making efforts, slated a black man as its candidate for mayor against the Democratic incumbent, Mayor Anthony B. Flask.

Hugh Frost, a two-hundred-fifty-pound former fullback at Bluffton College and director of a community center in a low-income ghetto, was confronted with two obstacles: his black skin in a city with only a 20 per cent black population and a preponderantly Democratic electorate.

Nevertheless, he polled a respectable 17,500 votes, or 31 per cent, out of some 54,000 votes cast. The mayor beat him by only approximately 10,000 votes and as Frost chuckled later in an interview, "They had predicted I would lose by 20,000 or 30,000 votes."

Not only did he pull the usual faithful, predominantly white Republican minority, but he attracted a considerable number of black votes to the Republican Party for the first time. Thus, a City Council which had long consisted of six Democrats and one lone Republican for the first time shifted to four Democrats and three Republicans due to Frost's pulling power in both the white and black communities. One of the Democrats is a black man.

The former athlete, who was the first black man to run for the board of education and led the ticket in his victory, plans to stay in politics. "Who knows, with all of these changes," he mused in an interview last February, "Youngstown could eventually elect a Negro mayor."

Philadelphia is a Democratic stronghold whose voters have been carefully nourished on the succulent patronage of the Democratic machine. When the party split over the designation of incumbent Mayor J. H. Tate, an affable Irish Catholic political mediocrity, the Republicans were convinced they could capture City Hall with an attractive, articulate, brilliant Jewish attorney, Arlen Specter. Considered by many to be more liberal toward black people than Tate, Specter also counted on a solid vote from the city's 100,000 registered Jewish voters.

Several black people also eyed the race as an opportunity to test their fledgling political wings in the black community for future leadership. One was Lenerte Roberts, a black real-estate dealer. But Roberts' candidacy was not viewed as a serious one by the black community. He had no widespread backing, and had not built up a large organization to challenge the Goliaths downtown. When the results were counted on primary day, May 16, 1967, Roberts ran a poor third with only 5593 votes, or 1 per cent of the total.

Two prominent civil-rights activists, fiery, mercurial, and flamboyant Cecil Moore, an attorney and popular president of the local NAACP, and the Reverend Leonard L. Smalls decided to run as independents in the November race. Moore ran on the Political Freedom Rights Party ticket and Smalls ran on the Consumers Party ticket.

Moore polled a feeble 8775 votes, or 1 per cent of the total, and Smalls did even worse, with only 6409 votes or .8 per cent of the total of 717,182 votes cast.

Both black men discovered a political fact of life that has plagued the progress and the capability of the civil-rights movement to achieve meaningful power: Civil-rights leaders can rarely transfer the popularity of their movement and personal leadership to the brass-knuckles arena of politics. This happened in Chicago when prominent civil-rights leader A. A. Rayner was soundly whipped by Congressman Dawson in the April 1964 Democratic primary, and three years later it had happened in Philadelphia.

History repeated itself in Chicago on April 4, 1967, when nationally known comedian and civil-rights activist Dick Gregory ran for mayor and polled only 20,775 votes, or 1.9 per cent of the total vote cast, 1,082,893. But Gregory's 20,775 votes represented a very respectable 19 per cent of the approximately 216,166 black votes cast in the predominantly black 2nd, 3rd, 4th, 6th, 8th, 17th, 20th, 21st, 24th and 29th wards. In addition to the usual stumbling blocks of running as an independent (built-in voter resistance, inability of voters to understand an independent's platform, lack of publicity, etc.), Gregory was confronted with the almost superhuman exercise of running as a write-in candidate.

Chicago is perhaps one of the most notoriously corrupt cities in America on election day (and the other 364 days of the year as well). When there is a way to steal votes, Chicago's political machines find it. No electoral system or ballot or machine has been invented that an imaginative Chicago precinct captain cannot successfully contaminate or "fix."

Write-in ballots require a precise method of writing in the candidate's name. Some election officials, with straight faces, told many voters seeking a ballot to write in Gregory's name that they were all out of ballots. Others required the voter to "Step aside, honey, for a minute and I'll take care of you. Got to get these folks in that election booth first." The voter ended up waiting an hour and leaving in disgust.

The other problem that crippled Gregory's final vote tally was the image of frivolity attending his campaign. A comedian must convince the voters he is sufficiently well qualified in the intricacies of government to successfully administer it. Gregory's reputation as a concerned and dedicated citizen attempting to rectify the gross racial injustices of the Daley administration was enough to substantiate his political candidacy. But Gregory spent as much time out of the city fulfilling speaking and entertainment engagements (and participating in civil-rights demonstrations) as he did in campaigning in Chicago. Consequently, a sizable number of people who might have been inclined to vote for any alternative to Mayor Daley shrugged their shoulders at Gregory's almost Alice-in-Wonderland candidacy, held their noses, and voted for Daley again.

The *Chicago Daily Defender*, one of the two black daily newspapers in the country, which has consistently backed black political independence in any place but Chicago, renewed its lease on the Daley plantation and endorsed Mayor Daley against Gregory.

Another city where black voters were to turn their backs on a black candidate was Memphis, Tenn. That brilliant political strategist Republican Robert R. Church, who ran black politics in Memphis in the 1920's and was one of the most powerful black politicians in America, would have turned in his grave at the thought of black people failing to support a black candidate for mayor some forty years later.

But the defeat of Tennessee State Representative A. W. Willis, Jr., in the Democratic primary on October 5, 1967, was due to only one fact: Black people did not vote for him.

Ever since Bob Church's regime, the vote in Memphis has always been roughly 66 per cent white and 33 per cent black. In 1967, there were approximately 78,000 registered black voters in the total of 235,000 registered voters.

In 1963, Willis, a forty-two-year-old militant civil-rights lawyer, won election to the state legislature, where there were already five black representatives. On August 8, 1967, he decided to run for mayor of Memphis, figuring that if he could win 90 per cent of the black vote and pick up at least 15 to 20 per cent of the white vote, he could be elected mayor. Willis was certain that the 90 per cent of the black vote he confidently expected to support his candidacy guaranteed him a sure place in the run-off. He could not have been more wrong.

Memphis, by the standards of Stone's Index of Proportional Equality, had not made the progress to which the black percentage of the electorate entitled it. There were no black persons on the city-wide elected five-member board of education; one criminal court judge out of the city's six judges was black; and the only black man heading a department within the city administration headed the department of hospitals. Its three black city councilmen represented 23 per cent of the thirteen-man city council (seven elected from districts and five elected at large).

While there has always been a political sophistication in the black community that was geared to the realities of Southern life, it had never been tested as an independent force. Ever since Bob Church first organized the black community to do business with the Democrats or the Republicans and the famed E. H. Crump machine ran the city as a personal extension of Crump's household, black people had dutifully voted as the machine wanted them to—and like Chicago's black voters, they were political slaves to the white man's political dogma.

Willis recognized this problem when he announced his candidacy. "This campaign is raising for the first time the real problems of racial inferiority," he declared in an interview on September 29 in the *New York Times*. "The Negro has been taught to be inferior." Then, in one of the most eloquently precise summations of the black man's subculture mentality, Willis declared: "He [the negro] thinks the white man's ice is colder, his sugar is sweeter, his medicine is better."

Willis was troubled with an additional problem besides the two of the black man's self-concept of inferiority and his expected limited percentage of the total vote. As the president of a savings and loan association and a realty and mortgage company, Willis evidenced all of the earmarks of the "black bourgeoisie." During some of his campaigns in the ghetto, opinions were expressed that "he's not really one of us" or "he's gotten so big and rich, he ain't a 'soul brother' no more."

Untrue, these statements still had their impact and were encouraged by the camps of Willis's two chief opponents, Mayor William B. Ingram and former mayor Henry Loeb.

Mayor Ingram had not only been popular among some black voters, but it was widely circulated among black people that even if Willis did win in the run-off, he never could be elected mayor, so casting a vote for Willis was a futile effort. Others resented the fact that the influential black-oriented Shelby County Democratic Club was headed by a prominent dentist, Dr. Vasco Smith. "It's gotten too big for its britches and it thinks it owns the colored vote," said one minister.

"Many ministers who had been on the fence in the contest became anti-Willis after Rep. John Conyers (D., Mich.) came in and scolded them for not showing more enthusiasm," wrote Moses J. Newsom, staff correspondent for the Afro-American newspaper chain, in an October 10 dispatch. Willis continued to campaign about the mayor's failure to appoint more black people to jobs. Using figures compiled by the Shelby County Democratic Club, Willis pointed out that as of June 30, 1967, black voters had but 246 jobs, or 8 per cent of the total, at City Hall, although black people comprised 40 per cent of the population.

On election day, the obstacles placed in Willis's path to City Hall tripped him. Of a total of 144,888 votes cast, he only won 17,744 votes, or a humiliating 12 per cent. He placed fourth in a field of seven, running far behind the former mayor who led with 47,778; the mayor with 36,074; and Shelby County Sheriff William N. Morris, with 30,979.

Both the mayor and former mayor garnered more black votes than Willis. According to Newsom:

Another interesting factor brought up repeatedly is the way Ingraham appears to have held the loyalty of colored voters and that of Bill (Bo) Turner, a taxicab owner who has friends in the White Citizens Council.

"The next day after Ingram named Tom Hayes (a colored businessman) to the transit authority, he put Bo Turner on the aviation commission," one complained.

Apparently members of the Shelby County Democratic Club did not realize how deeply divided the community was until the returns started pouring in there and at Willis's headquarters in the downtown King Cotton Hotel.

But, demeaning as Willis's crushing defeat was, his political baptism in the higher councils of power still left its imprint on the black voters. Willis made several mistakes—bringing in the abrasive and uninspiring Congressman Conyers to campaign for him, as well as not doing enough "nitty-gritty" campaigning among the "soul brothers." The educational benefits of this political exercise will not be lost on black people, and if the various factions in the black community can be unified under a Bob Church-type leadership, black people in Memphis may be able to elect themselves a black mayor in the near future. But, before that happens, they will have to clear their minds of cant and accept the fact that the white man's ice is not colder, his sugar is not sweeter, nor is his medicine better.

The Black Capital

One of the ironic political anomalies in the United States today is its capital, Washington, D.C.

In a country which has a national black population of 22,000,000 or approximately 12 per cent of the total, the District of Columbia is 66 per cent black. To most Southerners, D.C. is already a lost cause because of the saturation of so many niggers.

This black inundation has prevented Washington from being granted home rule—in the capital of the world's second largest democracy, the people cannot vote to govern themselves. Washington is ruled or "governed" by Congress. Because after hours Congress is invariably too busy attending to more important affairs of state such as frequent junkets abroad, late night parties in their offices, an endless series of Bacchanalian delights in private clubs, the business of the District is left to two committees and two subcommittees, the House Committee on District Affairs, the Senate Committee on District Affairs, the House Subcommittee on Appropriations for D.C. and the Senate Subcommittee on Appropriations for D.C.

This fact endows the chairmen of these committees and subcommittees with the power of life and death over the District budget and, in effect, the District itself.

Two Southern racists, Representative John McMillan of South Carolina and Senator Robert Byrd of West Virginia, a former organizer for the Ku Klux Klan, are the respective Chairmen of the House District Affairs Committee and the Senate Subcommittee on Appropriations for the District of Columbia. They are the most active watchdogs over the District budget and, as a result, exert enormous influence over their private plantation. It has been their long-standing opposition to home rule for Washington that has bottled up this democratic right in a galaxy of race hate, the belief that the nation's capital "belongs to all the people, i.e., the Congress" and the desire to maintain control for all of the personal favors and privileges Congressmen receive from District officials.

Unable to get a home-rule bill past the Southern-oriented House, although such a bill had passed the Senate three times in the last six years, President Johnson sent through an Executive Reorganization plan which, if not opposed by the House, would become law.

The plan went into effect, replacing the three-man Board of Commissioners, one of whom was its first black man, John Bonner Duncan. When President Kennedy came into power, he was dismayed by the ineffectual administration of the Board (actually, there was nothing wrong with the Board that three vital and courageous Commissioners could not have changed), and he appointed a Special Assistant with the implied power of the President's office to get things done.

Under a sensitive and intelligent President, this system worked, and many improvements in the operation of the District were effected. Under Johnson, a man of few sensitivities and questionable intelligence, the system broke down. Johnson finally came to the conclusion that a single commissioner or "mayor" was needed. His reorganizational plan made the change. In addition, the new plan provided for a nine-man city council with a chairman and vice chairman.

After the plan was finally approved, the great ethnic balancing act began. If the Commissioner was black, then the Deputy Commissioner should be white and vice versa. If the Council chairman was white, then the vice-chairman had to be black or vice versa. It was a comedy in the balance of ethnic equities.

Johnson then began the search for a Commissioner. As he had done with the Secretaryship of Housing and Urban Development, he offered the position to several nationally prominent white men (one of them, the former Republican Mayor of Baltimore, Theodore McKeldin, publicly stated he had turned the offer down because of his age). And just as he had also done with the HUD post, Johnson finally appointed a black man, Walter E. Washington, to the post of commissioner or "mayor" when he could not find the white man he had wanted to accept the post.

A white man, Thomas Fletcher, an urban renewal expert, was appointed deputy mayor. Continuing the interethnic balancing act, Johnson appointed a white man as council chairman and a black man, the Reverend Walter E. Fauntroy, the Washington representative of the Southern Christian Leadership Conference, as vice chairman.

Of the nine Council appointees, five were black—and four were criticized in many segments of the black community: "Unrepresentative of the black community," "Uncle Toms and Aunt Jemimas," "Unknown," "Little involvement in the leadership of the black community." Once again, Johnson only verified what he had slowly established in his administration—that he was only going to appoint black people who were so painfully conservative and submissive that they would become faceless blobs in the stagnant swamp of the Johnson administration. Fauntroy was the lone exception to this rule. But his involvement in an urban-renewal project in the area of his church required that even this courageous minister mute his militant statements.

After Walter Washington was appointed, the Senate committee which approves such appointments held hearings. Prominent civic, political, and religious leaders all endorsed Washington, a former executive director of the National Capital Housing Authority in D.C. and more recently the director of the New York City Housing Authority. The only opposition to Washington's appointment came from the Washington Committee for Black Power, which declared that Washington, an "Uncle Tom," would make no meaningful changes in the District government. The Committee pointed out, in its statement, that: 1) Of the forty major agencies that govern D.C., only five, or 10 per cent, were headed by black people; 2) As of June 1966 the 206 D.C. government jobs, GS 14 and above, employed only twenty-seven black people or 12 per cent of the total; 3) Of the five Federal agencies which have statutory responsibility for D.C., not one is headed by a black man. These agencies are the D.C. Redevelopment Land Agency, the D.C. Armory Board, the National Capital Planning Commission, the National Capital Transportation Agency, and the Washington City Post Office; 4) Of the 2081 skilled trades apprentices in the District of Columbia, only 384, or 18.5 per cent, were black, nor was there a single black journeyman glazier, lather, pipefitter, plumber, sheet metal worker, tile and terrazzo worker, machinist, photoengraver, or nonconstruction painter in Washington; 5) Of all the black people living in D.C. slums or substandard housing, 87 per cent are black, and of those families in the District earning $3000 or less, 83 per cent are black.

The Committee declared it did not believe Washington was either capable or would have the power to solve such critical problems. It also pointed out an indication of Presidential racism, the apppointment of J. C. Turner, secretary of the District Central Labor Federation, to the City Council. Turner, said the Committee, had been as responsible for black exclusion from labor unions in the District as any man in Washington. Nevertheless, Johnson appointed him to the Council. As expected, Washington's appointment was enthusiastically confirmed by the Senate, as were all of the other appointments.

The future of the "two Washingtons"—the city and the mayor—will depend upon the willingness of a balky Congress to loosen the tight purse strings with which it has strangled the District. The crisis in the 93 per cent black schools providing inferior education, the ongoing unemployment rate among black people, still two and one-half times that of whites, the continuing black migration from the South into D.C. in search of the promised land, and the worsening tensions between black and white in other major cities will determine whether the nation's capital will be permitted to join the exclusive club for "whites only" and govern its own affairs.

But, unfortunately, much of the city's development must still rely on Congressional good will. A slow-rising mood of racial antagonism in Congress does not augur a future of progress for this blackest of American cities.

The Charisma of Blackness

In the new revolutionary era of Black Power and black pride, black people have begun to develop an ethnic consciousness of their political capabilities that is rooted solely in blackness. No longer need a black man apologize for his black skin in a subconscious hope that white people, too, will be inclined to overlook its white-originated odium. And just as John "Honey Fitz" Fitzgerald as Boston's first Irish Catholic mayor could proudly refer in 1906 to "this Catholic city," black people over a half century later could finally discover a dignity and power in the color of the skin of a black mayor.

"Black," as applied to a race of people, covers any person who is not only black, but brown, light-skinned, fair-skinned, mulatto, café au lait, or even white. The last would require a public self-identification as a black man—as have done Adam Clayton Powell and the late Walter White, the blue-eyed and dove-skinned executive secretary of the NAACP, who looked more like a Scandinavian than a black man.

Thus, "black," as Powell has repeatedly said, is a way of thinking, not a skin color. Many are the fair-skinned, mulatto, or white negroes who are far more "black" in their thinking than many black men.

A one-company-dominated city of 175,000, Gary is the home of U.S. Steel, which employs over 16,000 workers. It is a depressingly typical American city with all the ethnic conflicts, race hate, and crises of air pollution, transportation, urban decay, and inferior education plaguing all cities. For years, it has been a balanced composite of Czechoslovakians, Poles, Hungarians, Irish, Greeks, Jews, Latin-Americans, and, more recently, blacks. A community where gambling and prostitution were carried on openly, Gary was known for its corruption, its stagnancy, and its hard-working population.

As rapidly as whites left the city, blacks moved in, and by 1966, black people were a majority of the population. This fact was not lost on the Democratic Party, which controlled the city, and there were whispers of a black candidate for mayor in the 1967 election.

The incumbent mayor, A. Martin Katz, had probably done more for black people than any previous mayor. Under his administration, every city commission was integrated for the first time, and black men were appointed as corporation counsel (third-ranking city official), superintendent of sanitation, deputy controller, assistant director of general services, and two assistant fire chiefs. Katz also appointed thirty-two black men as firemen, as many as had been appointed in the entire fifty-seven-year history of Gary. But this was still not enough, as far as many black leaders were concerned. Richard Gordon Hatcher was one of them. Gary was now a black city. Black people should control it or have a majority share in its administration.

By Stone's Index of Proportional Equality, Gary was more advanced than any other city in America, yet it still fell short of fulfilling an ideal pattern. Of the twenty-six city departments, only two, or 7 per cent, were headed by black people. Of Gary's four state representatives, none was black. In the nine-man city council, three, or 33 per cent, were black (including Hatcher, who had been elected as one of three at-large councilmen). Both the judges serving Gary, the City Court judge and the Criminal Court judge, were white, the former Jewish and the latter Irish. According to an Indiana Civil Rights Commission report which Hatcher used extensively in his campaign, only 28 per cent of the 2000 City Hall jobs were held by black people.

In the fall of 1966, Hatcher began to think seriously about running for mayor. He knew he would never be acceptable to the Gary political machine because of what many of the more conservative leaders regarded as his extremist views on many subjects. In an interview in the Black Muslims' newspaper *Muhammad Speaks* in the September 16, 1966, issue, Hatcher covered everything from black power to the war in Vietnam:

> As far as I'm concerned, the white community's interpretation of black power is irrelevant. Before a white man can talk to me about this, he'll first have to talk about white power which has been exercised so ruthlessly against black people. When he explains that, I'll talk about black power.
>
> If a man bombs my home, from a plane or any other way, and he is caught, I would demand that he be tried. Why can't the North Vietnamese try men who are bombing their homes? In any event, the United States should certainly find a way to get out of Vietnam. It's getting worse instead of better, and there is no way of winning against the huge forces of Asia.

The article, entitled "Struggle for Black Power in Gary," indicated that Hatcher had not decided to run for mayor then, but "modestly agrees that he would have an excellent chance of winning."

Hatcher's black militancy made him anathema to the essentially conservative political machine, and he knew that in 1971, when the Democratic Party was almost certain to slate a black man for mayor, he would not be that man. The favorite would more likely be Dr. Alexander Williams, a successful physician who had made history by becoming elected as the first black Lake County Coroner. Williams was as fair of skin as Hatcher was black. Had Williams had less integrity and a sense of honor, he would have been Gary's mayor today, instead of Hatcher. But Williams kept the faith, and it was a black man, not a white man, who broke it. What happened was a series of events that subsequently made Hatcher's election possible.

The behind-the-scenes political boss of Gary is George Chacharis, a well-read, friendly, burly Greek who had risen from a steel worker to become mayor of Gary. Convicted of income-tax evasion, Chacharis served time and then was released from the Federal penitentiary, returning to Gary to assume his former position as boss of the party. Chacharis had broken with Mayor Katz for political reasons and approached Williams in 1966 to run for election. With Chacharis' support, Williams would have won. But the coroner, who believed in fair play (an old-fashioned commodity in today's cauldron of corrupt politics), asked Chacharis for time to consider the request. He instead approached Katz, informed him of the offer and asked his reaction. Katz replied he knew Williams could defeat him with Chacharis' backing, but that he (Katz) strongly felt he deserved a second chance in adhering to the political tradition of Gary that "one good term deserves another." He also pointed out to Williams that the reason he (Katz) was in political trouble was because of his liberalism in racial appointments, which the white community deeply resented. Williams agreed, decided to support Katz for re-election, and so informed Chacharis, who in turn agreed to support Katz.

Hatcher subsequently announced his candidacy and put together a team of the strangest political bedfellows ever assembled. White radicals, black nationalists, upper-middle-class blacks, winos, black mothers on welfare, and wealthy Jewish businessmen, they were united in one cause—to defeat the machine and Katz. This could only be done by electing Hatcher.

Also announcing his opposition to Katz for the Democratic nomination was Bernard Konrady, who quickly became tagged as the white backlash candidate. The campaign was one of Gary's most violent in years. The tone was set when a top Hatcher aide, Jesse Bell, a public school teacher, was accused in a story in the *Gary Post-Tribune* on March 30, 1967, of having told an all-black audience in January: "All methods should be used to expose the Uncle Toms in this city and we should use whatever methods possible, including violence, in order to meet our goals."

Bell denied the charges, but they opened the floodgates for a wave of threats, intimidations of black people, and black party officials supporting Katz. Bricks were thrown through windows, tires of Katz supporters were deflated, and businessmen on the main thoroughfare of Broadway in the ghetto were told to put Hatcher signs in their windows or risk possible physical injury. Dr. Williams and his wife were threatened so often with personal violence by telephone calls and late night visitations that it became necessary for Williams to purchase a .38-caliber pistol, which he carried in the last couple of weeks of the campaign as he drove around the city speaking for Katz. April 19, in the early hours of the morning, a Molotov cocktail was thrown through the window of the pro-Katz black weekly newspaper, *The Gary Crusader*.

Katz campaigned hard in both the black and white communities, but he was like a man trying to keep his finger in the dike against white racism while the earthquake of black power was crumbling the earth beneath him. On May 2, 1967, Katz was chopped up between a defecting white vote for Konrady and a defecting black vote for Hatcher. The results were: Hatcher, 20,272; Katz, 17,910; Konrady, 13,133.

The voting was strictly along racial lines. Hatcher received 75 per cent of the black vote; Katz, 24 per cent (his headquarters had estimated that he needed to retain a minimum of 30 per cent of the black vote to defeat

Hatcher); and Konrady, 1 per cent. Among the white voters in the pre-
dominantly white 1st, 2nd, and 6th districts, Konrady captured 46 per cent,
Katz 45 per cent (doing far better than he anticipated among whites), and
Hatcher 7 per cent.

Hatcher did almost no campaigning, accurately concluding that Katz
and Konrady would decimate each other in the white community, and the
near solid black vote would elect him. After the election, Hatcher made no
effort to make his peace with the Democratic machine, which then announced it would not support him. Denied funds, Hatcher went on a national campaign and took out a full-page in the *New York Times* headlined,
"For God Sakes, Let's Get Ourselves Together," in which he appealed for
funds. He became the focus of national publicity, and Senator Robert
Kennedy gave a fund-raising party for him in New York City.

In the face of the now-united white vote against him and an informal
alliance of the Republicans and white Democrats, he knew he needed a
small percentage of the white vote to win. Many white Americans looking
for a peaceful antidote to the black violence overrunning American cities
saw in Hatcher a chance to stem the revolutionary tide and enthusiastically
supported his candidacy with financial contributions.

In Gary, just enough white Democrats remained loyal to the party for
Hatcher to win, and he defeated the Republican candidate, Joseph B.
Radigan, a very unimpressive businessman whose bland exterior as much
as his party affiliation cost him victory.

The final tally was: Hatcher, 39,330; and Radigan, 37,941.

The vote once again divided on racial lines, with Hatcher winning 91
per cent of the black vote and Radigan winning 83 per cent of the white
vote. The 6762 white votes Hatcher received were more than sufficient for
his 1389-vote margin of victory.

The City Council acquired another black man and is now divided, four
blacks, four whites, and one Latin American.

Hatcher's biggest campaign issues were corruption in Gary and "crime in
the streets," a phrase that has been useful for white reactionaries. But it
paid off, and white voters supported him in the hope that he could, indeed,
make the streets safe. Hatcher kept his promise to black voters that he would
make more black appointments and appointed as his administrative assistant
the firebrand Jesse Bell; as fire chief sixty-year-old Alphonso Holliday, a
forty-year veteran of the fire department, who had been appointed assistant
fire chief by Katz, but who nevertheless supported Hatcher during the campaign; corporation counsel Hilbert Bradley, replacing a black man, Laurence
Anderson, a Katz loyalist; and for the first time in Gary's history, a black
controller, forty-eight-year-old businessman Maurice Baptiste, the second-
highest ranking city official, who would succeed Hatcher were anything
to happen to him.

In line with his anticrime crusade, Hatcher appointed a white police department veteran who had headed the narcotics squad for twelve years, forty-one-year-old Detective Sergeant James Hilton. White men were appointed as city engineer and head of the city planning department. The Gary administration was finally and truly integrated.

Gary's future—and Hatcher's—will depend on the capacity of his administration to solve the rising crime rate, clean up corruption, and bring new urban renewal projects into Gary with Federal money (public housing is desperately needed, but has been vigorously opposed by whites since white areas are the only place such building construction could take place), and on his ability to tap U.S. Steel's till for more tax money (Hatcher claims it is not paying its way for the land it now occupies in Gary).

Problems of air pollution, downtown revitalization and slum eradication are all tied to the other, more pressing problems. It will take months and may take years before the scars of racial bitterness injected into the campaign are healed. Certainly, Hatcher, an early public advocate of black power whose attraction to many black people was based on his forthright advocacy of the new doctrine, was as much to blame for the hostilities engendered in both campaigns as any man. His silence on the violence of his followers and his subtle playing off of white radicals against black militants did not help.

How deeply Gary felt about this election was witnessed by the fact that of 103,077 registered voters, 77,271, or almost 75 per cent, turned out, exceeding the previous high of 72,890 who voted in the 1964 Presidential race.

Perhaps, in an unexpected way, the creative disorder of racial tensions is a revitalizing force for American democracy. When people feel passionately about something, they will get out and vote as they did in Gary. Black people obviously felt more strongly about electing Hatcher than white people did about defeating him, and the proportion of black voters was higher than that of whites.

If Hatcher can channel the black jubilation and the white fears into a workable alliance within the political crucible, it is possible he will have engineered a great experiment in American democracy. Hatcher, a taciturn, unattractive person, eventually will need to go beyond the emotionalism of his skin-black charisma and forge an administration to build Gary and not Hatcher. They go together, and the extent to which Hatcher can submerge his personal ambitions for the good of Gary will determine Gary's survival as a viable American city.

Shining New Black Star

In 1965, Cleveland, eighth largest city in America, was in search of an identity. Under the dull, unimaginative leadership of its mayor, Ralph S.

Locher, a machine-picked candidate of excruciating mediocrity, Cleveland was wallowing in the doldrums of political lethargy and civic indifference. No urban-renewal programs had been initiated, no planning undertaken (causing the Department of Housing and Urban Development to cut off Federal funds until such planning had been submitted), violent demonstrations had been mounted in protest against the school system's increasing de facto segregation, and racial tensions were so thick that they could almost be cut with a machete. The Democratic Party's apathy toward municipal black progress, as exemplified by Chicago's Mayor Daley, was taking a safe, stand-pat, do-nothing position on most civic problems.

A handsome, cultured, and successful attorney, Carl B. Stokes, was the first black man to be elected to the state senate from Cleveland. Stokes felt entitled to a place on the ticket in 1965 because of his outstanding vote-getting record and his quick rise in politics. The Democratic Party thumbed its nose at him, and Stokes announced he was a candidate for mayor. At first, nobody took him seriously, but they reckoned without Stokes's perseverance, which has marked his entire political career. He also did something that Hatcher did not do in the primary—Stokes campaigned in white neighborhoods. For the most part, however, he confined his campaigning to black neighborhoods in the belief that a split white vote against Locher and his opponents and a united black vote would win him the Democratic nomination. Even the very Republican weekly black newspaper, the *Cleveland Call-Post*, supported Stokes. Despite repeated newspaper stories that accorded him every chance to win, black voters stayed home and Stokes lost by 2458 votes.

Like Gary, Cleveland is an ethnic hodgepodge which embraces about 125,000 Polish-Americans, 75,000 Slovaks, 50,000 German-Americans, and sizable numbers of Italian and Czechoslovakians. (An Italian, Anthony Celebrezze, had been mayor before Locher and resigned to become HEW Secretary under President Kennedy).

After Stokes's defeat and Locher's re-election, Cleveland was watched closely for signs of racial progress. The city's race relations had been deteriorating slowly since April 7, 1964, when a white minister, the Reverend Bruce Klunder, had thrown himself under a bulldozer during a protest at a school site and was crushed to death.

In the summer of 1966, Cleveland experienced its first two violent holocausts. The first, on June 24, was only a mild prelude, when black teen-agers stoned white motorists, one of whom shot a black youth. Then, on July 18, Cleveland erupted into a five-day binge of violence in the ghetto known as Hough, with people attacking police and firemen with firearms and firebombs.

On April 16, 1967, more violence exploded in the Hough area. Cleveland was a city slowly sliding downhill. Once again, Stokes took the plunge. This time, however, he was viewed as a serious threat. The black community also was convinced he could win, and Stokes's election headquarters was in the building of the black Republican *Cleveland Call-Post*. The black community was united.

Unlike Hatcher, Stokes campaigned vigorously in the white community, for, unlike Hatcher, he needed white votes to win the primary. He sought them at meetings in the white enclaves and impressed whites with his logic, his brilliant analysis of the city's problems, and his program for progress.

On primary day, October 3, Stokes's strategy was rewarded. Whereas only 60 per cent of the white vote turned out, 74 per cent of the black electorate voted. Stokes won 52.4 per cent of the total vote, receiving 93,000 black votes, or 96 per cent of the black vote (compared to Hatcher's 74 per cent of the black vote in the Gary primary), and 17,000 white votes. Stokes's margin of victory was 18,736, when the city's 901 precincts reported the results as follows: Stokes, 110,769; Locher, 92,033; and Celeste, 8531. (Subsequently, a recount narrowed Stokes's victory margin to 18,231.)

For Stokes, the victory was not only over the County Democratic Party Chairman, Albert S. Porter, who had bitterly opposed Stokes, but it was also a triumph of his strategy to attract white voters. Large newspaper ads had proclaimed in huge letters: "Don't Vote for a Negro." And below that attention-getting line, the advice in smaller letters: "Vote for the Man." The Democratic organization did what it felt it could not do in Gary. It rallied behind Stokes and publicly declared it would support him. Some skeptics believed, however, that many Democratic precinct leaders were actively working for the Republican candidate, forty-four-year old Seth C. Taft, grandson of President William Howard Taft, nephew of the distinguished Senator Robert Taft, and a member of the one family whose name was almost synonymous with the city. Stokes knew he had to court the white vote this time and spared no effort. Although the statistics gave him a decided edge (40,000 registered Republicans compared to 326,000 registered voters), the ethnic realities did not. It was not a question of how many whites would vote for Stokes, but how many would desert the Democratic ship and go wading in the Republican pond.

Stokes made one mistake which many observers believed almost cost him the election. But it was a "mistake" that had been deliberately worked out in advance. Speaking in the auditorium of a high school in Cleveland's middle-class white West Side, Stokes declared: "I am going to be brutally frank with you. . . . The personal analysis of all competent political experts is that Seth Taft may win the November 7th election for only one reason. The reason is that his skin happens to be white."

The shocked white audience let loose a barrage of angry calls of disbelief and dissent. Undeterred, Stokes continued: "I brought it out in the open for you to see. Seth Taft has pretended to bypass this so-called black-white issue. But in practically every public utterance he has made in this campaign, he not so subtly points out: 'Carl Stokes has had more experience at being a Negro but Seft Taft has more experience at being a white man.' "

Taft, who was sharing the platform with Stokes, was visibly shaken. Standing up to respond to Stokes's charge, he nervously ran his fingers through his hair and replied weakly: "Well, well. It seems that the race issue is with us." Then, in an honest assessment of the dilemma he had found himself in as a white man who many believed had tried not to inject race into the campaign, he continued: "It now appears that if I say something on the subject, it is racism. If Carl Stokes says something, it is fair play."

That meeting was considered the second turning point in the campaign. The first was the prestigious *Cleveland Plain Dealer's* endorsement of Stokes in the Democratic primary, a big factor in giving him a city-wide respectability to white voters. (This was not done for unselfish reasons. The paper's publisher, Thomas Vail, had been reputed to be considering running against incumbent U.S. Senator Frank Lausche in 1968, and a strong ally in City Hall would assist that ambition.)

Despite the outrage the Stokes statement occasioned in both the black and white community (his campaign manager, Dr. Kenneth Clement, was reputed to be strongly opposed to it), most of his advisers defended it. Stokes's white public relations man, Alexander L. Ostrow, was one of the biggest supporters. "It was worth maybe 10,000 votes in the Negro community. They thought he had already won and they weren't planning to come out again. Sure everybody is moaning and groaning today. But we won through calculated risks before. It's the only way to go." (Ostrow, incidentally, was also the public-relations counsel to millionaire industrialist Cyrus Eaton, a client of Stokes's law firm.)

On election day, November 7, 257,157 votes, or 78 per cent of the total registration of 326,003, were cast. The final results: Stokes, 129,829; Taft, 127,328.

This time, Stokes's margin of victory was due solely to the white vote. Whereas he received 94.5 per cent of the black vote cast—86,669 votes—he needed a sizable white vote to defeat Taft, and he received 21 per cent of the vote in the largely white West Side and 20 per cent of the white vote in scattered ethnic pockets throughout the city. Stokes's primary day 18,231-vote margin of victory, of which 17,000 were white votes, could have been achieved without white votes. This time, the white vote was the balance of power.

After his election, Stokes moved—and some suggested a little too fast—to allay white fears by appointing a new white police chief, sixty-four-year-old Inspector Michael J. Blackwell. His new public safety director and his public relations secretary were also white. Disgruntled blacks began publicly, but quietly, accusing Stokes of caving in to the white power structure by appointing only whites to top positions in his administration. In two moves to head off that justified criticism, Stokes appointed a black man, Municipal Court Judge Paul D. White, as law director, the number-two man in the city administration and successor to Stokes should the latter leave office for any reason. Stokes also named a black woman, Mrs. Blanche Bolden, to the $15,652-post of Assistant to the Service Director.

Stokes's administration has gotten off to a shaky start because the understandably impatient mayor dismissed people before he found suitable replacements. But his sense of urgency is symbolic of the change that has affected Cleveland. He has run into some difficulties with the thirty-three-man city council (of which eleven are black—one of the highest percentages of black councilmen of any major city). But the affable politician whose easy-going charm has already endeared him to the electorate is expected to ride out the political storms.

If Stokes's election was a feather in Cleveland's civic cap, the new political headgear was long overdue. Cleveland blacks had been repeatedly gerrymandered out of a black Congressional seat since 1956, when a black Republican ran for Congress and lost. Only two years ago, the Congressional districts were gerrymandered once more to protect liberal Representative Charles A. Vanik's seat, which had a 50 per cent black constituency. In 1968, Congressional redistricting will finally ensure the election of a black Congressman from Cleveland.

Again, using Stone's Index of Proportional Equality as a measuring rod for the political power of Cleveland's black people (who, in 1967, constituted 35 per cent of the population), only the city council and the board of education have been successful areas of black political power.

Of the seven members of the board of education, two are black, and of the thirty-three members of the city council, ten were black prior to the 1967 election. Of the seventeen members of the state legislature from the Cleveland area, four, or 23 per cent, were black. Of the eleven positions in the mayor's cabinet, only one position, that of director of the welfare department, was held by a black man. Of the twenty-two judges on the Common Pleas Court, only one was black. Of the thirteen judges on the Municipal Court, only two, or 15 per cent, were black.

This was the political situation, as of 1967 B.C. (Before Carl).

Black people in Cleveland—and, far more important, white people—have a unique opportunity to make history. As the eighth largest city, Cleveland and its politics will be closely watched for the first racial tear as a result of Stokes's election.

Carl Burton Stokes is probably one of the most unusual black politicians in America. Considered a "soul brother" by the black militants, he is well liked for his ability to "rap" (communicate) with the "nitty-gritty" of the black citizenry. At the same time, Stokes's polished manner, sartorial nattiness, and sincere eloquence before the public have won him many friends in the white community. If any one man can hopefully mend that tattered city's race relations, Carl Stokes appears to be that man.

More Black Mayors?

The election of Stokes and Hatcher has had an electrifying effect on black communities around the country. A "me-too" mood has suddenly blossomed, and in several cities, aspiring young black politicians are planning to challenge the political machines for a prominent spot on city-wide tickets. In the next municipal elections in Chicago, Newark, Richmond, New York City, Philadelphia, Memphis, Baltimore, St. Louis, and Atlanta, black men can be expected to be serious candidates for the mayoralties, backed by formidable organizations in black communities and financial assistance from the white communities.

But to win they must have nine ingredients present in the Hatcher and Stokes campaigns but lacking in the Memphis, Philadelphia, Chicago, and Youngstown campaigns:

1) They must be regarded as serious candidates by the black community.

2) The black community must believe the black candidates honestly have a chance to win.

3) The black community must unite as a solid bloc vote.

4) The black candidate must have a strong organization and sufficient finances or develop imaginative techniques for unearthing them (Hatcher's *New York Times'* ad).

5) The black candidate must campaign for the white vote as assiduously as he campaigns for the black vote.

6) The black candidate must be a member of the political party which controls the community or which has the highest number of registered voters. (Youngstown's Hugh Frost's defeat was due as much to his Republican affiliation as it was to his race.)

7) There must be no other black candidate of significance or popularity in the race. (Hatcher really capitalized on this factor. As soon as he announced his candidacy, his followers began circulating public statements that any other black man who entered the race as a serious candidate was either an "Uncle Tom" or a paid black flunky of the white man sent to split the black vote. As a result, several black candidates who would have been infinitely superior candidates to Hatcher were frightened off.)

8) There must be a minimum of one-third registered black voters in the city.

9) The city's principal newspapers and radio and television stations must

either endorse the candidacy of the black candidate or remain neutral. (In Gary, they all remained neutral. This was a decisive factor in Hatcher's victory.)

As 1967 was a very good year for black people, there will be many more as more and more black men find their way into City Hall as principal occupants.

CHAPTER ELEVEN

The South Shall Rise Again— With Black Votes

Major General Oliver Otis Howard who was director of the Bureau of Refugees, Freedmen and Abandoned Lands from 1865 to 1874 was also responsible for the establishment of Howard University for black people in 1867, being its president from 1869 to 1872. During the year Howard was being developed, the general spoke to many groups of ex-slaves about the need for education. Speaking to one such group in a D.C. church, he told them he was going North for financial assistance. "What shall I tell them when I get there?" he asked the group. There was an embarrassingly long silence and finally, one young black man rose and said to General Howard: "Tell 'em, suh, we is a-risin'."

Ever since the Confederacy was reduced to rubble and humiliation by a superior Union war machine, Southern states have embraced the delusion that the South would rise again to its former greatness and walk with white Anglo-Saxon pride across the length of the land, carried faithfully on the backs of contented and loyal black servants. Plantations would be air-conditioned, farm production more abundant, wages higher, and prosperity would flourish; white men would be more courtly and white ladies more lovely.

In that dream, blacks would exist for beloved whims of white people. The two-class society would become the vital force for returning the country to the ideal of American democracy founded on the acceptance of black subordination and cultural separation. From the smoldering ashes of the Civil War, Southern white families have passed down from generation to generation the unextinguished flame of eternal white supremacy.

Even at its more extravagant moments, however, the fantasy did not reckon with the possibility that the South would rise again with black votes. Fear of black political restlessness eventuating into black equality and even black political domination had always lurked in the shadows of white repression, but it was never given substance or credibility.

In the mid-1960's the South has been rising as a "separate but equal" revolution slowly unfolds.

There have been black voting registration campaigns in Alabama, led by the Student Nonviolent Coordinating Committee.

There has been the fearlessly militant political activity of the Mississippi Freedom Democratic Party.

There has been the passage of the 1965 Voting Rights Act, resulting from the Reverend Martin Luther King, Jr.'s march from Selma to Montgomery, Alabama.

But none of these events, by themselves or cumulatively, would be meaningful unless black men and women could be elected to political office, no longer as "mere recipients from the decision-making process but participants in it." And that has been happening.

In Mississippi, a forty-five-year-old black man, NAACP official Charles Evers, led six white segregationist opponents in a special election for the U.S. Congressional Third District seat on February 27, 1967, by capturing 33 per cent of the total vote, but failed to win the seat itself because he had not won a majority of the votes cast. (The March 12 run-off between Evers and his white opponent Charles Griffith, who had come in second, was easily won by Griffith by a two-to-one margin. It took a united white vote to defeat a united black vote for Evers. But a Mississippi black man had made his point.)

In Charlotte, North Carolina, a prominent dentist and civic leader, Dr. Reginald Hawkins, filed his candidacy as an independent Democrat for the governorship of that state. The forty-four-year-old black man was the first in the state's history to file for the office. Although Hawkins lost in the Democratic primary, as had been expected, he nevertheless won 18 per cent of the total vote, a respectable percentage for a first bid for office.

In Selma, Alabama, a black minister, Rev. L. L. Anderson, announced his candidacy as one of three Democrats seeking to be mayor, and six other black candidates entered the race for the city's ten City Council seats.

In Mississippi, Louisiana and Virginia, black men were elected to the state legislatures in 1967 for the first time since Reconstruction.

In 84-per-cent-black Macon County, Alabama (which houses the famed black college, Tuskeegee Institute), a black man, thirty-five-year-old Lucius D. Amerson, was elected County Sheriff in 1966, the first black man to hold such a post anywhere in the South since Reconstruction.

In Miami, Florida, the city's first elected black woman Commissioner, Mrs. M. Athalie Range, was elected in 1967 as one of five Commissioners who govern the city, including the mayor. Mrs. Range carried all twenty-one of the city's precincts in her victory.

In Mississippi five black persons were elected to county-wide posts in the 1967 election for the first time. These posts were county supervisor, county constable and county justice of the peace. Of the six, four were political independents who had been sponsored or assisted by the Mississippi Freedom Democratic Party which is still influential in the Delta counties. Also for the first time since 1876, black delegates were named to the Mississippi state Democratic convention on July 2, 1968. In the eighty-two county Democratic conventions around the state, black delegates were named from at least ten counties. One of these was Charles Evers, who was elected chairman of the Jefferson County Democratic executive committee.

In South Carolina, five black persons were elected vice-chairmen of the State Democratic Party on March 4, 1968, and more than 100 black people elected as delegates to the state convention, March 28. At that convention, five black delegates and four alternates out of a total of sixty-two were elected delegates to the Democratic National Convention to mark the first time in this century black people would represent South Carolina at a national Democratic convention. The state convention also elected a black man, St. Julian Devine, a Charleston alderman, as convention secretary, an honorary position. Another index of change in South Carolina was the serious challenge mounted against South Carolina's L. Mendel Rivers by a thirty-nine-year-old black schoolteacher, George A. Payton, Jr. Rivers, chairman of the House Armed Services Committee, a Congressman of twenty-eight years and one of the most reactionary Southerners in the House, will easily defeat Payton in the Democratic primary. But the district is 36 per cent black, and with a strong Republican challenge there was so much concern that many white voters might switch to the Republican nominee that the state legislature tried to pass a bill permitting Rivers to run as a Republican, then revert back to his Democratic affiliation if elected in order to preserve his seniority in the House—and his chairmanship. The idea was shelved, but it demonstrated the extent to which a black man's political challenge had disturbed the state of South Carolina.

In two Deep South states, Georgia and Texas, black men and women now serve in the state legislatures (twelve in Georgia and two in Texas).

While there are a few Southern cities which have black city councilmen and members of the board of education, none of these black political breakthroughs compares in dramatic intensity and national impact with the election of a black sheriff (that office traditionally the most powerful symbol in the South of white oppression); a black man running for Congress in this nation's most anti-black state (and leading six white segregationists!); a black man running for mayor, and a black man running for governor.

In all of these political races, the candidates have been of sufficient stature in the black community to be regarded as major candidates and have polled sizable votes. With a strengthening of the black electorate and the increasing belief in its ability to either elect black candidates or decisively determine the outcome of important Southern contests, more black candidates will be encouraged to file for political office.

In this respect, 1968 closely parallels 1870 when the Federal government guaranteed the black electorate's use of the ballot. Today, acting under the 1965 Voting Rights Act, the Federal government again has not only provided similar protection, but has on more than one occasion been an administrative agent in the registration of black voters.

Voting Registration Figures for Southern Whites and Blacks (11 States)*
As of November 1966

STATE	WHITES REGISTERED	BLACKS REGISTERED		PER CENT OF VOTING AGE WHITES REGISTERED		PER CENT OF VOTING AGE BLACKS REGISTERED		PER CENT OF BLACKS IN TOTAL REG.	
	1966	1964	1966	1964	1966	1964	1966	1964	1966
Alabama	1,192,075	111,000	246,396	70.7	88.1	23.0	51.2	10.4	17.1
Arkansas	598,000	105,000	115,000	71.7	70.3	54.4	59.7	14.6	16.1
Florida	2,093,274	300,000	286,446	84.0	80.0	63.7	60.9	12.0	9.5
Georgia	1,378,005	270,000	289,545	74.5	76.7	44.0	47.2	16.8	10.9
Louisiana	1,071,573	164,700	242,130	80.4	83.1	32.0	47.1	13.7	18.4
Mississippi	470,920	28,500	139,099	70.1	62.9	6.7	32.9	5.2	22.8
North Carolina	1,653,796	258,000	281,134	92.5	82.4	46.8	51.0	11.7	14.4
South Carolina	718,061	144,000	190,609	78.5	80.2	38.8	51.4	29.3	20.9
Tennessee	1,375,000	218,000	225,000	72.9	77.3	69.4	71.7	14.9	14.0
Texas	2,600,000	375,000	400,000	53.2	53.3	57.7	61.6	11.7	13.3
Virginia	1,159,000	200,000	205,000	55.9	61.8	45.7	46.9	16.0	15.0
Regional Total	14,309,704	2,174,200	2,620,359	73.2	70.2	43.3	52.2	13.0	15.4

* Source: Voting Education Project of the Southern Regional Council.

As of November 1966, according to the Voter Education Project of the Southern Regional Council, there were an estimated 2,620,359 black registered voters in the 11 Southern states: Alabama, Arkansas, Florida, Georgia, Louisiana, Mississippi, North Carolina, South Carolina, Tennessee, Texas, and Virginia.

Only a quarter of a century before this, in 1940, one of the most authoritative studies ever undertaken in this area estimated that between 80,000 and 90,000 black people voted in that year's election in the eight Deep South states of Alabama, Arkansas, Florida, Georgia, Louisiana, Mississippi, South Carolina and Texas, out of a total black adult population of 3,651,256.*

Assuming a maximum of 90,000 black voters in 1940 as representing half of all black registered voters in those states or 180,000, that latter figure would represent an insignificant 4 per cent of all eligible black voters. Worse still, this means that approximately 2 per cent of all eligible black adults in the eight Deep South states voted in the 1940 general election.

America's "separate but equal" democracy had attained a perverse kind of excellence. It was the fourth stage in the black man's political development in the South. Southern black politics, as of 1968, is a history of six stages: 1) slavery; 2) Black Reconstruction; 3) black disenfranchisement; 4) black anonymity; 5) black litigation; and 6) the black revolution.

During Black Reconstruction, as has already been described, black people voted, elected U.S. Senators, Congressmen, lieutenant governors, acting governors, mayors, Speakers of the House and various state officials. This exercise of the franchise was newly acquired from the Reconstruction state conventions called together at the direction of the Union government to establish "loyalist" governments. In turn, the Federal government protected and enforced the right of all its citizens, white and black, to vote. The ten Deep South states at their Reconstruction conventions had the following racial compositions:

STATE	WHITES	BLACKS
Alabama	83	17
Arkansas	68	7
Florida	29	17
Georgia	133	33
Louisiana	52	40
Mississippi	68	17
North Carolina	107	13
South Carolina	34	63
Texas	81	9
Virginia	80	25
	735	241

Those figures destroy the myth that the Reconstruction state conventions or legislatures were "black-dominated." Only in South Carolina were a majority of the delegates black; in 1873, the entire Congressional delegation of three representatives was black.

Following the "Hayes Compromise" and the withdrawal of Federal troops from the South, white-dominated state legislatures went about the task of

* Dr. Ralph Bunche completed a seven-volume study titled "The Political Status of the Negro" for Gunnar Myrdal's An American Dilemma. Completed in 1940, the study has remained an unpublished manuscript and is one of the most detailed studies of Southern black voting habits up until 1940 ever compiled.

restoring white supremacy. This was the period of Black Disfranchisement or "political niggerism" when Southern states conceived some of the most intricate and imaginative extralegal devices to prevent black people from voting (the poll tax, the "grandfather clause," the eight-ballot-box law, etc.). So successful were these various devices, all buttressed by official approval and unofficial terrorism, that by 1890 the South's black people were effectively disfranchised. A period of black anonymity set in when, for all intents and purposes, black people, as voters, did not exist.

The Democratic party was responsible for this desecration of democracy.

"The Democratic one-party system, therefore, was the condition of continued Negro disfranchisement under the new constitutions; but the new constitutions also tended to preserve the one-party system, for they strengthened the hold of the Democratic machines in the face of any revolt which might occur over the admission of a Negro voting balance."*

The Southern Democratic Party's one-party system was able to effectively strangle black political development and prevent any substantial increase in the black electorate.

It cannot be definitely shown that Negro suffrage gained in the South between 1900 and 1930. No statistical evidence exists, and a certain number of Negroes always voted, under varying circumstances, from Reconstruction on. . . . There were four circumstances in which there might be an appreciable Negro vote in a Southern community. One was the case of the presidential election which may be dismissed as insignificant from the viewpoint of effective Negro political power. The two which were most significant were nonpartisan municipal elections and referenda. Cases under a fourth heading—unexpected contests for office—while most sensational, were exceptional; they depended on such accidents as some politician's resignation or removal, death, or courage to bolt from his party.**

Black people, however, were still determined to exercise the franchise as a matter of principle. National black organizations such as the National Association for the Advancement of Colored People—with its headquarters in the North, away from the terroristic pressures of Southern justice and white police brutality—went into Federal court to secure the right for their black brothers in the South. This began the period of Black Litigation.

The first breakthrough in the courts occurred in 1915 when the U.S. Supreme Court ruled in *Guinn* v. *United States* that the Oklahoma "grandfather clause" was unconstitutional. The second came in 1927 when the high court struck down a Texas law barring black people from voting in its white primary (*Nixon* v. *Herndon*). White primaries were banned altogether in 1944 by the Supreme Court.

Despite the U.S. Supreme Court's successive rulings, there was no sud-

* Paul Lewinson, *Race, Class and Party*, p. 196.
** Lewinson, p. 162 and p. 198.

den upsurge in the registration of black voters. The Southern governments continued to condone lynchings, floggings, bombings, murders and various forms of harassments of black people which cumulatively obtained the same effect as the former unconstitutional laws—barring black people from the polls.

Beginning slowly with the May 17, 1954, U.S. Supreme Court decision outlawing segregation in public schools, what was to become known subsequently as the "Negro Revolt" or the "Negro Revolution" or the "Black Revolution" took shape.

From the courts in 1954 to the "sit-ins" in 1960 to CORE's "Freedom Rides" through the South in 1961 to the demonstrations and protest marches in Birmingham and other Southern cities in 1963 which culminated in the gigantic "March on Washington" to the 1964 black insurrections in the summer of 1964 in Harlem, in Watts, Los Angeles, in 1965 to the beginning of the era of black power in the summer of 1966 and finally the raw explosions of Newark and Detroit in the summer of 1967, a black cataclysm of incredible dimensions had shaken the foundation of white American complacency about its mistreatment of black citizens.

Most of the early phases, the strategies and the organized political activity within the black revolution occurred in the South. The Student Nonviolent Coordinating Committee (SNCC) was one of the first groups to recognize the need and value of black voter registration. SNCC's organizational work in 1965 in Lowndes County, Alabama, did not result in the election of its Black Panther Party candidates, but it did instill in black people in other Southern communities the political courage to register in larger numbers as Federal laws made less hazardous the road to the courthouses. Whereas SNCC's Lowndes County political experience did not result in any immediate change in the political status quo in Alabama, subsequent events in the surrounding communities where black people registered and even dared run for office can be traced back to SNCC's 1965 voter registration campaign.

Mississippi Freedom Democratic Party (MFDP)

The Student Nonviolent Coordinating Committee was equally responsible for one of the most revolutionary political programs ever attempted in the South—the formation of the Mississippi Democratic Freedom Party (MFDP).

Not only did the MFDP have a profound effect on Mississippi politics, but it nearly split apart the 1964 Democratic National Convention in Atlantic City, N.J., caused a reevaluation of what is possible in Southern politics, destroyed the timetable of gradualism and created an atmosphere of political sensitivities facilitating Evers' campaign for Congress in 1968.

MFDP had the unheard-of audacity to challenge the entire segregated Mississippi Congressional delegation in 1965, and came within 85 votes in the House of Representatives of having the five-man delegation unseated.

Not since 1920 when the NAACP successfully led an army of national protest to defeat President Hoover's nomination of U.S. Circuit Court Judge John Johnson Parker for the U.S. Supreme Court had a civil rights organization played such a decisive role in national politics. (In that year, the NAACP rallied every one of its branches, sympathetic religious, civic and labor officials as well as a mountain of support from prominent politicians to oppose Parker's nomination which Hoover had sent to the Senate on March 21, 1930.)*

MFDP was formed with the intention of remaining sufficiently independent of close party ties so that it could embarrass the Democratic Party nationally, hopefully take it over locally and provide the impetus for a sorely needed new radical political thrust among black people in the South. MFDP dared to organize a political party in the deepest of the Deep South that placed black people in control and focused attention on black people

---

* Quoting Parker's 1920 statement on accepting the North Carolina Republican nomination for governor that ". . . the participation of the Negro in politics is a source of evil and danger to both races . . . ," the NAACP lined up friends who also had a vested interest in defeating Parker. (For example, the normally conservative and anti-black American Federation of Labor joined the NAACP's ranks because they had been offended by Parker's upholding the constitutionality of the "yellow dog" contract which compelled a worker to waive his right to join a union for collective bargaining.)

Public opinion supported by favorable editorials built up rapidly against Parker's confirmation and on May 7, 1920, the Senate shamed Hoover by rejecting Parker's nomination, 41 to 39.

According to Henry Lee Moon in *Balance of Power: The Negro Vote*, p. 111: "To the unyielding President it was a humiliating defeat; to the Negro, it was an indication of his political maturity and a demonstration of the value of organization."

But if the black man was to unveil his political sophistication in Parker's defeat he was to sit back and let it wither away in the succeeding years. The NAACP soon forgot the merits of organizing black people into a powerful instrument of effective political activity. Instead, the NAACP shifted all of its energies to assaults on the legal bastions of racial segregation, a painful, slow and gentle approach to integration when it should have been directing its resources to the nitty-gritty to black self-help in politics. Had the NAACP chosen this role, it might have encouraged black politicians into more militant and productive activities on behalf of black people. If nothing else, it might have made black politicians more independent.

Gunnar Myrdal, in one of his few accurate assessments of the political needs of black people, recognized the value of an independent organization acting outside the immediate sphere of politics, but nonetheless actively engaged in politics:

". . . the Negro leader is in a dilemma. If he pleads allegiance to a political party he will lose in bargaining power. If, on the other hand, he keeps outside the parties, he loses some of the influence he could exert by being in the inner circle of one of them. Out of the dilemma there is only one possible and rational escape: a division of labor and responsibility among Negro leaders, so that the Negro politicians proper and the party workers identify themselves with political parties and work with them, while other Negro representatives, invested with superior prestige among their people, remain independent of close party ties and do the important collective bargaining." (*An American Dilemma*, p. 507.)

as the most prominent representatives of the party. That, in itself, was an amazing departure from the submissive accommodation that Southern black people had made with both the Democratic and Republican parties.

MFDP's genesis flows from SNCC's first voter registration project in McComb, Mississippi, in 1961. As Stokely Carmichael and Charles V. Hamilton point out in their book, *Black Power: The Politics of Liberation in America:*

> Voter registration schools were established to urge and assist people to register to vote. SNCC believed that in order to break through racist Mississippi society, black people must awaken their potential political power. . . . The Mississippi Democratic Party kept black people from power; it saw to it that black people never entered the political arena. In the fall of 1963, SNCC worked to build parallel political structures to challenge that stranglehold. The "Freedom Vote" held in November of that year tested the possibilities of parallelism. Over 80,000 people in the black community cast ballots for two "freedom" candidates as Governor and Lieutenant Governor.
>
> After passage of the 1964 Civil Rights Law, SNCC decided to devote its resources to building grass-roots political strength. The decision was finally made in February 1964 to establish a new political entity in the state of Mississippi. Formally constituted on April 26 in Jackson, it took the name of the Mississippi Freedom Democratic Party (MFDP).*

From its inception, MFDP plainly did not intend to be a mere voter registration program for black people. MFDP was dedicated to the pursuit and acquisition of political power in Mississippi for black people. MFDP seriously hoped to take over the political structure of the Democratic Party in Mississipi, if not today or next week or next month, certainly within the foreseeable future.

Consonant with its concept of black political parallelism, MFDP decided to send its own "open delegation" to the Democratic National Convention in Atlantic City, N.J., in August of 1964. It submitted a legal brief to the Credentials Committee of the Convention, outlining in detail how the Mississippi "regular" Democratic Party had maintained a lily-white slate, operation and delegation. MFDP saturated the Convention with legal arguments and case histories, and ran a high-powered press relations operation that provided the only excitement at one of the dullest and most boring national conventions the Democratic Party had ever held in its history.

Even though MFDP supported the platform of the Democratic Party (Mississippi's regular Party did not), was integrated (the regular state Party was not) and was willing to sign a loyalty oath, the Democratic Party opted to remain with the white segregationists as it has throughout its history, and turned down MFDP's application for recognition as the true Democratic delegation from Mississippi.

Under the heavy-handed pressure of white political racism at the Con-

* Pp. 87-88.

vention, directed by Lyndon B. Johnson and marshaled by Hubert H. Humphrey, a compromise was worked out which would allow two MFDP delegates to be seated as non-voting "delegates-at-large."

MFDP delegates quickly held a caucus and agreed unanimously to turn down the perfumed white racism, accurately calling it an offer of "the back of the bus." Although most of the sympathetic white liberals, under intense pressure from Hubert H. Humphrey (whose selection as Vice President resulted from his potential to deliver the liberal "sell-out"), withdrew their support one by one, MFDP remained firm and indicated it would accept a different compromise in which the loyal Democrats of the rival Mississippi delegations would have been seated as well.

Losing this battle, MFDP was still determined to press for a cleansing of the Mississippi Democratic Party. Marshaling an unbelievably impressive and formidable array of statistics, witnesses and notarized sworn statements, MFDP challenged the right of the Mississippi Congressional delegation to be seated in January 1965, as provided by the House rules. The issue was effectively stalled by the House Administration Committee whose chairman, Representative Omar Burelson of Texas, was openly sympathetic to the incumbent delegation.

MFDP's challenge was based on the easily documented proposition that the five members of the Mississippi Congressional delegation had been elected unconstitutionally and illegally because of a variety of legally sanctioned repressive techniques that denied black people the right to vote.

The United States Congress, custodian of the nation's laws and its legislative morality, heard nothing. President Johnson refused to speak out on the issue and the Democratic Party closed ranks to protect its white Congressional racists.

On September 17, 1965, the House adopted by a 228 to 143 roll-call vote the resolution (H.Res 585) dismissing the MFDP challenge. A key proponent for dismissal was Representative Frank J. Thompson of Trenton, N.J., chairman of the allegedly liberal Democratic Study Group, the labor movement's "man in the Congress," an occasional liberal on civil rights and the leader of the move to strip Representative Adam Clayton Powell of his chairmanship in the Ninetieth Congress.

Thompson stoutly defended the right of the regular Mississippi delegation to be seated and it was his key support that swung many Northern liberals over to the cause of Mississippi white racism.

If MFDP had lost a narrow battle in the House of Representatives, it won a tremendous moral victory in the councils of black opinion. Both the Atlantic City and Congressional battles taught black people that they "would have to organize and obtain their own power base before they could begin to think of coalition with others. To rely on the absolute assistance of external, liberal, labor forces was not a wise procedure."*

* Carmichael and Hamilton, p. 96.

In retrospect, it can be understood why, in the light of the desertion of the MFDP by organized labor and "white liberals," Black Power developed; the consciousness of blackness and the modus operandi of going-it-alone, without the help of whites, was a result of bitter experience, of many bitter experiences.

Charles Evers' 1968 race for Congress was made possible by the fact that his campaign manager was Lawrence Guyot, the portly and tough strategist who was head of MFDP. By joining two disparate forces in the black community—Evers' which believed that white allies were necessary for progress in the South and Guyot's which operated under the premise that white allies were irrelevant and that the important fact of life was to get black people together first and *then* form a coalition—Evers was able to make a creditable showing.

But, once again, the MFDP assessment of the white mentality in the South was correct. Evers received almost no public support from either labor or white liberals. As one campaign worker phrased it, "they really deserted us."

Which Way into the Future?

With voter registration programs now underway throughout the South, such as South Carolina's outstanding black-dominated "Voter Education Project," and the relative guarantee of black voters' right to register and vote, the black electorate ultimately is going to be the critically important segment of the national electorate for black political power. There are many Southern counties where blacks are 50 per cent or more of the total population.

According to the 1960 Census, the following racial compositions in the ten Deep South states existed:

STATE	PER CENT OF BLACKS IN POPULATION
Alabama	30.0
Arkansas	21.8
Florida	17.8
Georgia	28.5
Louisiana	31.9
Mississippi	42.0
North Carolina	24.5
South Carolina	34.8
Texas	12.4
Virginia	20.6

Clearly, the key states to watch in this group are Alabama, Georgia, Louisiana, Mississippi and South Carolina.

Two philosophies, however, will be competing for the loyalty of black voters—one, the Evers philosophy which attempts to forge an alliance of white liberals, labor and blacks, and the MFDP philosophy which conducts its own voter registration drive among black people and runs its own slate of black candidates, regardless of what the white liberals want or believe politically possible.

Given a measure of black sophistication or even black ambition, it is the MFDP philosophy that seems likely to prevail in a nation that now recognizes that it must live with the fact of black nationhood in spirit, if not in fact. While he was not sponsored or materially assisted by MFDP, a black man, Lucius D. Amerson, decided by himself to run for Sheriff without worrying about what it would do to the tender political balance between whites and blacks in Macon County, and in this instance, the MFDP philosophy once again prevailed.

The South will be the true battleground for the test of black political power because of the numerically high proportion of black people in Southern states and counties. For example, of the seventy-six Congressional Districts that had a 25 per cent or more black population as of 1960, only twenty-six or 34 per cent were in Northern states. Mississippi's Third Congressional District, which still has only half as many blacks registered as whites, is nonetheless 65.5 per cent black. North Carolina's Second Congressional District is 50.5 per cent black. Mississippi's Second Congressional District is 49.6 per cent black.

In many instances, black political activists may not be able to win the race for Congressman, governor, mayor or even U.S. Senator. But they can be the decisive factor in the outcome of those elections.

The extent to which the black electorate in the South can both determine the outcome of all political races and elect black officials in proportion to their percentage within the total population is the extent to which the South will "rise again."

In the North, black people can only hope to elect an occasional mayor, state or city official, or U.S. Congressman when the white-dominated state legislators and the gerrymandering of a black district permit.

In the South, black people will soon be able to elect governors, U.S. Senators and state legislators as they are able to fearlessly embrace Black Power and make it work for them.

The black North in 1968 is today the most sophisticated and the most curried political force among black people. But in ten years, the black South is going to be the leading political force among black people and, as was true during Black Reconstruction, spawn a race of brilliant and articulate black men whose capacity for innovative social legislation may well help to save America from the self-destruction of its own white racism.

CHAPTER TWELVE

The Future of Black Political Power

The present position of the Negro has been pointed, but what of his future? Upon one thing many Negro leaders agree: that there must be an effective organization of the colored votes; and this, of course, presumes a proposal of some sort of plan or program for his national political advancement.
—WILLIAM F. NOWLIN, *The Negro in American National Politics*, Boston, Mass.. The Stratford Co., p. 140

I believe the future is only the past again, entered through another gate.
—SIR ARTHUR WING PINERO in *The Second Mrs. Tanqueray*

People will not look forward to posterity who never look backward to their ancestors.
—EDMUND BURKE, *Reflections on the Revolution in France*, 1790

The future of black political power must be discussed against the backdrop of a possible future civil war between the black and white races or, at best, a legally instituted system of racial apartheid in Northern ghettoes.

The future of black-white relations has never been more grim, more bleak or more ominous. Black power and the black rebellions or "race riots" have frightened the white community into a near total alienation from black people.

Two diametric social forces in the black and white communities are working against each other and, ironically, toward the same goal—separation of the races.

In the white community, the frightened response to the riots of the last three summers and the expectation that more massive onslaughts of violence are coming has been to construct a wall of white exclusiveness. The white retreat into lily-white suburbs which will encircle predominantly black cities appears to be accelerating faster than the urban renewal upper-class high-rises designed to bring whites back into the inner city.

The white community has, in turn, sought a sociological cop-out. Rather than attempt to address itself to the root causes of racial unrest—unemployment, continuing exclusion of black people from labor unions, dilapidated housing, deficient educational facilities, police brutality and a pervasive iron curtain of non-communication—the white community instead appears to be relying upon a national get-tough policy that will substitute force for understanding, firearms for employment, concentration camps for better housing and containment for integration.

In the black community, a new mood of black pride—a "look backward to their ancestors"—and an organized drive for total black control of all-black communities has begun to counteract the movement toward racial integration. Young black people are now asking themselves: of what value is an integrated society if black people remain essentially powerless?

The frustration, the bitterness and the anger in the ghettoes have intensified as the alleged Great Society has increased its material munificence for whites, yet shrunk the horn of plenty for blacks. Black Power has struck a responsive chord in the innermost recesses of black thought.

While there is a variety of respectable interpretations of black power current—political power, economic power, organized community power, educational improvement power—there remains a hard-core group in the ghetto who seek a violent confrontation between the races as the only solution. Out of this confrontation we can expect to emerge a new society of two nations—black and white—co-existing as co-equals.

Such a view is quickly condemned as naive, irresponsible and impossible by the black intellectual mercenaries of the white establishment—the Kenneth Clarks, the Whitney Youngs, the Roy Wilkins and the Bayard Rustins. But it is a view that appears to have captured the imagination of not a small number of black youths and started white America to wondering whether true integration is possible or even desirable. Many white racists now believe a racial confrontation is inevitable and many black nihilists are suicidally hoping for it.

The March 1968 issue of one of the country's leading magazines, *Esquire*, headlined its featured story:

How WASHINGTON, D. C. is Preparing for
THE SECOND CIVIL WAR—
Blacks vs. Whites
The Weapons . . . The Strategy . . . The Leaders

Inside was a restrained and sober analysis of the very real possibility of a full-scale race war. The author, Garry Wills, conducted extensive, in-depth interviews with black militants, black revolutionaries, white police officials, white vigilante organizers and the advocates of the most advanced and sophisticated techniques of mob containment (various types of gas, modern weaponry and detention camps). Wills quoted a distinguished writer, Richard Rovere:

I can imagine the coming to power of an American deGaulle or even of someone a lot more authoritarian than deGaulle. Much of the trouble-making in the months and years will be the work of Negroes and I can even imagine the imposition of some kind of American apartheid—at least in the North, where Negroes live in ghettoes that are easily sealed off. If there should be the will to do it, it could be done quite "legally" and "Constitutionally." There are enough smart lawyers around to figure out how.

Wills himself then writes:

The threats of police blitzkrieg, on one side, of guerilla terrorism on the other are reaching that "unthinkable" stage which made atomic weapons, in Churchill's estimate, maintain the world peace throughout the Fifties. The Second Civil War is not a possibility but the present reality—anyone who denies that is not telling it like it is.

With a gloomy forecast of such racial tensions and potential racial warfare, what is the role of the Negro politician? Will he move toward the center of blackness or toward the edges of integration? If he chooses the latter, can he remain effective in the black community and how effective? Will the white community permit him to maintain rapport with the black militants? Will the white community make distinctions between conservative or safe "house niggers" and radical, tough "field niggers," or will it simplistically lump them all together for its peace of mind and bar all black people from white communities?

It is safe to predict that black political power in the major urban centers will continue to expand as these cities become more black. The election of black mayors, the increase of black representatives in state assemblies and the proliferation of black officials in top-level government positions will whet the appetites of black political aspirants. More black challengers will run for the offices now held by white men, and where a white elected official represents a black district or one which has even a slight majority of black people (such as Chicago's West Side Sixth Congressional District, now estimated to be 53 per cent black, yet represented by an Irishman), black people will demand that job.

For the next few years, however, black politicians who run for office and are elected will realistically tone down any blatant appeals to blackness. They will, in all likelihood, conduct their campaigns in a manner that minimizes offending white-controlled political machines. Just as Cleveland's

Carl Stokes and Gary's Richard Hatcher were able to maintain a close and intimate rapport with the black militants in their communities and still passionately appeal for white votes, future black politicians will campaign along similar lines. This is based upon the candid recognition that no black politician, unless he represents a predominantly black district, can win any city-wide or state-wide post without white votes. Consequently, the "new breed" of black politician must be militant enough to attract the support of black militants (or they will split and form separate parties as have white liberals and white conservatives) and still not alienate white voters. Furthermore, black politicians who aspire to city-wide or state-wide office know that at some point they must go to the Federal government or state legislatures for financial assistance for black improvement programs, and both are controlled by heavily white majorities. Nothing sobers the intoxicated black militant more quickly than the political realities of public office.

Consequently, it is possible that the ability of black people to significantly strengthen their political representation in the Congress, in the Federal government, in state assemblies, in state governments and in local public offices and, most importantly, in the judiciary at all levels, will be a mollifying influence on the violent stridency of black militancy.

The success of the black politician in maintaining a posture of reasonableness and attempting to work closely with the white political community will depend largely on that community's willingness to meet the justifiable demands for greater black representation, black jobs and the elevation of the black community to the comparable levels of comfort and excellent services enjoyed by the white community.

For years, there has been no black Congressman from Baltimore, St. Louis, Brooklyn's heavily black Bedford-Stuyvesant, the Bronx and Cleveland because the state legislatures, at the hard insistence of white Congressmen and white political bosses, have gerrymandered these Congressional districts to restrict black representation.

If the state legislatures of this country, both in the South and in the North, can move to meet black demands for more political representation, the smooth transition can be peacefully effected.

If, however, the state legislatures resist the legitimacy of increased black representation, the illegitimacy of black violence will flourish. It would appear, as of now, that white resistance to black progress in America is going to influence the legislatures to obstruct the rise of black political power.

If this occurs, it is entirely possible that a Black Third Party will evolve.

Myrdal, in his *An American Dilemma*, pompously predicted the opposite:

> If we focus our attention only on Negro voting in those parts of the country where Negroes have, or will have, the unhampered right to the ballot, it can, with reasonable security, be foretold that *there is not going to be a "Negro party" in American politics.* . . . Negroes in America are further bent on cultural assimi-

lation to the fullest degree allowed by the white majority and are careful to abstain from every move in the political sphere which might be interpreted as group exclusiveness.*

Myrdal, because he was white and had projected in his monumental studies many of the prejudices and wishful thinking of white sociologists rather than a realistic assessment of the options open to black people in the future, has proved to be wrong in both statements above.

There is the very real possibility of a Black Third Party which will be a response to two factors: (1) the extent to which the "Black Power" and new mood of blackness grows in the black communities and captures the imagination and followship of black people and (2) the speed and depth with which both major political parties are able to accommodate black demands for a proportionate share in the decision-making positions in the political parties and the government and a larger slice of the patronage pie.

If neither fact occurs with a more accelerated rapidity than has been evident to date, black people will form a third party in the conviction they can do no worse politically than they have by trying to work within the two-party system.

Not a third party, but a second party—the "Black Panther" Party of the Lowndes County Freedom Organization in Alabama—was formed in March 1966 to run black candidates for county offices. Most of the organizational work and voter registration was done by Student Nonviolent Coordinating Committee workers. Their goal was the November 1966 elections in which they ran candidates. All of the "Black Panther" candidates were defeated, but there were two accomplishments: (1) in a county which was 81 per cent black and which, as of March 1965, did not have a single registered black voter, SNCC was able to register 3900 black voters; and (2) this organizational job of registering and voting was accomplished under the aegis of an all-black political organization. This latter fact defied Southern convention and the Southern white tradition of negro docility.

In a sense, LCFO's "Black Panther" Party was a Third Party concept because it was all-black. If it was able to attain its limited success in a hostile white political climate in the deep South, it could conceivably perform more successfully in a Northern or upper South community.

Lately, there has been a growing discussion among black people of the feasibility of a predominantly black Third Party which would gain vicarious impetus from the third party organizational efforts of whites disenchanted with the Vietnam War and the absence of any real differences between the two parties on many domestic and foreign issues. In 1968, "Peace and Freedom" Parties and slates of candidates are being formed in several states and cities. Any degree of success for these slates would have the net effect of encouraging a Third Party among blacks.

* Myrdal, p. 505.

But any coordinated national black effort toward a Third Party does not appear at this writing to be under formation. It is not, however, an impossibility and must be considered within the range of future alternatives, again depending upon the response of the two major parties to black demands for more proportionate political power.

Myrdal's second statement in his quotation that black people "bent on cultural assimilation" will not make any political moves which contravene the thrust toward integration by establishing islands of political exclusiveness has also been proved historically erroneous by the National Conference of Negro Elected Officials.

Conceived by an articulate and militant young California state senator named Mervyn M. Dymally from Los Angeles, the Conference met in Chicago for three days, from September 29 to October 1, 1967.

Of an estimated 603 black elected officials in 33 states and the District of Columbia, approximately half, or 300, attended. The overwhelming majority of them were Democrats. Co-chairing the Conference were Manhattan Borough President Percy E. Sutton, one of the brightest and fastest-rising black politicians in America, and Dymally.

The important fact about this conference is that it was held. Here were a large group of black public officials meeting together on the basis of one fact—their black skin. They were *not* being "careful to abstain from every move in the political sphere which might be interpreted as group exclusiveness." On the contrary, they were asserting that this "group exclusiveness" was as necessary for their political survival and advancement as it was for the Irish, the Italians, the Jews and the Poles.

Ordinarily, neither the Democratic nor the Republican Party wishes to publicly admit there is such a thing as an ethnic vote (although both maintain "minorities" or "nationalities" divisions within their national headquarters). But the successful formation of the Conference of Negro Elected Officials and informal efforts among some elected black officials to maintain constant contact did have its effect, at least, upon the Democratic Party.

Thus, during the previous year, a Workshop Conference of Negro Elected Democratic Officials was held on June 3, 1966, in the Rayburn House Office Building under the honorary chairmanship of Rep. William L. Dawson of Chicago, dean of the six black Congressmen. Convening the Workshop was Louis Martin, Deputy Chairman of the Democratic National Committee, a former editor of several negro newspapers and one of the few politicians who had been hired in the Kennedy administration and managed to survive in the Johnson administration. It has been suggested by some of Martin's critics that a great amount of dexterous "Uncle Tom-ming" was necessary to retain his position. Martin's role has remained that of the political court jester in race relations for the Democratic Party with very little power either to implement good black appointments or prevent bad ones. Johnson has relied mostly upon his white advisers for suggestions of black appointments and when he was uncertain about a name, then and only then has he checked with Martin.

It is clear that there will be more meetings of elected black officials, particularly as their number increases. In the 1967 election, it is estimated that approximately fifty more black people won elective office. This includes the two black mayors of Cleveland and Gary as well as the several breakthroughs of negro legislators in Southern states.*

It can be comfortably predicted that whites will continue to resist black political advancement, not solely on the basis of race, but also because no group enjoys the surrender of political power. If race tensions escalate because of black violence, then black political breakthroughs will be resisted by both the white population and the white politicians who now serve predominantly black constituencies or districts with a significant percentage of black people. In the South, particularly in the Southeastern states of North Carolina, South Carolina and Georgia, black candidates running as "independents" or possible Third Party candidates will multiply far out of proportion to their ability to get elected.

But the mere fact of their participation in political races will both educate and encourage black people to a greater sensitivity to political activity as well as stimulate demands for expanded black representation. The day has almost passed when a white candidate will be able to campaign anywhere in the South and appeal to anti-black prejudice. As black people increase their voting registrations and step up the threats of independent candidacies or Third Party movements, Southern white politicians may move to head off such developments by slating more black people for office.

A Black Man on the National Ticket

In the early months of 1967 when negro Senator Edward W. Brooke was looking his attractive best and not appearing to be too much of a negro or sounding too civil righteous while letting everybody realize that he was still colored, there were occasional flirtations by some newspaper columnists with the idea of a Republican Presidential ticket of Governor Romney of Michigan and Brooke. This was known as the perfectly balanced ticket—a moderate Midwesterner, symbolic of the essence of patriotic Americana,

* According to the statistics compiled by Dymally, the 603 negro elected officials included, as of 1967, prior to the November elections: 195 city councilmen, 119 state representatives, 112 school board members, sixty-two judges, thirty-three state senators, twenty-one county commissioners, nine mayors, eight state college governing board members, six U.S. Congressmen, five city clerks, one U.S. Senator, and thirty classified as "other." While the total number may appear to be impressive, it represents less than one per cent of all elected officials in America.

and a moderate Eastern negro Republican whose views on civil rights were sufficiently conservative not to alienate white voters, but whose skin color was just enough of an emotional magnet to win black votes.

Subsequently Romney withdrew, and by early 1968, following Romney's withdrawal from the Presidential race, former Vice President Richard M. Nixon emerged as the almost certain winner of the Republican nomination. During the early months of 1968, one of the most widely discussed topics in official Washington was the possibility of a Nixon-Brooke ticket. Several nationally prominent columnists hinted at this prospect and one syndicated columnist actually outlined the possibility.

Ironically, the entry of the more liberal Republican New York State Governor Nelson A. Rockefeller into the Presidential race would all but kill Brooke's chances since a negro would no longer be needed to balance the ticket. Rockefeller's nomination as the Republican Presidential nominee in November 1968 would require a conservative Midwestern or Western Republican to offset his Eastern Liberalism.

There is the possibility that in the not too distant future a negro, under a combination of unpredictable circumstances, will be chosen for the Presidential ticket. More than likely, it will be Republicans who have the ability and the style to orchestrate radical progress without being labeled radicals. As suggested in previous chapters, Republicans have done this in several elections and Democrats have jumped on the political bandwagon afterward.

But black people must wait their turn in the ethnic pecking order of succession, and until a Jew and possibly an Italian are nominated for the national ticket of either party, black people will not be seriously considered by either party.

As the ugly mood of white America moves toward a posture of more racial hate and resistance to black progress, as the violence in the ghettoes and "crime on the streets" increase, there always remains the possibility of enough white Americans coming to their senses and recognizing that the only solution to eventual racial togetherness is more, not less, black political progress. Despite three "long, hot summers" of racial rebellions, Americans still elected a black U.S. Senator, defeated a "white backlash" candidate for mayor of Boston, elected two black mayors of major cities and made notable political progress for black people in several states and cities.

Consequently, a remote possibility does exist that a potential "Civil War" between the races will not preclude black political progress. While such an eventuality is indeed remote, it nonetheless exists. The nomination of a negro for Vice President would also be the most dramatic and racially unifying gesture that could be made in these troubled times.

In New York State, in the last two Senatorial races, Dr. Ralph Bunche's name figured prominently in the discussion of potential Democratic candidates to oppose Republican Senator Javits in 1962 and again in 1964, before the late Robert F. Kennedy virtually purchased the nomination.

A black lieutenant governor in New York State is an imminent possibility, and the election of an attractive, bright and vote-getting black person would not only place him in the national spotlight for consideration, but would also deliver the clout delegates to the national political convention from the country's largest state.

The 1968 Presidential Election

As of this writing, the 1968 Presidential campaign has been turned upside down by the withdrawal of President Johnson as a candidate for re-election, the withdrawal of Republican Governor George Romney of Michigan, the entry of Republican Governor Nelson A. Rockefeller, and finally the shocking assassination of New York Senator Robert F. Kennedy in Los Angeles on June 5th just after he had won California's Democratic primary. Winning the Indiana, Nebraska and California primaries, Kennedy demonstrated that he was enormously popular with black voters. There was a special affinity for him, partly because of the association with his late brother, President John F. Kennedy, whom black people revered, and partly because of Kennedy's ability to communicate with the black masses.

Neither Humphrey nor McCarthy possesses this quality. In McCarthy's case, it is a function of his reserved philosopher-king posture. Humphrey, a worn-out liberal who believes that running-off at the mouth is a substitute for genuine liberalism, has no strong following in the black community. Depending upon what kind of campaign the Vice President runs and the candidate of the Republican Party, the Presidential race for black people will not command the excitement or interest which Kennedy's activities had brought to it.

Whether Johnson would respond to a genuine massive national draft is unknown. If he were able to achieve a reasonable settlement of the Vietnam War, he would surely be a national hero. Yet, it is also equally likely that he sincerely wishes to step down from the burdensome responsibilities of the Presidency and turn them over to his Vice President, Hubert H. Humphrey.

These are the imponderables in the 1968 Presidential race.

Johnson's decision not to seek re-election must be considered as an augury of hope for racial reconciliation in America. His re-election would have been for black people one of the great political tragedies of this era.

Slowly retrogressing to the racial prejudice that had characterized his career in the House and the racial conservatism that was the hallmark of his Senate career, Johnson, with his shrewd sensitivity to the political winds of change, had given every indication that he intended to ride the back of the "white backlash" tiger toward re-election. Had the Republicans nominated a conservative who decided as a matter of strategy not to campaign for the black vote, Johnson would then have been pushed toward the same aggressive hunt for the middle-class white vote. Johnson had already begun catering to "white backlash" sentiment and was becoming the "real Lyndon Johnson," no longer politicking for civil rights as he did when the country was on the emotional binge that followed John F. Kennedy's assassination. The true Johnson, the white Southerner with parochial tastes and narrow expectations, would have conducted his campaign in this framework.

His appointment of his Special Assistant, W. Marvin Watson of Texas, as Postmaster General is one more major indication that Johnson had turned his back on the black vote. No one man has been more hostile to black aspirations in the Johnson administration that Watson. A conservative businessman with ties to Texan H. L. Hunt, one of the wealthiest political reactionaries in the country, Watson established an early reputation for being unsympathetic to labor unions and to black people. It was this conservative reputation that endeared him to Johnson.

Should, however, the Republicans nominate Rockefeller, it is safe to predict that the black vote, for the first time in twenty years, will come close to a split down the middle. Black disenchantment with Johnson is widespread. The basic distrust of a man who has been able to talk out of both sides of his political mouth has grown in the black communities. Rockefeller has few of these liabilities as far as black people are concerned. While his record as governor has not produced the proportion of jobs in the state that civil service black people believe they deserve, nevertheless Rockefeller is recognized and accepted by black people as an honest liberal on civil rights. Most black people feel he can be trusted, and that Johnson cannot.

Also, Rockefeller's spectacular move to construct a state office building in the center of Harlem at the corner of 125th and Seventh Avenue (a corner that has come to be regarded as the "Crossroads of Black America") has captured the imagination and affection of Democratic Harlem. His nomination would result in a large number of prominent black people, black militants and even some well-known black Democrats endorsing his candidacy and supporting him against Johnson.

Only the election of a liberal Republican like Rockefeller or Eugene McCarthy can forestall America's inexorable march toward a racial civil war. Johnson's re-election would hasten it.

The Assassination of the Reverend Martin Luther King, Jr.

No political event in 1968—unless the war in Vietnam should suddenly end—will have a more dramatic impact on the 1968 Presidential race than the assassination on April 4th of the Reverend Martin Luther King, Jr.

As of this writing, following his funeral and a period of national violence, looting and angry denunciations of whites by many black militant leaders, no one can predict the extent his death will continue to divide this nation or encourage its unity. Black militancy, of course, will quickly fill a vacuum, and the ascendancy of black political solidarity could have either detrimental or salutary effects on the body politic. More black politicians, following the increasing black militancy, might be encouraged to seek a black together-ness that would alienate, yet insulate the black community from white political domination, and in turn achieve greater black political power.

On the other hand, it is equally logical to expect some black politicians to continue to maintain channels of communication between black and white. Which will prevail, no one knows. Only one fact is certain: The United States of America stands on the threshold of the most critical period in its history since the first shot was fired on Fort Sumter in 1861.

Americans have yet to come to grips with the problem of the black man, his aspirations, his desire and demand for the good life and, although many militant blacks will not admit it, his full inclusion in a bi-racial American society.

No longer can the question be asked: "What does the negro want?" The question now must be: "How is America going to accord him every eco-nomic, political and educational right possessed by whites?" Now.

The black political advances of 1967 are reminiscent of those of 1870. Following the 1870 election of the first black U.S. Senator and two black Congressmen and other officials, there was a halcyon period of racial progress when America elected twenty black Congressmen and two black Senators, as well as countless state public officials. The Federal govern-ment's sympathetic attitude and its support of black progress with Federal troops kept the peace (and the faith) in Southern states, facilitating the black man's climb up the political ladder. Then, America turned another corner. It became expedient to trade the black man's future and security for selfish political gains. The period of the next eighty years was one of grinding poverty, political repression, officially sanctioned brutality and agonizingly slow progress for black people.

America has come to another corner in 1967. The dramatic achievements of a black U.S. Supreme Court Justice, a black man in the Cabinet and other political advances at the state and local levels presage a new era of escalated freedom.

Yet, just the opposite can occur, and indeed, as Pinero has observed, the future may well be the past again, "only entered through another gate." Under a second Johnson administration, it is far more likely that there would be a period of the most severe official repressions. A new kind of McCarthyism that equates any form of Federal assistance for Negroes as "coddling lazy niggers" has opened the door of the era of unmerciful politics.

America found no Constitutional impediment, suffered no official em-barrassment, or experienced no national shame when it evacuated 126,000

Japanese-Americans from the greater portion of Washington and Oregon, all of California and southern Arizona, beginning on March 2, 1942. The establishment of internment camps by the War Relocation Authority to house Japanese-Americans viewed by many Americans as potential enemies because of America's war with Japan is one of the most obnoxious chapters in American history.

It was a time of national emergency, a time of war, and during such periods a nation can lose its head and the people will support it in the most irresponsible display of reckless mistreatment of its own citizens.

In the era of unmerciful politics which could be expected to exacebate racial tensions if Johnson were re-elected, black Americans could well find themselves in similar internment or detention camps. The intensifying of a national emergency that pins down a nation's military resources in Vietnam, and perhaps throughout South-East Asia soon, will diminish that nation's tolerance and patience for domestic insurrections. A national fatigue may set in and a national exasperation with conflict may expedite concerted calls to crack down unrelentingly on black insurgency. This is how the "race riots" and black rebellions in urban centers can conceivably lead to a national policy of preventative detainment for black people as a means of controlling future outbreaks. America did it with the Japanese. It can do it again with black people.

Whether history will repeat itself for black people and once again tread the same paths of racial suppression that began in 1877 for black people and again in 1942 for Japanese-Americans cannot be prophesied with any certainty now.

But the political survival of black people will depend upon a new courage of black politicians and an enlightened, painstakingly planned unity of black people. This latter may take the form of a new national organization, displacing the conservative and outmoded NAACP, and welding black people into a powerful political phalanx. Or it can come in the form of a third political party organized by black people to act as the balance of power which decides elections, as the Jews have done with the Liberal Party in New York State.

Black political power has just begun to come of age. Whether it can grow from the gangling adolescent into a mature adult with all of the prerogatives of power possessed by other ethnic groups will be determined by the extent to which bitterness or sympathetic understanding predominates in the black-white relationship. The future of American democracy as a civilization and as a viable force in world affairs is wedded to the manner in which this nation can solve this problem by energizing itself to a new sense of national responsibility and finally discovering some lasting merit in the ancient creed of racial brotherhood.

Bibliography

Bell, Daniel, *The End of Ideology*, The Free Press, Glencoe, Ill., 1960.

Bennett, Lerone, Jr., *Before the Mayflower*, Johnson Publishing Co., Chicago, 1962

Carmichael, Stokely and Hamilton, Charles V., *Black Power: The Politics of Liberation*, Random House, New York, 1967

Coleman, Emmett, *The Rise, Fall and ? of Adam Clayton Powell*, Bee-Line Books, New York, 1967

Cox, Oliver Cromwell, *Caste, Class and Race—A Study in Social Dynamics*, Doubleday & Co., Garden City, N.Y., 1948

Daniels, John, *In Freedom's Birthplace*, Houghton Mifflin Co., New York, 1914

Du Bois, W.E.B., *The Souls of Black Folk*, Fawcett World Library, New York, 1961

Educational Heritage, Inc., *Negroes in Public Affairs and Government*, Educational Heritage, Inc., Yonkers, N.Y., 1966

Evans, Rowland and Novak, Robert, *Lyndon B. Johnson: The Exercise of Power*, The New American Library, New York, 1966

Fager, Charles E., *White Reflections on Black Power*, William B. Eerdmans Publishing Co., Grand Rapids, Mich., 1967

Glazer, Nathan and Moynihan, Daniel P., *Beyond the Melting Pot—the Negroes, Puerto Ricans, Jews, Italians and Irish of New York City*, The M.I.T. Press, Cambridge, Mass., 1963

Golden, Harry, *Mr. Kennedy and the Negroes*, World Publishing Co., Cleveland, Ohio, 1964

Lewinson, Paul, *Race, Class and Party—A History of Negro Suffrage and White Politics in the South*, Grosset and Dunlap, New York, N.Y., 1932

Lubell, Samuel, *White and Black: Test of a Nation*, Harper & Row, Publishers, New York, 1964

Machiavelli, Niccolo, *The Prince*, The New American Library of World Literature, New York, 1952

McCune, Wesley, *The Nine Young Men*, Harper & Brothers, New York, 1947

Moon, Henry Lee, *Balance of Power: The Negro Vote*, Doubleday & Co., Garden City, N.Y., 1948

Musmanno, Michael A., *The Story of the Italians in America*, Doubleday & Co., Garden City, N.Y., 1965

Myrdal, Gunnar, *An American Dilemma*, Harper & Brothers, Publishers, New York, 1944

Nowlin, William F., *The Negro in American National Politics*, The Stratford Co., Boston, Mass., 1931

Salk, Erwin A., A *Layman's Guide to Negro History*, Quadrangle Books, Chicago, Ill., 1966

Shannon, William V., *The American Irish*, Macmillan Co., New York, 1963

Shoup, Earl L., *The Government of the American People*, Ginn and Co., 1946

Stone, Chuck, *Tell It Like It Is*, Trident Press, New York, 1967

White, Theodore H., *The Making of the President 1960*, Atheneum Publishers, New York, 1961

White, Theodore H., *The Making of the President 1964*, Atheneum Publishers, New York, 1965

Index

Abner, Willoughby, 173
Abolitionists, 27
Adamowski, Benjamin, 172
Addonizio, Hugh, 125
Adkins, Thomas I., 13
Adonis, Joe, 121
Alabama, 77, 226, 228, 229, 235
Alexander, Clifford L., Jr., 69, 75, 198
Allen, Ivan, Jr., 48
Allston, J. Henderson, 13
Alsop, Joseph, 22
American Dilemma, An (Myrdal) 37-38, 54-55, 229, 232, 240-41, 242, 249
American Federation of Labor–Congress of Industrial Organizations (AFL–CIO), 90
American Irish, The (Shannon), 111, 112, 116-17, 250
American Jewish Congress, 130
American Labor Party, 120, 132, 153
American ("Know-Nothing") Party, 111
Amerson, Lucius D., 236
Amsterdam News, 184, 185
Anastasia, Albert, 121
Anastasia, Tony, 121
Anderson, Jack, 131
Anderson, L. L., 226
Anderson, Laurence, 217
Anderson, Marian, 5, 7
Annunzio, Frank, 121
Appalachian conference of 1953, 121
Arkansas, 77, 228, 229, 235
Arvey, Jacob, 10, 136, 137
Atlanta, Ga., 48, 81, 223
Atlanta Enquirer, 48
Attucks, Crispus, 165

Aurelio, Thomas, 194-95
Austin, Samuel, 205

Bailey, John M., 125
Balance of Power: The Negro Vote (Moon), 35, 44-47, 55-57, 82, 86, 232, 249
Baltimore, Md., 54, 64, 108, 135, 137, 157, 223, 240
Baltimore Sun, 137
Baptiste, Maurice, 217
Baruch, Bernard, 133
Bassett, Ebenezer Don Carlos, 35, 95
Bayonne, N.J., 142
Beame, Abraham, 132
Bedford-Stuyvesant, see New York City
Before the Mayflower (Bennett), 13, 249
Bell, Daniel, see End of Ideology, The
Bell, Jesse, 216, 217
Belotti, Francis X., 124
Bennett, John J., 122
Bennett, Lerone, 4; *see also Before the Mayflower*
Bernstein, Benjamin, 180
Bethune, Mary McLeod, 87-88
Beyond the Melting Pot (Glazer and Moynihan), 112, 114, 119, 121, 132, 133, 134, 249
Birmingham, Ala., 231
Black and White: Test of a Nation (Lubell), 79, 86-87, 249
"Black Cabinet," 87-88
Black codes, 28-29
Black Panther Party, 231, 241
Black Power, 9, 12, 13, 14, 16, 17, 18, 19, 20, 21, 22, 23, 24, 25, 31, 41,